A Breed Apart

The History of the Texas Rangers

Eddie Michel

24/12/12

To Fiona and Michael

Merry Christmas!

Best Wishes
Eddie Michel

outskirtspress
DENVER, COLORADO

The opinions expressed in this manuscript are solely the opinions of the author and do not represent the opinions or thoughts of the publisher. The author has represented and warranted full ownership and/or legal right to publish all the materials in this book.

A Breed Apart
The History of the Texas Rangers
All Rights Reserved.
Copyright © 2012 Eddie Michel
v2.0

Front Cover Image - Texas Rangers on horseback patrolling the Big Bend in 1940.
"Courtesy of Texas State Library and Archives Commission." All rights reserved - used with permission.

This book may not be reproduced, transmitted, or stored in whole or in part by any means, including graphic, electronic, or mechanical without the express written consent of the publisher except in the case of brief quotations embodied in critical articles and reviews.

Outskirts Press, Inc.
http://www.outskirtspress.com

ISBN: 978-1-4787-2031-7

Outskirts Press and the "OP" logo are trademarks belonging to Outskirts Press, Inc.

PRINTED IN THE UNITED STATES OF AMERICA

Table of Contents

Chronology v
Introduction..xi

1823-1865
1 Humble Beginnings 1
2 The Crucible of War..5
3 Los Comanches and the Indian Troubles 11
4 Los Diablos Tejanos 23
5 To Arms for Dixie: The Corps and the Confederate years 36

1874-1935
6 The Frontier Battalion and the Indians..........................46
7 The Special Force..53
8 Feudists and the Outlaw Breed..59
9 Tools of Big Business:
   the Cattle Kingdom and Industrial Growth 68
10 Bandidos, Sediciosos and the Plan de San Diego 76
11 The Roaring Twenties 82

1935-Present day
12 The Department of Public Safety: A New Era Begins 120
13 Challenges: Old and New 129
14 Los Cincos Candidatos, La Huelga
   and the Swinging Sixties 154
15 Approaching the New Millenium....................................182
Reflections: Deep in the Heart of Texans 205
Glossary 215
Notes...219
Bibliography 241

"They knew their duty and they did it."

Captain John S. 'Rip' Ford

Chronology

1690 - First colonization of Texas by Spanish settlers.

1821 - Mexico achieved independence from Spain.

1821-24 - Stephen F. Austin and the 'Old Three Hundred' colonized the region between the Brazos and Colorado rivers.

1823 - Austin called for a force of ten Rangers to defend the frontier against Indian raids.

1835-1836 - Texan Revolution.

1835 - Permanent Council of Texas passed an ordinance calling for three companies of Rangers.

1836 - Siege of the Alamo, Battle of San Jacinto, Texas becomes an independent nation.

1840 - Council House Fight, Comanche raids on Victoria and Linnville, Battle of Plum Creek.

1841 - Santa Fe Expedition.

1842 - Mexican forces twice invade Texas and capture San Antonio, Battle of Salado, Mier Expedition.

1845 - Texas joins the United States and is granted full statehood.

1846-48 - U.S.-Mexican War.

1848 - At the Treaty of Guadalupe-Hidalgo, Mexico ceded California, New Mexico and its claim to Texas north of the Rio Grande in exchange for fifteen million dollars.

1858 - Battle of Antelope Hills.

1859-60 - First Cortina War
1860 - Battle of Pease River.
1861 - Texas seceded from the Union and became the seventh state of the Confederacy.
1861-65 - Civil War between Union and Confederacy.
1862 - Army of New Mexico seized Albuquerque and Santa Fe before retreating back to Texas.
1865 - Confederacy is defeated, Battle of Palmito Hill, Rangers disbanded on federal orders.
1870-71 - Twenty companies of Rangers formed for a twelve month enlistment to protect the frontier.
1874 - Formation of the Frontier Battalion and the Special Force, Battle of Palo Duro Canyon.
1875 - Quanah Parker, the last free Comanche chief, surrenders at Fort Sill, *Las Cuevas* Affair.
1877 - El Paso Salt War.
1881 - Battle at Sierra Diablo.
1883-88 - Fence Cutting War.
1891-93 - Garza Revolution.
1915 - Plan de San Diego.
1915-16 - Bandit War.
1918 - Massacre at Porvenir.
1919 - The Eighteenth Amendment was ratified signaling the beginning of the Prohibition Era, race riot in Longview.
1920 - Longshoremen strike in Galveston.
1930 - Race riot in Sherman.
1934 - Bonnie Parker and Clyde Barrow killed near Gibsland, Louisiana.
1935 - Formation of the Department of Public Safety comprising of both the old Highway Patrol and the Texas Rangers, *The Texas Rangers: A Century of Frontier Defence*, written by Walter Prescott Webb, was first published.
1938 - Homer Garrison Jr. appointed Director of DPS.
1941-45 - World War Two.

1941 - Strike at the Rogers-Wade Furniture Factory in Paris.
1943 - Race riot at Beaumont.
1955 - Riot at the Maximum Security Unit of Rusk State Hospital.
1957 - Lone Star Steel Strike in Daingerfield.
1957-60 - Rangers clean up the gambling mecca of Galveston.
1962-78 - *Tejanos* challenge Anglo-Texan political control of Crystal City and Zavala County.
1963 - President John F. Kennedy was fatally shot in Dallas.
1966-67 - 'La Huelga' agricultural workers strike near Rio Grande City.
1967 - Construction began of Fort Fisher, a Ranger company headquarters and Ranger Museum on the Brazos River.
1968 - Death of Homer Garrison Jr. who had served as DPS Director for nearly thirty years.
1969 - Jailbreak at Carrizo Springs. Arturo Rodriguez Jr became the first Hispanic in the modern Ranger force.
1970 - Several thousand University of Texas students protesting the Vietnam War take over the Capitol building in Austin.
1973 - Building work began on Texas Ranger Hall of Fame at Fort Fisher.
1974 - George Parr, the 'Duke of Duval', commits suicide after a conviction for tax evasion and the Parr political machine subsequently collapses. Fred Gomez Carrasco and two other inmates seize control of the Walls Unit of the state prison in Huntsville.
1987 - Ranger Stan Guffey is killed in a gunfight while serving in the line of duty.
1988 - Lee Roy Young Jr. became the first African-American Ranger in the twentieth century.
1993 - The Branch Davidians, led by David Koresh, engage in violent confrontations with both the ATF and FBI. Two women, Cheryl Steadman and Marrie Reynolds Garcia become the first female Rangers.
1995 - Former Ranger Steadman and State Trooper Lisa Shepherd engaged in a federal lawsuit against the Ranger Division on the grounds of discrimination and prejudice.

1997 - Rangers besiege the Republic of Texas (ROT) militia compound in Jeff Davis County.

1999-2000 - Rangers provide security for presidential candidate George W. Bush.

2000 - The U.S. Supreme Court ruled in favor of the Texas Rangers in the Steadman/Shepherd lawsuit ending the legal action.

2008 - Rangers lead a law enforcement raid on the Fundamentalist Church of Jesus Christ of Latter-Day Saints (FLDS) ranch in Schleicher County.

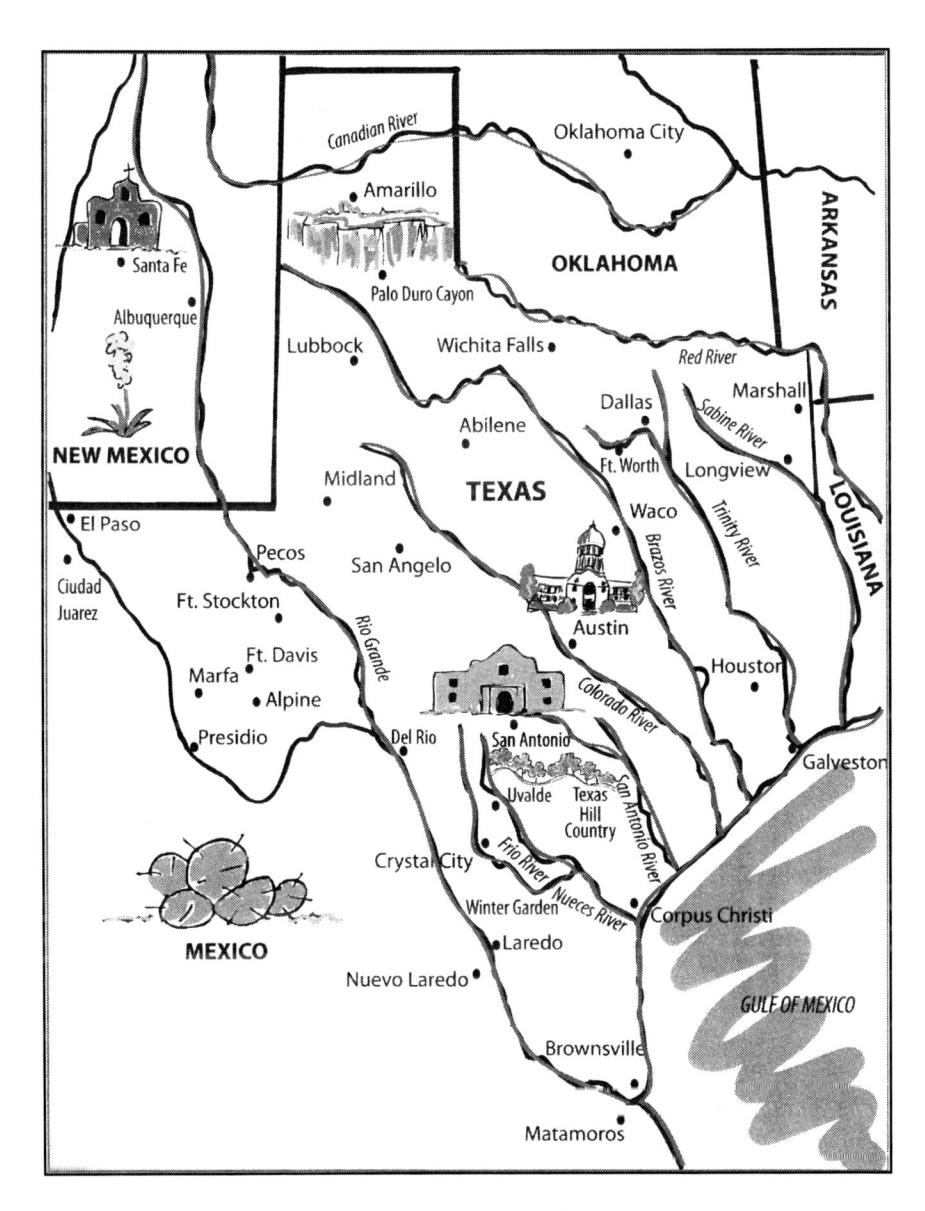

© Melissa Moulton

Introduction

In popular culture the Texas Ranger is an iconic figure who epitomizes the spirit of the American West. The heroic lawman who swaggers across main street his spurs clinking on his boots, the immortal warrior who from under his broad brimmed cowboy hat stares down the desperadoes before delivering justice with his six-shooter. In a lawless and dangerous era the Ranger has been portrayed as a defender of liberty and justice and a guardian of society who protected the civilized frontier from the depredations of American bandits, Mexican outlaws and Indian warriors. A Texas Ranger was a breed apart, a man who stood alone as a barrier between society and her enemies.

This stereotypical image of the Ranger corps has been reinforced, in a less dramatic fashion, in numerous academic publications. Notably, renowned Texan historian Walter P. Webb, in his classic work *The Texas Rangers*, published in 1935, stated that a ranger "could ride like a Mexican, trail like an Indian, shoot like a Tennessean, and fight like a devil"[1]. Webb highlighted Ranger captains as exceptional men who typically commanded respect, possessed intelligence, good judgment, and a complete absence of fear.[2] Webb further enhanced the aura of the Rangers by comparing the inevitably courageous Anglo-Texans to cruel and cowardly Mexicans and the primitive and ferocious native savages, who were incompatible with civilized

Anglo Saxon culture.³ Webb and other Texan historians including T.R. Fehrenbach have thus helped give scholarly authority to the popular heroic image of the Texas Rangers.

The Rangers, however, while idolized by some have also received significant criticism notably from the *Tejano* or Texas-Mexican community. The Rangers, it is claimed, acted as the law enforcement arm of the Anglo-Texan society as a tool to maintain white supremacy. *Tejanos* notably those who lived in the Rio Grande Valley frequently suffered from racial profiling and violence especially during the brutal suppression of the Plan de San Diego in 1915. '*El Corrido de Gregorio Cortez*' a popular Mexican-American folk ballad, glorifies a Mexican farm worker who killed a Texas sheriff in self-defense before eluding the hundreds of cowardly and incompetent Rangers who are unsuccessfully searching the chaparral country for a single Mexican fugitive.

Many Chicano and revisionist academics have also questioned the 'myth' of the ranger as genuine frontier heroes. Chicano intellectuals including Americo Paredes, J.T. Canales and Julian Samora have undertaken critical reexaminations of the historical role of the Texas Ranger corps and exposed a darker side to the ranger corps including brutality, corruption and the indiscriminate killing of potential suspects based solely on race. A classic example of this scholarship is *Gunpowder Justice*, first published in 1979, in which Julian Samora, Joe Bernal and Albert Pena sought "to shed some light on the long dark shadow behind the image."⁴ A number of more recent publications, while perhaps less critical of the ranger corps have nonetheless questioned their noble image. Benjamin Heber Johnson, writing in 2003, commented that the rangers represent the "embodiment of the Texan version of the American frontier myth."⁵ He acknowledged that the Ranger units acted courageously in protecting the white pioneers from Indians and outlaws but points out that a key function of the corps was to keep *Tejanos* as second class citizens throughout the 1800s.⁶ In *Policing the Great* Plains, by Andrew R. Graybill, published in 2007, the author compares the Texas Rangers to the Royal

Canadian Mounted Police. Both forces operated during the same time period in borderland regions of the Great Plains and both were tasked with pacifying the frontier for the benefit of larger national entities engaged in state building.[7] The key difference between the two corps when fulfilling this mission, Graybill maintains, was the exceptional levels of violence used by the Texas Rangers compared to the restraint shown by the Canadian Mounties.[8]

A Breed Apart: The History of the Texas Rangers, traces the origins of the Texas Rangers back to the 1820s and explores the organization's history from the years before Texan Independence through statehood, Civil War, Reconstruction and the modernization of the corps during the 20th century. The Texas Rangers were forged during the brutal War of Independence from Mexico and tempered by the fires of further conflicts with Native-Americans and the U.S. Mexican War. During the 1800s the Rangers protected the settlements against marauding Indian raiders and defended the international border from Mexican *bandidos*. The methods they used were frequently both morally and legally dubious but they operated in a dangerous and turbulent era that cannot be fairly judged by modern standards. In the late 19th and early 20th centuries the corps became increasingly corrupt and beholden to economic and political interests. The bloody counterinsurgency waged against the Mexican community during the Plan de San Diego was an exceptionally dark stain on the record of the Rangers.

In 1935, the corps was reorganized and incorporated into the newly formed Department of Public Safety. The newly formed DPS faced a range of challenges, yet under the astute leadership of Homer Garrison became a widely respected law enforcement agency. Although the Rangers received negative publicity for their alleged oppression of Tejano political activism in the sixties by the seventies Texans had virtually universally rallied around their cherished lawmen. By 2000, the Rangers were no longer a band of Anglo-Texan brothers, Hispanics and African-Americans were well represented in their ranks although few women had been deemed worthy to wear the *Cinco Peso*. In spite of repeated accusations, some merited, of the Rangers as a tool of Anglo economic interests and persistent questions over the continued need for a Ranger force the Texas Rangers remain an integral part of Texan law enforcement as well as a vibrant historical emblem of the American frontier.

In writing *A Breed Apart: The History of the Texas Rangers*, my intention is to explore and assess the fascinating yet at times controversial history and legacy of the Texas Rangers. In order to achieve this, I have primarily but not exclusively relied on previous scholarship on the Rangers, Texas, and a number of other academic fields including borderlands, military and Native-American histories as well as broader work on the American West. Every author, however, brings a different set of assumptions based in part on their personal beliefs and social or cultural milieu in which they live. I intend and hope to achieve the production of an accurate and unbiased narrative. With that aim in mind, I have sought to incorporate, wherever possible, a selection of works from authors whose differing viewpoints can only serve to strengthen my own understanding of the Texas Rangers and their history.

I am particularly indebted to the work of the following individuals. Renowned Texan historian Walter P. Webb, whose landmark book *The Texas Rangers* remains in my mind a masterpiece of historical scholarship. *Gunpowder Justice* by Julian Samora, Joe Bernal and Albert Pena along with Americo Paredes' *"With His Pistol in His Hand": A border ballad and its hero* provide useful insight on the *Tejano* perspective regarding Ranger history. *Lone Star: A History of Texas and the Texans* by T.R. Fehrenbach provided a wealth of material while the biographies of former Texas Ranger Joaquin H. Jackson, *One Ranger: A Memoir* and *One Ranger Returns*, are fascinating and insightful acccounts of Ranger operations in the mid to late 20th century. *Time of the Rangers* by Robert Cox along with both *Lone Star Justice* and *Lone Star Lawmen* authored by Robert M. Utley proved to be a vast resource of information on the history of the Texas Rangers.

1823-1865

1

Humble Beginnings

The history of the Texas Rangers begins with the arrival of Anglo-American settlers and their citizen soldier tradition in the then Mexican province of *Tejas*. Texas was first colonized by the Spanish in 1690 as a strategic imperialist move to counter the growing French presence in Louisiana. Missionaries provided the first wave of colonists but by 1718 a civilian settlement had been constructed at San Antonio. Cattle ranches known as *rancheros* sprang up in the chaparral country and the Nueces Strip north of the Rio Grande paving the way for the future Anglo-Texan cattle kingdom of the mid to late 1800s.[9]

The *Tejano* population remained low, however, a mere four thousand colonists in 1804, prompting Spanish concerns over the security and viability of the province. In 1821 Mexico achieved independence from Spain after an eleven year armed struggle. In the Constitution of Mexico of 1824 the new government combined Texas with the more heavily populated region of Coahuila to form a new province of *Coahuila y Tejas*. The Texan settlements remained isolated and underpopulated. The Mexican government concerned about both continued American expansion westward following the Louisiana Purchase of 1803 and Indian raids turned to immigration as a solution.

Empresario grants were offered to well-connected individuals who would develop and administer settlements which in the view of the Mexican authorities would provide a buffer zone against both the

Indian tribes and the rapid spread of the American republic. Settlers were permitted to take up to 4438 acres of irrigable land with additional grants for those raising cattle. The *empresarios*, however, were exempt from these restrictions.[10] In 1825 Mexico enacted the General Colonization Law which allowed all heads of household, regardless of nationality or race or to claim land in Mexico.[11]

Stephen F. Austin was the first *empresario,* his settlers, known in Texan lore as the 'Old Three Hundred', colonized the region between the Brazos and Colorado rivers in the years between 1821 and 1824. The majority of the *empresarios* were Anglo-American, only one, Martin de León, was born in Mexico. Officially Mexican law required immigrants to learn Spanish, practice Catholicism and emancipate their slaves.[12] In practice these laws were frequently ignored. By the same standard many Anglo-American settlers both legal colonists and illegal squatters often ignored the injunction to request permission from local Mexican authorities before settling in the region.

The new arrivals colonized the humid woodlands and coastal plains of eastern Texas. The settlers were generally Southerners, wealthy planters grew cotton on large scale plantations around the coastal plains while frontiersmen established small farms and ranches growing corn and raising cattle. Both groups brought with them key elements of Southern culture including defending a masculine honor and a penchant for violence. The settlers were further aware that emigration to Texas could lead to conflict with native tribes and in this they were not mistaken.[13]

During the 1820s a number of Native-American groupings considered Texas to be their home. The Caddo Confederacy of the eastern woodlands were primarily agriculturalists cultivating crops such as corn and maize. The Caddo Indians for the most part offered the hand of friendship to the European settlers. The colonists early interaction with other tribes proved to be less convivial and frequently resulted in violence. The Karankawas of the coastal region, while not numerous, proved to be ferocious fighters who proved adept at attacking and disrupting the maritime trade.

In the region between the eastern forests and the Great Plains dwelt a variety of tribal groups including the Tonkawas, Tawakonis, Wichitas and Lipan Apaches. To varying degrees these tribes both farmed and also hunted the buffalo herds for subsistence. These groups frequently raided the Anglo settlements in search of horses or other stock. In time, however, it would prove to be the Comanche who would pose the greatest threat to Anglo settlement of Texas. The Comanche bands followed the vast buffalo herds and engaged in raid/trade relationship with other groups. whether native of European. The Comanche through the adoption of a horse based culture developed into feared raiders and warriors who had formed a barrier to both Spanish and Mexican imperial aspirations in the Southwest.[14]

As *empresario*, Stephen F. Austin was granted considerable authority over the colony's security and military defense. Austin himself was endowed with the title of Lieutenant Colonel of militia. The danger of Indian raids was omnipresent and magnified by the lack of military support from the Mexican authorities. The immediate concern for Austin was to ensure the safety of the settlements and thus secure their growth and more importantly continued viability to exist. In August 1823, Austin called for a force of ten Rangers to defend the frontier and screen the settlements from hostile attacks. Austin offered fifteen dollars a month in land to those who enlisted as Rangers. The empresario, was influenced by both the Mexican governor, José Félix Trespalacios, who gave permission for a paid volunteer militia and the example of Lieutenant Moses Morrison who had formed a unit of ten men in May 1823 for community protection. There is little evidence, however, that any Rangers supplemented Morrison's tiny force and the nascent corps was disbanded in the fall of 1823 after the Mexican authorities failed to provide pay or supplies.[15]

The growth of the colony between 1823 and 1826 sparked an increase in native hostilities leading Austin to issue a new call for a Ranger company. Austin himself, led an 1823 militia against Tonkawa horse thieves preying on the Colorado river settlements. The Karankawas were responsible for the vast majority of fatal attacks until 1824 when a strong militia action forced the tribe to agree to remaining west of the San Antonio river. The Tawakonis posed the greatest problem for the colonists after 1824, together with the Wacos, they possessed a force of over two hundred warriors. In 1826 a Tawakoni horse raid deep into the settlements was only defeated by the actions of militia Captain James J. Ross who gathered a thirty-one man force which killed eight and wounded five Tawakonis. In August of that year Austin met with leaders of the six militia districts and proposed a permanently mounted corps to guard the frontier and screen the colony from potential Indian attacks. It was agreed that a force of twenty to thirty mounted Rangers would be permanently in the saddle to protect the settlements. Every Texan landowner or a substitute was required to serve for at least a month for every half league of land they owned.[16]

The Rangers, as envisaged by Austin, stemmed from the historical roots of the citizen soldier tradition in North America. The first English settlers had formed militia units or posses to defend their families and communities from native tribes, outlaws and later during the American Revolution, the British redcoats. As the frontier expanded westwards into Ohio, Kentucky and the 'old Southwest' of Mississippi and Louisiana the citizen soldier became the key defender of the settlements and American liberty. In Texas over the following decades the Ranger corps attracted a variety of men. Frontier farmers joined the corps to protect their families in times of danger while a number of rangers were young men who coming from the Southern martial tradition enlisted for the thrill of battle as much as for the low wages.[17]

The immediate impact of Austin's call for a Ranger unit is less clear. The lack of documentary evidence impedes our knowledge of this corps leading historians to wonder when and where it was formed, if it ever engaged in battles and even whether it was actually implemented as an irregular frontier force. Until 1835 we have no records to indicate Ranger activity or lack thereof. Ironically, it would be the fire of revolution and not the Indian threat that would lead to the true *naissance* of the Texas Rangers.

2
The Crucible of War

On March 2 1836, at Washington-on-the Brazos, Texan delegates formally declared independence from the Mexican Republic. A little over two months later on May 14th the Mexican Presidential dictator, General Antonio Lopez de Santa Anna, a prisoner of the Texan army following the decisive victory at San Jacinto signed the Treaty of Velasco guaranteeing Texan independence and an end to the war. The brutal and bloody revolution made Texas a nation, bequeathed a legacy of further conflict with Mexico, immortalized the defence of the Alamo as a Texan Thermopylae and most importantly in the context of this book, initiated the dawn of the Texas Rangers.

The Texan War of Independence or Texas Revolution stemmed primarily from tensions between the growing tide of Anglo-American immigrants and the Mexican Federal Republic. By 1834 Texas was home to over thirty thousand Anglos, both legal immigrants and illegal squatters, compared to less than eight thousand *Tejanos*. Anglo-Texas was prepared to accept the Mexican flag and live under the umbrella of the Mexican nation but for all intents and purposes it remained a self-reliant mini republic.[18] The inherent tensions in such structural model soon became clear. Most American immigrants rejected Catholicism and few made an effort to learn the Spanish language. Many were Southerners determined to transplant the cotton plantation culture dependent on slave labor to a Mexican Texas where slavery had been abolished in 1823 by federal decree. Race also played a major role, Anglo-Texans regarded the Mexican nation with distaste and disrespect considering them to be a degenerate *mestizo* race of mixed native and Hispanic ancestry.[19] The failed Fredonian rebellion of 1826-1827 when *empresario* Haden Edwards attempted to create a Republic of Fredonia near Nacogdoches is seen by some historians as a precursor to the Texan War of Independence.[20]

The actions of the Mexican Government combined with the growing political instability in Mexico aggravated the situation. The Edict of 1830 passed by the Mexican Congress primarily forbade any further American immigration into Texas as well placing customs duties and taxes on the previously exempt Anglo communities, ordered the settlement of Mexican convicts in Texas and placed the region under greater federal control. The edict was viewed with great consternation by the Anglo-Texan communities as it placed intolerable regulations on a fiercely independent pioneer people and the suspension of further immigration threatened the very survival of their communities.[21]

The collapse of the Mexican political system into anarchy further exacerbated the situation. *Yorkinos*, liberal federalists who supported greater autonomy for the regions clashed militarily with *escoceses* who favored a strong centralized government.[22] In 1834 General Santa Anna seized control and assumed dictatorial powers included the abolition of the Mexican Constitution of 1824.[23] A number of Mexican states including *Querétaro, Tamaulipas, Yucatán* and *Zacatecas* rebelled against Santa Anna engulfing Mexico in the flames of civil conflict. The *Tejanos* also harbored a number of federalists in their communities resulting in the Mexican government dispatching troops, many of whom were former convicts, north of the Rio Grande. The Texans, unused to and deeply despising of military rule, were angered by the swaggering and insulting behavior of the Mexican soldiery who flouted their authority and power regardless of Texan sensibilities.[24]

The Anglo-Texans were divided into two camps; the War Party comprised primarily of illegal immigrants who held no allegiance to

Mexico. They sought the annexation of Texas to the U.S. and viewed the *Tejanos* with a mixture of suspicion and racial prejudice. The so called Peace Party headed by Stephen F. Austin and supported by many legal colonists shared much in common with the *Yorkinos*. Their leaders sought greater political and economic autonomy from the central government including Texan separation from Coahuila which was far more heavily Hispanic and held a different economic agenda. The Peace Party, however, did not seek Texan independence merely a degree of self-rule within the Federal Republic of Mexico. The swift escalation of hostilities, however, dictated an alliance between both elements of the Anglo communities and the *Tejano* federalists.

The spark that set Texas ablaze occurred in Gonzales on October 2 1835. Captain Francisco Castañeda supported by approximately two hundred Mexican soldiers demanded the return of a brass six pound cannon which had been previously issued by Mexico for the purposes of frontier defense. Future Ranger captain John H. Moore, the leader of the Texan forces at Gonzales, refused and ordered his men to open fire. A brief skirmish ensued before the Mexican military retreated back to San Antonio.[25] By December of 1835 the Texan rebels had captured both Goliad and San Antonio including the strategic *presidio* or fortress known as the Alamo.[26]

General Santa Anna, stung into action by the earlier defeats, rapidly assembled an army of over six thousand men in northern Mexico before advancing into Texas and laying siege to the Alamo on February 23 1836. The defense of the Alamo has achieved near mythical status in Texan history, for twelve long days around two hundred Texans commanded by William Barret Travis and including in their number legendary Western figures Davy Crockett and James Bowie held out against a force of approximately five thousand Mexicans. Santa Anna had won the battle but it was a pyrrhic victory, nearly sixteen hundred Mexican soldiers had been killed and the general had wasted nearly two weeks attacking the old fortress. Significantly, the brutal butchering of the surviving defenders including Davy Crockett and subsequent execution of over three hundred Texan prisoners at

Goliad angered not only the Anglo-Texan community but also the United States helping to stimulate a flood of volunteers to the Texan cause.[27]

Santa Anna believing that victory was won and the Texan resistance broken divided his army into five columns with orders to drive the Anglo population back into the U.S. and destroy everything in their path. During next weeks known as the 'Runaway Scrape' virtually the entire Anglo community fled east even abandoning Gonzales to Santa Anna's army. Sam Houston, the military leader of the Texan forces, mirrored this retreat and maneuvered his forces back towards Louisiana.[28] On April 21 1836, prodded by the eagerness of the rank and file soldiers, Houston attacked and decisively crushed a Mexican flying column led by Santa Anna himself, the Mexican dictator was captured hiding in a swamp wearing the uniform of a private. The bitter war for Texan Independence was over. [29]

The fires of the revolution signaled the official creation of the soon to be legendary Texas Rangers. On November 20 1835 the permanent council of Texas passed an ordinance calling for three companies of Rangers, each company comprised of fifty-six men commanded by a captain supported by a first and second lieutenant. A major in command supervised Ranger operations and reported to the Texan commander in chief. The Ranger privates enlisted for one year and were paid one dollar and twenty-five cents daily. Eight days later on November 28 the officers of the corps were elected. R. M. Williamson was elected major while Isaac W. Burton, William H. Arrington and John J. Tumlinson became captains.[30] A year later, on December 10 1836, the congress of the Republic of Texas enacted legislation providing that all officers and privates employed as Rangers since July 1835 shall receive pay from their time of enlistment. Essentially, the law ensured that July 1835 would be formally recognized as the date that established the beginning of the Ranger corps.[31]

The new Ranger force only played a minor role in the revolutionary era. In February 1836, during the 'Runaway Scrape', Major Williamson ordered the company of John Tumlinson to Bastrop.

Tumlinson and his rangers played an important role covering the military retreat and protecting the fleeing civilian population. Williamson himself joined Houston's army as a private and saw action at San Jacinto.[32] The Rangers' most notable feat during the war was the capture of three Mexican ships with supplies valued at twenty-five thousand dollars. Captain Isaac W. Burton had been dispatched to the gulf coast with twenty men to keep watch for Mexican naval activity. On June 3 1836, Burton and his tiny force assaulted the *Watchman*, a Mexican vessel before luring the officers of two other ships, the *Comanche* and the *Fanny Butler* into a trap and seizing their boats and cargo. The bold Captain Burton and his Rangers were subsequently known as and glorified in the title of 'horse marines'.[33]

The Indian tribes were a major concern for the newly formed Texan council who rightly feared the specter of simultaneous military conflict with both the numerically superior Mexican forces and the native peoples. The council sought to develop of policy of friendship with the Texas-Indians at least for the duration of the revolution. Notably the Texan leadership dispatched peace commissioners to the Cherokee, new arrivals in East Texas following their tragic removal from their homeland in Georgia, and passed a resolution to engage in a treaty of friendship and trade with the Comanche people. For the most part, these efforts bore fruit, there exists little evidence of significant Indian depredations during the war for independence.[34] One glaring exception was January 1836, when Captain Tumlinson, based out of Brushy Creek to prevent Comanche raids, engaged in the hot pursuit of a Comanche raiding party. The band had taken captive a Mrs. Hibbons and her three year old boy after murdering her husband, brother and baby son. The redoubtable Mrs. Hibbons escaped her Comanche captors and fortuitously stumbled upon the Ranger unit who immediately gave chase and caught the Indians at camp on Walnut Creek killing one and rescuing the young child.[35]

The Texan War of Independence was the spur that stimulated the creation of a Ranger corps. Faced by a dual need to screen the civilian population from a powerful invading army bent of eliminating every vestige of Anglo Texan society while concurrently protecting the frontier from marauding Indians the Texan council opted for an irregular body of mounted horsemen independent from both the army and the militia. The Texas Rangers were born into a crucible of war and would be hardened by the decades of violence yet to come.

3
Los Comanches and the Indian Troubles

The years following the revolution were far from peaceful, the Texans had won their de facto independence from Mexico but still faced formidable foes in the form of the native tribes determined to defend their land and way of life. The Texans had been able to placate many Indian groups, including the Comanche, during the conflict by offering treaties of friendship and trade but in the aftermath of independence the flames of war once again engulfed the young nation. Time and time again the Texan frontier witnessed the atrocities of rape, murder and torture. The military defeat or eradication of the native tribes thus became the primary task of the newly formed Ranger corps.

While Ranger operations would be conducted against a variety of tribes including the Apache, Keechis, Tawakonis and Wacos, it was the Comanche who posed the most potent threat to the expansion of Anglo civilization. The Comanche are a Shoshonean speaking people who emerged as a distinct ethnic group shortly before 1700, when they broke off from the Shoshone people and moved south from the upper Platte River in Wyoming towards present day Texas. By the mid 18th century the Comanche had pushed the plains Apache west into New Mexico and forced the Utes to retreat into the Rocky

Mountains. At the pinnacle of Comanche power their homeland, the *Comancheria*, consisted of present-day eastern New Mexico, southern Colorado, southern Kansas, parts of Oklahoma, and most of northwest Texas.

The Comanche were a warrior people whose whole ethos and way of life was based primarily on war and a system of war honors. From a very young age Comanche boys were brought up to engage in and respect the warrior codes. The prestige gained by war honors was integral to Comanche existence. The military nature of Comanche society led to Comanche warriors becoming the most deadly and efficient horseman on the southern plains.[36] The tribe also used warfare for economic purposes, specifically the lucrative trade in slaves and plunder.[37] Comanche war bands often raided as far as three to four hundred miles from their bases.[38] northern Mexico was a favored target of Comanche war parties who frequently rode south by the light of a full moon, leading to the term a 'Comanche moon'. Brian DeLay in *The War of a Thousand Deserts*, argued that in the decade before the U.S.-Mexican War the impact of large scale and systematic Comanche raids into northern Mexico turned the region into a desolate 'desert' which both promoted and facilitated American conquest.

The Comanche system of war honors however, also led to a penchant for brutal killing and horrific torture of captives. According to T. R. Fehrenbach, the war parties would massacre all those they had no need for including old men and women and children too old to be useful slaves. Adult captives were frequently tortured, and due to the Comanche belief in male courage rites, men suffered particularly painful and degrading forms of torture.[39] As a result of this belief system many settlers both Hispanic and Anglo as well as numerous other Native Americans suffered the most appalling and horrifying torments before dying. The native art of warfare and the brutalities committed on Anglo Americans led to in the words of Fehrenbach; "the total dehumanization of the native race in the American mind."[40]

In the classic revisionist work, *The Comanche Empire*, published in 2008, Pekka Hamalainen argued that Comanche were a major historical actor who used diplomacy, economic exploitation and military force to dominate the colonial Southwest. The tribe possessed an advanced economic political and social structure ranging from a separation of powers between civil chiefs and war chiefs, elite military cults, a structured integration policy that allowed the assimilation of other nations, religious beliefs, a malleable system of social slavery and a market-oriented system of animal husbandry that led to a highly profitable trade network.[41] Furthermore, according to Hamalainen, the Comanche also possessed a highly elaborate foreign policy in their dealings with neighboring peoples whether Indian or European. Grand alliances were made and broken as required and when negotiating with the Spanish or Mexican authorities in New Mexico and Texas the Comanche operated from a position of military and economic superiority and as a result the nature and length of the alliances was formulated for Comanche interests and on Comanche terms.[42] If Hamalainen is to be believed, the Texans were not confronting a primitive nomadic people they were engaging in conflict with a mighty Native-American empire.

The decades of the 1830s and 1840s saw spiraling levels of violence between the Comanche and the newly independent Republic of Texas. Sam Houston, the first president of the Republic of Texas sought to address the Indian conflict through treaties of peace and trading relations. Texan emissaries concluded treaties with several native tribes including the Southern or *Penateka* Comanche in May 1838. What Houston tragically failed to realize was that the *Penateka* chiefs could only speak for their own tribal grouping not the Comanche nation and even within the Southern Comanche the loose authority that the leaders held over the tribe could not prevent individual warriors from engaging in raids.[43]

Furthermore, the Comanche resented the appearance of surveyors on the Pedernales River recognizing their presence as the harbinger of Anglo-Texan encroachment on their land. The treaty also failed to resolve the thorny issue of territorial boundaries, the Comanche sought a permanent frontier between the *Comancheria* and the Anglo

Texans while the Republic of Texas was not prepared to entertain any Comanche claim to her land. The accession of Mirabeau Bonaparte Lamar to the Texan presidency in December 1838 ended any chance of a negotiated peace. Lamar detested both Houston and Indians, in his inaugural address he demanded the "total extinction or total expulsion" of the Texas Indians.[44]

The Comanche were also not prepared to end their raids through Texan territory into northern Mexico, an excellent source of trade wealth especially horses and mules.[45] Between 1830 and 1846 it is estimated that the Comanche stole over 100,000 horses from northern Mexico alone.[46] The trade in captives was also lucrative for the Comanche, many were taken to the *Comancheria* as slaves, other captives were used as economic pawns and were ransomed often to *Comanchero* traders from New Mexico.[47]

The peace treaties that the Comanche made with neighboring tribes indirectly led to a major increase in Comanche raids. In 1834 the Comanche made peace with the Osage, a traditional rival and also settled their differences with the newly relocated eastern tribes such as the Cherokee. Six years later in 1840 the Comanche, Arapaho and Cheyenne agreed the so called 'Great Peace'.[48] The peace pacts not only provided security for the Comanche homeland while the warriors were raiding, but the new allies also became trading partners thus increasing the incentive to obtain plunder.

During this period the Rangers served as the primary defenders of the fledgling Texan nation and developed an inherent animosity and enmity to the Comanche. The Texans and later the Americans fundamentally failed to comprehend the codes that the Comanche lived by which permitted them engage in ferocious warfare, but then sit down and negotiate peace. A culture of frontier ignorance and hatred thus permeated the corps leading on occasion to atrocities being committed. The Texan war against the Comanche proved to be exceptionally violent and characterized by brutality on both sides.

Following Texan Independence the first notable clash between Rangers and Indians occurred on November 10 1835, the so-called

Battle of Stone Houses. The opponents were not the feared Comanche but the Keechis, who ignoring their treaty obligations, raided Fort Smith on the Little River. Lieutenant A. B. Van Benthusen and seventeen rangers caught up with the Keechi band just south of present day Windhorst but the tiny ranger force was routed by the Indians who killed nine Rangers and stole the all the mounts forcing the remaining Rangers to make a slow and humiliating journey to the Sabine River.

The Cherokee also posed problems for the Republic of Texas. On May 18 1839, Ranger lieutenant James O. Rice and seventeen men engaged in a battle with a mixed party of around twenty five Indians and Mexicans. One of the dead was a Mexican citizen by the name of Manuel Flores, on his body the Rangers found documents revealing negotiations between the Cherokee and Mexico planning a joint military campaign against Texas which if successful would lead to the creation of an Indian buffer state between the Mexico and the expansionist United States.[49] Evidence was also uncovered of correspondence between Flores and 'The Bowl', a prominent Cherokee chief and Vincente Córdova, a Mexican agent who two months earlier had instigated a failed Kickapoo uprising around Nacogdoches.[50] Texas Rangers led by Captain Mathew Caldwell had pursued a wounded Córdova but failed to apprehend the fugitive.

The Córdova Rebellion and the evidence linking the Cherokee nation to Mexican intrigues provided President Lamar with the justification he sought to expel the Cherokee from Texan territory. In July 1839, followed failed negotiations over the exact terms of the Cherokee removal, a force of over five hundred men including two Ranger companies commanded by Captains James Ownsby and Mark B. Lewis moved against the Indians. The Battle of the Neches lasted over two days and when the shooting stopped over a hundred Cherokee including 'The Bowl' lay dead.[51] The Texans completed the removal process by driving out eight other tribes including the Kickapoos and Seminoles. While morally unjustifiable, on a political and military level the expulsion policy of Mirabeau Lamar was a clear success, at least in dealing with the eastern tribes.

The Comanche, numbering close to thirty thousand, the undisputed lords of the southern plains who controlled a vast region between the Arkansas River and the Balcones Escarpment would prove to be far more challenging opponents.[52] The first years of Lamar's presidency were marked by near constant raiding by Comanche war parties. In March 1840, however, a delegation of *Penateka* Comanche led by Muk-war-rah came to San Antonio to negotiate peace. The *Penateka* bands were more vulnerable to Texan retaliations and had been weakened by devastating smallpox epidemics.[53] The chiefs were also well aware of the value that the Texans placed on Anglo captives and sought to exploit this to achieve favorable terms.

The sixty-five Comanches who attended the peace conference brought with them a Texan captive, a young girl by the name of Matilda Lockhart. Her scarred and mutilated body angered the Texan delegates who were then driven into a fury by her report of other captives held by the Indians who were intending to ransom them individually as bargaining chips. The outraged commissioners then ordered the chiefs to remain as prisoners until the all the captives were released in accordance with previous pledges. At this point pandemonium broke out both inside and outside the council house. When the shooting stopped, thirty-five Comanche were dead, including twelve chiefs. The Council House Fight, was understandable from a Texan angle, the chiefs had been acting dishonestly and sparked the violence by aggressively resisting arrest. From the Comanche perspective, however, it was an act of unforgivable treachery.[54]

Comanche culture demanded an appropriate retaliation, six months later in August 1840, the *Penateka* war chief Buffalo Hump, who had scorned the peace talks in San Antonio, led a party of over six hundred warriors on a mission of revenge. The huge Comanche force sacked and burned the town of Victoria before plundering the port of Linnville. The warriors, by this point, laden down with booty, then turned their horses back to the *Comancheria*.[55] The Texans reacted swiftly to the attacks on Victoria and Linnville. Ranger captains Mathew Caldwell and Ben McCulloch helped to assemble a combined Ranger and militia force of approximately two hundred men which confronted the numerically superior Comanche host at Plum Creek. The Ranger captains, experienced in Indian warfare, called for a mounted charge which broke the Comanche lines and led to a decisive Texan victory. Captain John H. Moore raised two companies of volunteers who pursued the fleeing raiders and in October attacked and destroyed a Comanche village on the Colorado River.[56]

The Battle of Plum Creek was a staggering defeat for the Comanche. Nearly one hundred and fifty warriors were killed and the raiders lost virtually all their plunder. The Comanche would never again attempt to burn down large towns or confront the Texan forces en masse. The battle also demonstrated the growing competence and spirit of the Texas Rangers when confronted by Indian foes. Rangers such as Edward Burleson, Mathew Caldwell and Ben McCulloch were developing into skilled and hardened Indian fighters who exhibited both extraordinary fighting ability and leadership. Notably, the future ranger legend, John "Coffee" Hays, a twenty-four year old newcomer to Texas demonstrated sufficient courage and skill at Plum Creek to be given the captaincy of a company based in San Antonio.[57]

Hays' name echoes through Texan lore as the Ranger captain all future rangers would seek to emulate. Hays was born in Little Cedar Lick, Tennessee and trained as a surveyor before joining the Ranger corps. Under his leadership the company he commanded, which included the renowned Indian fighter, William A. A. 'Bigfoot' Wallace, epitomized the very best of the Ranger tradition. Hays instigated vigorous training routines to improve both marksmanship and horsemanship. He was particularly determined that his men would become the equals of the Comanche when in the saddle and borrowed elements of Mexican *vaquero* equipment and Comanche techniques to achieve his goal.[58]

In 1841, Hays' Rangers though outnumbered, won victories over the Comanche at the battles of the Llano and Bandera Pass. Notably during the Battle of the Llano, under the leadership of Captain Hays, twenty five rangers put to flight over two hundred Comanche braves.

In 1844 Hays equipped his company with Paterson Colt revolving pistols from surplus Texan navy materiel.[59] On June 8th at Walker Creek, fourteen Texas Rangers armed with Paterson Colts and commanded by "Coffee" Hays routed a Comanche force comprised of seventy warriors who left over twenty-three dead on the battlefield.[60]

On December 29 1845 Texas was formally annexed by the U.S. and admitted to the union as the twenty-eighth state. The Comanche threat, however, remained unresolved and in fact during the years following Texan annexation the new state saw a dramatic increase in Comanche raids. It has been argued by some historians including Walter P. Webb that the increased Comanche attacks between 1848 and 1858 were the product of ineffective federal military and Indian policies. Webb suggests that the Rangers, could have handled the escalating violence but were given no financial support and limited legal status by the federal government.

There is certainly more than a degree of truth to this analysis. By 1850 the U.S. Army had stationed only fifteen hundred soldiers garrisoned in a handful of forts to protect a four hundred mile frontier between the Red River and the Rio Grande as well as a turbulent international border with Mexico that stretched over a thousand miles. Furthermore, approximately eighty percent of the soldiers in Texas were infantry wholly unsuitable to defend against or pursue mounted raiders.[61] Needless to say, despite fortifying the Texas frontier with artillery, dragoons, infantry and even camels, the U.S. military presence was totally inadequate and entirely unable to protect the Texan frontier.[62]

The federal government's policy of annuities and reservations for allegedly peaceful tribes aggravated the situation. The Comanche treated the Americans and Texans as two separate peoples and the northern bands saw no hypocrisy in signing a peace treaty with the U.S. government but continuing to engage in violent raids into Texas. In 1855, Indian agent Robert Neighbors noted that every fall the Northern Comanche and their Kiowa allies would receive ten thousand dollars in gifts from the federal government yet this huge sum did not equate with the vast plunder the tribes had looted from the Texans each summer. Neighbors also observed that during the 1850s Indian bands known to be ravaging the Texas settlements were being issued guns and ammunition by the U.S. itself.[63]

American traders based on the Arkansas River and within Indian Territory proved to be willing trading partners of the Comanche stimulating further bloodshed in Texas. Furthermore, the federal policy of relocating eastern tribes to the Indian Territory exacerbated the situation by both leading to further competition for dwindling resources and providing new trading partners for goods stolen in Texas.[64] Especially aggravating for the Texans was the fact that federal law prohibited incursions by state forces onto the Indian reservations giving marauding bands a safe haven from retaliation.

An inherent tension, however, also existed over the differing Texan and federal philosophies regarding Native-Americans. While the U.S. promoted a policy of peace treaties and reservations, Texans preferred the less tolerant option, of simple expulsion, by whatever means, of hostile tribes from the Lone Star state.[65] The Texans were somewhat hypocritical in expecting the federal government to adopt the expenses of frontier defense yet accept that Texan institutions would be responsible for the implementation. The army and the Rangers as the representative military arms of the U.S. and Texas respectively thus held deeply different convictions of how to deal with the Indian threat. While the U.S. Army sought to police the borderlands and prevent breaches of the peace, the Rangers, who possessed an innate hostility to the Texas Indians, rode to avenge or punish and did so with lethal ferocity.[66]

As early as 1849 the U.S. government and army leadership recognized the need for a federalized Ranger force. In spite of his serious misgivings over the effectiveness of Ranger operations and inherent mistrust of the corps, Brevet Major General George M. Brooke, in September of that year, federalized three ranger companies. A fourth company, led by 'BigFoot' Wallace, was mobilized in March 1850. These four companies joined the eight Ranger units in state service in guarding the frontier. The federal ranger units, however, only remained in state service until late 1851.[67] From statehood to secession Texan governors and legislators continuously barraged Washington with demands for federalized Rangers. For the most part, however, the requests fell on deaf ears.

Nevertheless, the Texas Rangers played an important role in combating the Comanche threat during the years before the Civil War. The mid to late 1850s were marked by escalating levels of violence as the line of settlement inexorably expanded towards the Comanche homeland, the *Comancheria*. On January 27, 1858, Governor Hardin Rummels appointed John "Rip" Ford as captain and supreme commander of a combined Texas Ranger, Militia, and Indian Force.[68] Ford, like John "Coffee" Hays, was originally from Tennessee. An individual with many talents, Ford had studied law, practiced medicine, engaged in politics and edited an Austin newspaper before becoming a Texas Ranger captain in 1849 at the age of thirty four. Ford proved to be an exemplar Ranger captain who reduced the Comanche threat on the frontier in part by the vigorous training of his men giving special attention to the techniques of Comanche warfare.[69] Governor Rummels who had campaigned on a political platform of ending Comanche raids ordered Ford to carry the battle to the Comanche in the heart of their homeland on the *Comancheria*.

On May 12 Ford's Rangers supported by around a hundred Indian allies including Tonkawa warriors attacked several Comanche villages including one controlled by the allegedly invulnerable chief known as Iron Jacket due to the Spanish armor that he wore. In the ensuing attack, known as the Battle of Antelope Hills the Rangers engaged over three hundred Indians killing seventy-six including Chief Iron Jacket and capturing over three hundred horses. The remaining Comanche villages in the vicinity were saved by the intervention of Chief Peta Nocona whose warriors delayed the Texans allowing the villages along the Canadian to swiftly retreat.[70] The Battle of the Antelope Hills dealt a significant psychological blow to the Comanche, for the first time in history the Texans had penetrated deep into the *Comancheria* destroying villages and decisively defeating a Comanche force. The operation also served as a model for the regular Army, General Twiggs, inspired by Ford, ordered Brevet Major Earl Van Dorn and four companies of the Second U.S. Cavalry across the Red River into Comanche territory. At Rush Springs and Crooked Creek Van Dorn achieved significant victories over the Comanche.[71]

Sam Houston, 'the Old Lion', won the gubernatorial election of 1859. A cornerstone of his Indian policy was peace with the Comanche. Although his long standing principles inclined Houston to use diplomatic means, the desperate pleas for frontier protection led the new governor to authorize a major military offensive. Between January and March of 1860, Houston ordered seven companies of Texas Rangers to patrol the frontier and within two months the governor had deployed nearly one thousand men to combat the Comanche threat.[72] Houston also subjected the fiercely independent Ranger units to severe oversight including moral guidelines that forbade drinking, gambling and horse racing.[73] In March, Houston appointed Middleton T. Johnson a wealthy cotton planter as commander of the ranger regiment. Johnson, however, proved to be an utterly incompetent commander, during the summer of 1860, he located no hostile Indians, provoked a confrontation with the U.S. Army, and drained the Texas treasury.[74] In August the Ranger regiment led by Johnson was disbanded by gubernatorial order.

Houston was able to claim one notable success. On December 18 1860, newly appointed Ranger captain Sul Ross discovered and attacked a Comanche village at Mule Creek. Virtually the entire band including women and children were slain by the Rangers and reputedly Ross himself killed Chief Peta Nocona in single combat although this is disputed by a number of historians who believe that in fact Nocona was out hunting at the time of the battle. The attack which has become known as the Battle of Pease River is renowned for the liberation of Cynthia Ann Parker who had been captured as a young girl twenty four years earlier during the Fort Parker Massacre of 1836. During her years with the tribe Cynthia Ann had married Peta Nocona and their son Quanah Parker would be remembered as the last great Comanche chief.[75]

The record of the Texas Rangers as frontier defenders during this era is mixed. When led by captains such as John "Coffee" Hays and "Rip Ford" the Ranger corps achieved notable victories over the Comanche and proved to be far more competent guardians of the settlements than the U.S. Army. Under incompetent or weak leadership, however, Ranger units proved to be ineffective as citizen soldiers. In the late 1850s ranger companies commanded by John H. Connor, Neill Robinson and Thomas C. Frost achieved nothing of any positive note.[76] The failings of Middleton T. Johnson despoiled the luster of the Ranger image and embarrassed the Texan leadership. Most significantly, however, is the salient fact that despite the bravery and heroism exhibited by many rangers and the victories that they won, the Comanche remained a potent danger and would continue to pose a threat until the 1870s.

4
Los Diablos Tejanos

The Alamo laid the seeds for the myth of *Los Diablo Tejanos* in Mexican lore. When the fury of the battle had passed and the dust settled over the Mexican army the church bells of San Fernando rang a terrible toll. Over fifteen hundred crack soldiers, the cream of Mexican military lay dead. Another five hundred were grievously wounded. A mere two hundred Texans based in a crumbling fort had not only delayed a five thousand strong professional army by twelve crucial days but had inflicted a morale sapping and soul destroying number of casualties.[77] The Texas Rangers over ensuing decades would cement the legend of the Texan Devils in Mexican history. The corps became renowned for both incredible courage but would also leave a darker legacy of violence and brutal atrocities.

Following Texan Independence in 1836, Mexico remained a powerful threat to the young republic. The Treaty of Velasco which formally acknowledged Texan independence was never ratified in Mexico. Following the debacle at San Jacinto, Santa Anna had been deposed as president of Mexico and his centralist successors claimed that he had no authority to represent the Mexican government. Following his return to power, Santa Anna himself reneged on his promise and threatened to re-conquer the new nation. Although the Republic of Texas received diplomatic recognition from the United States, in Mexican eyes Texas remained a province in revolt.[78]

Furthermore, a festering territorial issue dogged Texan-Mexican relations. In 1836, the Texan Congress asserted that the Rio Grande would form the southern and western border of the republic despite the fact that the under both Spanish and Mexican rule the Nueces river had designated the southern boundary of the province. Mexico rejected the Texan claim and the Nueces Strip located between the two rivers remained a hotly contested region patrolled by both Mexican soldiers and Texas Rangers. The imperialist ambitions of President Lamar also escalated tensions between the two nations. Lamar coveted the Mexican province of New Mexico especially the lucrative trade between Santa Fe and Missouri. He envisaged stimulating the Texan economy by rerouting the trail southeast to Houston and dreamed of swelling the republic's empty coffers with the substantive customs fees.[79]

Anglo-Texans also harbored a deep seated conviction of their racial superiority over the mixed race *mestizo* nation of Mexico. This prejudice inflamed by the violent legacy of the Texan Revolution and the atrocities at the Alamo and Goliad embedded in the Texan mindset a vicious animosity towards both Mexicans and *Tejanos* which aggravated socioeconomic tensions and planted the seeds of future conflicts.[80]

It was in fact aggressive Texan actions which sparked the first of several clashes between the two nations. President Lamar, as noted earlier, sought to incorporate New Mexico into Texas and in 1841 initiated a bold scheme to seize the Mexican province. In June of that year the grandiosely named Santa Fe Expedition departed from Brushy Creek near Austin with the intention of negotiating a peaceful conquest.[81] In spite of the Texas Congress repeatedly refusing to provide funding President Lamar simply removed eight-nine thousand dollars to pay for the expedition. The column of over three hundred men included a military contingent, merchants and official delegates of the Texan Republic. While not an official Texas Ranger action many Rangers participated in the undertaking. Ranger captain Mathew Caldwell commanded one of the military companies.[82]

History has judged the Santa Fe Expedition to be a total fiasco. The ill advised, badly equipped and poorly led column endured great hardship as it straggled across plains and desert to Santa Fe. Upon arrival in New Mexico the starving and broken survivors were promptly arrested by Mexican authorities.[83] The Texan captives were forced to march on a brutal trek to El Paso before suffering months of cruel torture in Perote Castle near Mexico City.[84]

In March 1842 Mexico retaliated by dispatching General Rafael Vasquez to recapture San Antonio. Vasquez with an army of approximately seven hundred including regulars, militia and Indians reached San Antonio on March 5th and defiantly flew the Mexican flag from the cathedral of San Fernando. Ranger captain Jack Hays opted to withdraw his force of a hundred and seven men from the city rather than surrender. From the hills nearby Hays could do little more than watch as the Mexicans plundered San Antonio before withdrawing back to the Rio Grande. Three months later a band of two hundred Texan volunteers including a ranger company commanded by Captain Ewen Cameron clashed near *Lipantitlán* with a significantly larger Mexican force of seven hundred led by General Canales. After a brief battle the Mexicans retreated leaving behind three dead on the battlefield.

The most serious Mexican attempt to re-conquer Texas occurred in September 1842. Brigadier General Adrian Woll, a French citizen in the Mexican military, led an invasion force of well over a thousand soldiers and militia across the Rio Grande and once again seized San Antonio after only a brief skirmish with the Texan defenders.[85] Ranger Mathew Caldwell, recently released from Perote castle, rapidly gathered together a group of volunteers and united with a small Ranger force under Jack Hays. The handful of Rangers comprised of some of the most competent men in the corps, including Ben and Henry McCulloch, Sam Walker and William 'Bigfoot' Wallace. On September 17, a decoy force led by Hays lured the Mexican army onto Salado Creek. After several hours of inconclusive fighting General Woll launched a full scale assault on the Texan positions but was beaten back and withdrew to San Antonio.[86]

Three days later, on September 20, the Mexican invasion force left the city and began a retreat towards the Rio Grande. Mathew Caldwell, leading the Texan forces, received reinforcements including two separate groups under Colonel John H. Moore and Major James S. Mayfield swelling his numbers to around five hundred. At the *Arroyo Hondo*, Hays with around fifty men charged the Mexican rearguard but a rare lack of cohesion among the Texan commanders prevented a decisive assault and Woll was able to slip away. A strong and decisive command structure had enabled the Texans to achieve victory at Salado Creek but the quarrelling between Caldwell, Moore and Mayfield during the ensuing pursuit of Woll allowed the Mexican general to escape across the border.[87]

Texan hostility to Mexicans was exacerbated by the massacre of Captain Nicholas Dawson and over thirty men during the Battle of Salado. Dawson and around fifty volunteers from LaGrange had hurried to join Caldwell on Salado creek but were surrounded by a mixed force of Mexican artillery and cavalry retreating from the battlefield. At first Dawson defied the Mexican call to surrender but as cannon fire and cavalry sabres shredded his men he literally raised an improvised white flag but was shot down. Mexican cavalry then slaughtered the remaining Texans, few were able to escape.[88]

President Houston, despite personal misgivings, succumbed to appeals from his vice president, Edward Burleson, as well as public calls for retaliation and dispatched Brigadier General A. Somervell to San Antonio. Somervell took command of a militia of rangers, adventurers and freebooters that had originally been mustered to protect the city but would serve as an invasion force of northern Mexico which would become known as the Mier Expedition.[89] The brigadier general proved to be an inept leader; desertion, drunkenness and logistical delays plagued the 'army' which finally reached Laredo in December 1842. Unable to keep control, Somervell could do little as his men pillaged the town. The expedition ably guided by Hays' Rangers did successfully cross the Rio Grande and camped near Guerrero in northern Mexico. At this point, however, Somervell fearing the potential arrival of Mexican soldiers ordered the force back to Texas.[90]

Around three hundred Texans, including Rangers Ewen Cameron, Sam Walker and 'Bigfoot' Wallace, dreaming of booty, riches and vengeance refused the order. On Christmas Day, the band led by William S. Fisher unwisely attacked the desert town of Mier protected by Mexican General Pedro Ampudia and fifteen hundred infantry. During the desperate fight the outnumbered Texans killed several hundred Mexican soldiers before surrendering. The prisoners were taken to Mexico City, a mass escape en route somewhat delayed their Mexican guards but the majority of the Texans were recaptured.[91]

Santa Anna at first decreed that all the captives would be executed but under pressure from the Americans and British he decreed that every tenth Texan would be killed. The prisoners were presented with a large jar containing one hundred and seventy six beans seventeen of which were black those who drew a black bean would be executed. 'Big Foot' Wallace noted that the black beans had been poured in on top and in his words "dipped deep" and received a white bean. Ewen Cameron also received a white bean but on the insistence of General Canales, who had fought the Ranger captain at *Lipantitlán*, Santa Anna ordered him to be shot.[92] The surviving Texans suffered confinement in Perote castle and endured brutal punishments notably removing carts full of dirt to which they were harnessed like horses. Apparently, 'Bigfoot' Wallace did not prove to be a willing worker and would frequently take off with the cart in tow knocking over pedestrians and damaging the adobe houses.[93]

Anglo-Texans were infuriated by the treatment of the Mier prisoners. The black bean affair especially rankled. The fact that Fisher and his men had deserted their military commander and had invaded a foreign country in search of plunder was conveniently ignored by most white Texans.[94] Nevertheless, the inhumane conduct of the Mexican authorities regarding the Mier episode combined with the Dawson Massacre and the memories of the Alamo and Goliad exacerbated Texan hatred of Mexicans and spurred a burning desire for vengeance especially among the Texas Rangers. The outbreak of hostilities between the United States and Mexico would provide just such an opportunity.

On April 25 1846, a U.S. Army patrol numbering seventy men commanded by Captain Seth Thornton was attacked by a two thousand strong Mexican cavalry force near an abandoned *hacienda* in the contested territory of the Nueces Strip. Sixteen American soldiers were killed in the skirmish and forty nine men including Captain Thornton surrendered and were taken as prisoners to Matamoros, *Tamaulipas*. U.S. President James Knox Polk condemned the incident, expressing outrage at the Mexican 'invasion' which had spilled American blood on American soil. Congress swiftly passed a war resolution and called for fifty thousand volunteers and ten million dollars to fund the conflict. Polk signed the declaration of war on May 13th and in so doing provided the rangers with a chance to exact revenge.[95]

The 'Thornton Affair' may have been the ember that ignited the war but deeper underlying factors lay behind the conflict. The U.S. annexation of Texas in 1845 outraged the Mexican government who perceived the 'Colossus of the North' as engaging in an outright theft of Mexican territory. Polk was an expansionist who cast covetous eyes on the Mexican province of California and believed that it was the 'Manifest Destiny' of Anglo-Americans to spread their nation's borders all the way to the Pacific Ocean. As early as November 1845, Polk had sent John Slidell to Mexico City with an offer of $25 million to purchase the Mexican provinces of *Alta California* and *Santa Fe de Nuevo México* as well as acceptance of the Rio Grande border.

The volatile political situation in Mexico, four presidents in 1846 alone, meant that the Slidell was unable to undertake fruitful negotiations with the Mexican Government. Furthermore, the Mexican public, the wounds of Texan independence and annexation still fresh in their minds, would not permit any political faction to further tarnish the national honor by giving up more land to the U.S.[96] Tensions between America and Mexico were further heightened by the Mexican failure to pay the debts of around three million dollars owed to American citizens for damages caused by the Mexican War of Independence and by the continued Comanche raids into northern Mexico from bases in Texan territory.

When Polk ordered General Zachary Taylor to the disputed region north of Rio Grande, it is highly probable that he was scheming to provoke an international incident that would serve as a ruse for war. The 'Thornton Affair' provided the perfect pretext, Polk's machinations to incite conflict with Mexico had come to fruition.[97]

The Mexican American War (1846-48) was a resounding success for the U.S. and a military humiliation for Mexico. The war was fought on four fronts; California, New Mexico, Texas and central Mexico. The noted explorer John C. Fremont, in northern California at the outbreak of hostilities, raised an army of frontiersmen and captured Sonoma in June and declared an independent 'Bear Flag Republic.' One month later the commodore of the U.S. Pacific Fleet John D. Sloat sent troops ashore to raise the U.S. flag, by August, American forces, under a new commodore, Robert F. Stockton had defeated Mexican resistance in southern California. Meanwhile, on August 18, Colonel Stephen Watts Kearny with sixteen hundred soldiers had occupied Santa Fe, New Mexico and installed an American civilian government. Kearny then pushed west with three hundred men linking up with Stockton at San Diego in time to suppress an abortive *Californio* revolt.[98]

General Zachary Taylor, based in Matamoros, delayed his advance until he received what he deemed adequate numbers and munitions. He finally headed south in September 1846 and captured the strongly fortified city of Monterrey. Polk, suspicious of Taylor's growing political popularity, ordered the general to wait outside Matamoros. Taylor, however, unhappy with his orders moved west and attacked a powerful Mexican force at the indecisive Battle of Buena Vista. In the meantime, General Winfield Scott with over ten thousand troops had set sail for the port city of Vera Cruz which was captured in March 1847. Scott then defeated a Mexican army at Cerro Gordo before seizing Puebla and Mexico City in May and September respectively, the war was over and the U.S. had emerged victorious.[99] In February

1848, at the Treaty of Guadalupe Hidalgo, Mexico ceded California, New Mexico and its claim to Texas north of the Rio Grande in exchange for fifteen million dollars.[100]

The history of the Texas Rangers during the Mexican-American War is a tale of both heroism and dark deeds. Upon arrival in Texas, General Zachary Taylor enlisted Rangers to scout and guard the frontier. Samuel H. Walker was commended for his boldness and courage eluding a large number of Mexican troops when carrying a vital message to Fort Brown. Following the 'Thornton Affair' Taylor asked Texan governor James Pinckney Henderson for Texan regiments to supplement his Army of Occupation. Henderson mustered a Texan division including two cavalry regiments commanded by Colonel John 'Coffee' Hays and Colonel George T. Wood. The Texan volunteers, notably Ranger Ben McCulloch and his company, provided vital scouting services for General Taylor including the mapping out of the most functional route to Monterrey and pursuing the Mexican partisans who harassed the American forces.[101]

The 'federalized' Texas Rangers demonstrated enormous courage and played a key role during the siege of Monterrey. Ranger units led by Hays, Wood and McCulloch were at the forefront of the U.S. forces which stormed the bloody heights of *Loma Federacion* and the strategic Bishop's Palace located on *Loma Independencia*.[102] The duration of the Texans' enlistment expired following the Battle of Monterrey and subsequent truce, the majority of the rangers returned to the Lone Star State. Taylor, however, shrewdly exacted a promise from Ben McCulloch to return if hostilities recommenced.[103]

In January 1847, McCulloch led his band of twenty-seven men, a company of the Texas Mounted Volunteers, into Monterrey to report for service. In the days preceding the Battle of Buena Vista it was McCulloch himself who not only located the Mexican army but remained close by, at a considerable risk to his own life, to gather an estimate regarding the enemy strength before conveying the report to Taylor. The subsequent American victory at Buena Vista owed much to information gleaned by the skill and daring of Ben McCulloch.[104]

One month later a mixed force of Mexican soldiers and irregulars launched a devastating attack on an American wagon train in northern Mexico killing and mutilating over a hundred teamsters. General Taylor requested rangers to protect his supply lines and Texan companies under captains Mabry B. Gray, Walter P. Lane and Major Michael Chevallie fought a vicious campaign against local partisans to ensure the supply route remained open. The record of Ranger successes against the guerrillas is mixed but it is perhaps telling that General Taylor insisted on maintaining the Texans in field service until June 1848.[105]

As General Winfield Scott advanced towards Mexico City he also experienced extreme difficulties with Mexican *guerrillas*. His ever lengthening supply line followed the National Road from Vera Cruz, over two hundred miles through rugged mountain ranges and the Mexican central plateau. Following the capture of Mexico City the Mexican military joined the partisans to continue a brutal form of *guerrilla* warfare.[106] Ranger companies led by captains Sam Walker and John Hays operated as highly mobile counter-*guerrilla* units delivering an unforgiving justice. Walker routed *guerrilla* forces at Las Vegas and La Hoya Pass in June before being shot down leading a mounted charge during the Battle of *Huamantala*.[107] In November, Hays and thirty rangers armed with repeating pistols repulsed over two hundred Mexican lancers. The Treaty of Guadalupe-Hidalgo did not end the *guerrilla* attacks and in February of 1848 a U.S. force of four hundred and fifty men including two hundred and fifty rangers commanded by Hays struck the mountain town of *Zacualtipan* winning a decisive victory and destroying *guerrilla* power.[108]

Ranger successes during the war, however, were marred by incidents of brutality, excessive violence and mass murder. While serving as scouts for General Taylor the Rangers had earned a reputation as troublemakers especially at Reynosa where many of them had been mistreated as prisoners following the Mier Expedition.[109] Taylor himself noted that the Rangers rarely returned to camp without having killed at least one Mexican in dubious circumstances. Under Mabry

"Mustang" Gray, a Ranger force murdered the entire male population of a village near Ramos in retaliation for the earlier wagon train atrocity. In Patos, a Ranger detachment shot an unspecified number of villagers after a drunken Ranger was flayed alive for dragging a church crucifix behind his horse and riding down an elderly priest.[110]

It was in Mexico City that the Texas Rangers earned the title *Los Tejanos Sangrientes*. The city was a dangerous place for the occupying Americans and almost every night an unwary soldier lost their life. The Rangers, however, lived by a different code and operated under the law of an "eye for an eye and a tooth for a tooth". An insult, theft or stone hurled in their direction all elicited the same answer, the distinctive booming thud of a Walker Colt revolver. When Ranger Adam Allsens foolishly wandered into a dangerous quarter of the city known as 'Cutthroat' he was cut to shreds by a murderous mob.[111] The Rangers exacted a bloody retribution, after a long night of violence over eighty Mexicans were found slaughtered in the streets of 'Cutthroat'.[112] When confronted by General Scott, Captain Hays defended the Ranger response and audaciously told the general that no authority could impose on the corps.[113]

The Mexican-American War aptly demonstrated both the Rangers skill and daring when confronted by regular or irregular forces but also their penchant for brutality and staggering levels of violence. In the words of Robert M. Utley; "the Texas Rangers ended the Mexican War with the twin legacy of combat excellence and vengeful excess."[114]

In the subsequent decade relations remained tense between Anglo Texans and the Mexican communities on both sides of the border. This was especially the case in the trans-Nueces region and along the Rio Grande. White Texans spurred by the memories of the Texas Revolt began to classify Hispanics, whether *Tejano* or *Mexicano*, as second class citizens. Even Juan Seguin, a hero of the War for Independence, who had fought alongside Travis at the Alamo and saw action at San Jacinto, was forced to flee San Antonio in 1842.[115] Following U.S. annexation and victory over Mexico a flood of Anglo Americans poured into the border region seeking land and wealth.

The newcomers dominated the border trade and dispossessed many *rancheros* and villagers through a variety of quasi-legal mechanisms including property taxes, legal fees and 'suits for partition'. The Anglo community in the border region, numbering around twenty-five hundred in 1850, compared to eighteen thousand *Tejanos*, set in place a socioeconomic order based on race that both oppressed the Hispanic majority and ensure white elite control of the economic system and the apparatus of government.[116]

The turbulent international frontier led to further tensions and violence. The continuing conflict between the Centralists and Federalists in Mexico ensured that the northern border provinces remained embroiled in political and military conflict. Bandits, both American and Mexican plagued the region with little regard for the nationality or ethnicity of their victims. Slavery also remained a source of contention between Texas and Mexico. Ever since the early days of Anglo settlement chattel slavery had remained a cornerstone of the Texan economy but the prospect of freedom across the Rio Grande tempted many African-Americans to abscond and flee to the dubious sanctuary of Mexico. The recovery of fugitive slaves on Mexican territory often by force became a contentious issue in relations between Texas and her southern neighbor.[117]

During this period the Texas Rangers served as both representatives of law and order as well as the enforcement tools of the Anglo politico economic establishment. Two events involving the rangers are of particular note. On October 1 1855, Ranger Captain James H. Callahan with one hundred and eleven men crossed into Mexico just below Eagle Pass. Officially, the objective of the mission was to pursue Mexican Indians who had raided Texan settlements, in reality, the expedition was a slave hunting adventure with the possible aim of seizing Mexican territory. The Texans clashed with a superior Mexican force, looted and burned the town of *Piedras Negras* before retreating across the Rio Grande when confronted by the Mexican military. Although the incident created a diplomatic crisis for the U.S., in Texas, the Anglo community praised Callahan and the legislature even voted to pay for the expenses he had incurred.[118]

The so called 'First Cortina War' in 1859 most aptly demonstrates the tension along the border and provides a good example of both the best and worst in Ranger competence and conduct. Juan Nepomuceno Cortina was a wealthy landowner from a prominent family who dabbled in numerous nefarious activities including horse theft. He was, nevertheless, a Mexican patriot proud of his ancestry and angered by the discrimination suffered by his people. On July 13th, in Brownsville, Cortina witnessed Robert Shears, the city marshal, pistol whipping a drunken Mexican who had once worked for Cortina. Attempting to remonstrate, Cortina was insulted by Shears whom he promptly shot, wounding the marshal in the torso, before bearing the injured Mexican out of town.[119]

The incident had pushed Cortina to breaking point. Two months later, at the head of around a hundred men, he returned to Brownsville killing four men, including two who he alleged had murdered Mexicans but had gone unpunished. The *Cortinistas* also freed all the prisoners in jail, raised the Mexican flag and terrorized the community. It should be noted, however, that Cortina engaged in no wanton plundering or killing in Brownsville. Cortina then issued a *pronunciamento* or proclamation calling for a rising against Anglo Texan tyranny and subsequently defeated the 'Brownsville Tigers' a force assembled to pursue Cortina following the raid.[120]

In November a body of Texas Rangers commanded by William G. Tobin finally reached Brownsville. Allegedly, Tobin's force contained one good Ranger but he broke his neck falling from a carriage shortly after arrival. One of the first acts of the Rangers was to permit an angry mob to break into the jail and lynch Tomas Cabrera, an elderly lieutenant of Cortina's. Tobin continued to demonstrate staggering incompetence throughout the month of November. A group of Rangers sent by Tobin to meet Captain Donaldson of the U.S. Army failed to locate the officer but were ambushed in the chaparral with three fatal casualties.[121] The ambush prompted Tobin to attack Cortina's base, the fortified Rancho del Carmen. Upon arrival, however, he concluded that it would be unwise to assault the fortifications and ordered a withdrawal to Brownsville.[122]

Meanwhile, Governor Hardin R. Runnels, appointed 'Rip' Ford as major and ordered him to Brownsville. Ford's Rangers, however, arrived to late to participate in the victory at El Ebonal. A U.S. Army force of a hundred and sixty men commanded by Major Samuel P. Heintzelman with reluctant support from Tobin's Rangers had defeated Cortina.[123] Ford, however, together with Heintzelman achieved a decisive victory over the *Cortinistas* at Rio Grande City before crushing Cortina at La Bolsa Bend where Ford, Tobin and only fifty Rangers routed an enemy numbering around two hundred.[124] In the months that followed, Ford and U.S. Army Captain George Stoneman conducted several expeditions into Mexico including a confrontation with a combined *Cortinista* and Mexican *Guardia National* force at La Mesa. The operations in northern Mexico failed to capture the elusive Cortina but did bring an end to his cross border uprising. The ineffectual Tobin continued to underperform, until his retirement in early 1860, his Rangers looted the Mexican communities along the Rio Grande.[125]

The legend of *Los Diablos Tejanos* neatly encapsulates the Texas Rangers during this era. On one hand the courage and effectiveness of many Ranger units in the service of both the Texan Republic and the United States is without question. At the Battle of Salado, the storming of Monterrey and when confronted by brutal Mexican guerrillas the ability and heroism of men like John 'Coffee' Hays, Ben McCulloch and Sam Walker exemplifies the highest ideals any Ranger could aspire to. Nevertheless, the needless filibustering typified by the Santa Fe and Mier Expeditions as well as the raid on Piedras Negras when combined with the brutality and violence exhibited by the Rangers during the war with Mexico have left a indelible dark stain on the Ranger legacy.

5
To Arms for Dixie: The Corps and the Confederate years

The Civil War (1861-65) was a defining period in American history. The Union victory reunified the nation and the passage of the Thirteenth Amendment abolished the inhumane and brutal system of chattel slavery. Over six hundred thousand Americans died during the conflict and the war is viewed by many historians as the first 'modern' war in terms of weaponry, tactics and effect on civilian populations.

The immediate spark that set the nation ablaze was the shelling of Fort Sumter, in Charleston harbor, by Confederate forces in April 1861. This action led to President Abraham Lincoln issuing a War Proclamation and the subsequent secession of four more states to the fledgling Confederacy.[126] The long term causes of the Civil War, however, were an irrepressible economic and political sectional divide on the issue of slavery and the blundering handiwork of a generation when dealing with the issue of Western expansion.

Beginning with Vermont in 1777, the northern states had begun the gradual abolition of slavery.[127] In the South, however, slavery had developed into the engine of the southern economy. By 1861 the dollar value of southern slavery outstripped the net worth of all the nation's banks, railroads and factories combined. Politically, the southern planters were determined to maintain chattel slavery. Southern leaders had forced the three fifths compromise into the U.S. Constitution whereby a slave counted as three fifths of man for taxation and voter representation. This gave the southern states an undue amount of electoral power.[128] Southern political leaders were also determined to protect slavery by maintaining a balance of power in the senate. Economically, southern dependence on an agrarian slave based economy led to tensions with the rapidly industrializing north.[129] While the South favored low tariffs on manufactured goods northern industrialists preferred high tariff rates to protect their fledgling industries. The growth of the abolitionist movement in the 1830s enraged white Southerners who correctly perceived abolitionism as a threat to their way of life, but incorrectly linked the movement to slave uprisings.[130]

The growing sectional divide was exacerbated by the actions of a blundering generation in dealing with the question of slavery and westward expansion. Following the American victory in the war with Mexico, the Treaty of Guadalupe-Hidalgo, gave the U.S. a vast swathe of western territory. The debate whether the new territories would be 'slave or free' led to sectional tensions. Southerners, in particular, feared the creation of free states that would undermine the political balance of power. The Wilmot Proviso, Compromise of 1850 and especially the 1854 Kansas Nebraska Act fragmented the Whigs and Democrats along sectional lines and boosted the emergence of a Republican Party comprised of so called free soilers and abolitionists.[131] The election of Lincoln in 1860 on a purely sectional vote directly led to secession. Although Lincoln was no abolitionist he opposed the western expansion of slavery and was not even on the ballot in ten southern states. The South, already shaken by John Brown's Raid a year earlier and mistaking Lincoln for a radical abolitionist, seceded from the union beginning with South Carolina in December 1860.[132]

Texans had voted for John C. Breckinridge in the 1860 election and following Lincoln's victory public opinion in the Lone Star

State swung in favor of secession. On February 1 1861, the special convention on secession voted to adopt an Ordinance of Secession from the United States and to return to full sovereignty on March 2nd. Texans then ratified the decision in a state wide referendum held on February 23 in which secession was approved by a majority of 46,129 to 14,697 votes. In March 1861, Texas ratified the Constitution of the Confederate States of America becoming the seventh state of the fledgling Confederacy.[133] The Ordinance of Secession showed that Texans supported 'disunion' on a variety of grounds including cultural solidarity with the other Southern states, a desire to maintain slavery for both economic and social motives, a perception that Lincoln was an extremist determined to ruin the South and intriguing because the Union had failed to protect Texans from the depredations of Mexican bandits and Indian tribes.[134]

The Ordinance of Secession was opposed by a Unionist minority including James W. Throckmorton and most notably Sam Houston. Houston, a giant in Texan history, had spent nearly fifty years advancing the cause of U.S. expansion and fundamentally opposed secession especially annexation to the Confederate States. Houston campaigned furiously to turn the popular vote against secession and refused to take an oath of allegiance to the Confederacy which precipitated his removal as Texas governor. It should be noted, however, that when the flames of conflict finally arrived, the majority of Unionists chose Texas over the United States preferring to fight for their land and their people as opposed to any loyalty to the Union. James Throckmorton became a Confederate brigadier while Sam Houston refused President Lincoln's offer to use the U.S. Army to retain his gubernatorial powers.[135]

Anglo-Texans, whatever their political affiliations, rallied in large numbers to the Southern cause. Between sixty to seventy thousand men served under the Confederate flag out of a total white male population of ninety two thousand. In 1861, Richmond, the new seat of the Confederate government, asked for twenty companies of Texan infantrymen to serve in the eastern theater, thirty-two companies answered the call.[136] Texans were consistently at the forefront of the Civil War battles playing major roles at Antietam, Gaines Mill and Gettysburg.

A number of Texas Rangers enlisted individually in the Confederate forces seeing action across numerous battlefields. Notable examples include Ben McCulloch who rose to the rank of brigadier general, leading impressively at Wilson's Creek, Missouri and also in Arkansas before a Federal sharpshooter claimed his life at the Battle of Pea Ridge in 1862, ending an illustrious career.[137] Thomas S. Lubbock and Walter P. Lane, the latter a Confederate general, had also served time in the Rangers corps. Future Ranger captains John B. Jones and Leander H. McNelly both enrolled in the Confederate forces. The Eighth Texas Cavalry, a regular Confederate regiment, nonetheless became known as 'Terry's Texas Rangers' and included past and future Rangers among their number. It is of note that the regiment would choose to be known as 'Rangers', attesting to the already revered and renowned reputation of the corps.[138]

In 1862, the Army of New Mexico, a Texan force commanded by General Henry H. Sibley advanced north along the Rio Grande into New Mexico Territory. The move marked an ambitious Confederate attempt to establish a 'Southern Empire' stretching west to California. Rebel sympathizers had established the Confederate Territory of Arizona in August 1861 and the Southern leadership hoped to seize the mineral wealth of Colorado, Nevada and California. While the Texas Rangers played no official role in the operation, Sibley's army included three regiments of Mounted Rifles and it is likely many recruits were drawn from the Ranger corps. The Confederates defeated a Union army at Valverde on February 2nd before occupying Albuquerque and Santa Fe in March. The Texan dream of westward expansion to the Rio Grande became, albeit briefly, a reality. The Texans, thousands of miles from their bases and low on supplies began to forage off the land leading to local resentment.[139] Federal troops based in Denver, Colorado headed south to Fort Union and confronted a Confederate force at Glorieta Pass. In the subsequent battle, despite the fact that the Confederates took the field, a Union detachment under John M.

Chivington destroyed the Texan supply train forcing the rebels to retreat back to Santa Fe.[140] The lack of supplies and munitions enforced a Confederate retreat, first to Albuquerque followed by a horrific long march back to San Antonio.[141]

In 1861, the Secession Convention assigned famous Texas Ranger John 'Rip' Ford as a Colonel of State Cavalry and dispatched the old warrior, now nearing fifty, to the Rio Grande.[142] Even before the booming guns at Fort Sumter signaled the beginning of a bloody and prolonged war Ford achieved two noteworthy successes. The Ranger persuaded Union commander Fitz-John Porter to abandon Fort Brown despite his strong garrison in order to avoid bloodshed. In April, when an uprising against the Confederacy led by a Mexican named Ochoa occurred between Brownsville and Laredo, Ford's cavalry crushed the insurgents and in so doing technically won the first battle of the Civil War.[143]

By 1863, the Union forces sought to strengthen federal control of the Lower Rio Grande. This effort blocked the stream of Confederate cotton bales to European ships waiting in the Gulf of Mexico. Arms, medical supplies and other merchandise bound for Texas were also delayed by the presence of around four thousand Union troops. Under increasing pressure from business interests the Confederate authorities requested Ford to raise a cavalry regiment to campaign along the Rio Grande.[144] In March 1864, the Cavalry of the West, commanded by the grizzled old Ranger, clattered out of San Antonio and rode south to battle. Over the next few months Ford conducted a highly successful *guerrilla* war against the Union culminating with the capture of Brownsville.[145] In July 1865, as the agony of the Civil War drew to a close, and more than a month after the surrender of Robert E. Lee at Appomattox, newly- arrived Union officer Colonel Theodore H. Barrett broke the truce on the Rio Grande and attacked the Confederate camp. At Palmito Hill, the Cavalry of the West, boldly led by Ford, drove the federal forces from the field. Thus the last encounter of the Civil War ended in the same manner of the very first, the Texans, commanded by the celebrated Ranger Captain, once again emerged victorious.[146]

The war took a terrible toll on the Indian frontier. Following secession Union garrisons abandoned the army posts and their Texan replacements were mostly withdrawn to the eastern theaters. The Comanche and their Kiowa allies profited from the chaos by launching a new wave of raids intended to drive back the line of Anglo-Texan civilization. The Comanche were also angered by the failure of the Confederate government to fulfill its promises. The Confederate Indian Agent, Albert Pike, had agreed in August of 1861 to pay various goods to the Comanche in exchange for peace. The Confederacy, habitually short of finances, reneged on the agreement infuriating the Comanche.

The duty of protecting the Texan frontier, from the Red River to the Rio Grande, once again became the responsibility of the Texas Rangers. In 1861, the Committee of Public Safety appointed Ranger Henry McCulloch as colonel of a frontier force mustered to protect the settlements. In April the same year, the Confederate government in Richmond, Virginia, was convinced that frontier protection was their responsibility and McCulloch's men were placed on the payroll of 'Dixie' as the First Texas Mounted Rifles. One year later the First Texas was disbanded and replaced by the Frontier Regiment this time reporting to and paid by the state of Texas. The Confederacy, as was the case with United States over a decade before, was not prepared to finance indefinitely Ranger units which operated outside the regular command structure.[147]

The Frontier Regiment was first led by the inept and unpopular Colonel James M. Norris. In 1863, Governor Lubbock replaced Norris with the James E. McCord supported by the experienced Ranger James B. 'Buck' Barry as lieutenant colonel. Although the new leadership proved more effective at tracking down and confronting Indian raiders the border settlements were continuously pillaged and burned by Comanche and Kiowa war parties. The Confederacy did provide a border regiment commanded by Texas Ranger James Bourland and in August 1863, concerned about a potential Union invasion from the Indian Territory, dispatched army units to Bonham under the command of Brigadier General and former Ranger Henry McCulloch.[148]

McCulloch faced not only Indian warriors and Union forces but the growing threat posed by bands of draft dodgers and Confederate renegades who plundered and terrorized the civilian population. The Brigadier General, by offering amnesty, recruited five hundred fugitives and formed the Brush Battalion. The force, however, proved inept and unreliable leading to its disbandment in 1864. Moreover, none of the 'guardians of the frontier' were able to prevent a major Comanche raid before Christmas 1863. Approximately three hundred warriors ravaged the farming communities northwest of Fort Worth.[149]

That very same month Richmond finally acceded to Texan demands that the Rangers serve on the Confederate payroll. The flaw in the agreement, at least from a Texan perspective, was that the newly named Frontier Organization was subject to the military whims of the Confederate government. Almost immediately six companies of Rangers until Colonel McCord were transferred to new postings elsewhere and the frontier was further weakened by the withdrawal of Barry's contingent in August of 1864. Two months later a combined Comanche and Kiowa offensive, numbering up to six hundred Indians, swooped down the Brazos massacring men, women and children and burning the settlements.[150] By the end of the Civil War era the Anglo-Texan frontier had retreated over one hundred miles due to the determination and ferocity of the Indian attacks and lack of protection from either Confederate or state forces.

The Rangers ended their wartime duties on a low note that would further stain their legacy. On January 8th of 1864, a combined Ranger and militia force whose leaders included Captains Buck Barry and Henry Fossett attacked a peaceful camp of Kickapoos on Dove Creek. The slipshod assault and strong Kickapoo resistance, however, led to a demoralizing defeat and the deaths of twenty six Rangers.[151] The Rangers of the Civil War era failed to stem the Indian aggressions or protect the boundary of Anglo-Texan settlements. It should be remembered, though, lest history judge the corps too harshly, that the wartime Rangers were grievously undermanned and operated under confusing and ever shifting lines of authority. Furthermore, even the most competent Rangers before them, legendary figures such as Hays and Ford were also unable to fully stem the violence of the Comanche threat.

Following the Union victory in the Civil War, the federal government, forbade any state to possess a force of armed men for any function and in the case of Texas dispatched the federal army to patrol the frontier. For the next five years the Texas Rangers vanished from the historical record.[152] The increasing lawlessness in the Lone Star State, however, prompted newly elected Republican 'carpetbagger' governor E. J. Davis to organize a State Police of two hundred men who possessed extraordinary judicial powers and who reported directly to the governor's office. The State Police enjoyed little support from the Texan populace, in part due to the enrollment of African-American officers, which sparked the resentment of Anglo-Texans most of whom had fixed racist beliefs of white supremacy, but primarily due to the inefficiency of the force and the use of the organization by the Davis administration as a tool of intimidation and oppression against political opponents.[153]

Chaos also reigned on the frontier in the post Civil War era. The Comanche and Kiowa, despite signing a peace treaty at Medicine Lodge Creek in 1867, continued to raid Texan settlements, often using the reservation in Indian Territory as a sanctuary between forays. Lipan Apaches and Kickapoos attacked communities in South Texas stealing horses and cattle before fleeing south across the Rio Grande into Mexico. Military authorities proved incapable of maintaining security and Governor Davis, in response, authorized twenty companies of Rangers for a twelve month enlistment in June of 1870.[154] Despite tensions with the U.S. Army and the limited timeframe the Ranger record was exceptionally impressive. Notably Captain's John W. Sansom and H. J. Richarz proved highly competent while Sergeant Edward H. Cobb with only ten men pursued and confronted a much larger Indian raiding party in the process killing two Comanche and

Kiowa chiefs. Nevertheless, the Rangers were mustered out in June 1871 and the task of protecting the frontier lay with the army supported by a corps of minutemen.[155]

For the next three years, notwithstanding an improved and vigorous military presence, the Texan frontier was continually devastated by Indian incursions while the Rio Grande borderlands remained mired in disorder and violence. In 1874, the State of Texas would once again turn to the Texas Rangers to bring stability and security to a land marred by brutal conflict.

1874-1935

6

The Frontier Battalion and the Indians

The Texas gubernatorial election of December 1873 marked the end of Reconstruction in the Lone Star State. The newly elected Texas Governor, Richard Coke was a Democrat and Southern 'Redeemer' who had routed Republican incumbent Edmund Davis.[156] Coke, a former Confederate veteran, represented the re-ascendancy of the deeply conservative Anglo-Texan order and took office determined to expunge the Radical Republican legacy.[157]

The perennial concern over the frontier, however, was a paramount issue on the new governor's agenda. The Comanche and their Kiowa allies, although weakened by smallpox and constant warfare, remained a potent danger to travellers on the Great Plains. Numerous cases of horse theft, scalping, murder and the kidnapping of children were reported along the line of settlement. Apache raiding parties also caused havoc in the south western regions of the state.[158]

On May 2 1874, Governor Coke appointed John B. Jones major of the newly formed Frontier Battalion of the Texas Rangers. The major's command was comprised of six companies of twenty-five men led by a captain and two lieutenants.[159] Jones, born in South Carolina in 1834, had displayed both bravery and military skill during his service as a Confederate officer. A man of slight stature but possessing intelligence, tact and dignity, the major held himself and his men to high martial standards.[160]

The Rangers of the Frontier Battalion were mostly unmarried young men from across Texas drawn to the corps by a desire for adventure as much as for the pay. The Rangers remained citizen soldiers, furnishing their guns and horses and dressing as they pleased in a variety of colorful clothes. The men, many of whom possessed little Indian fighting experience, were opposed to formal military discipline and preferred a relaxed camaraderie with their commanding officers. Nevertheless, Major Jones succeeded in constructing a military style organization based on order and diligent attention to duty through a style of strong leadership as opposed to strict martial control. The inexhaustible Jones not only organized and implemented Ranger operations but also juggled the copious logistical, economic and political issues of Ranger management in Austin.[161]

On July 12 1874, the Rangers engaged in their first foray against Indian foes. While inspecting the Ranger Company of Captain G. W. Stevens, a scout reported with news of a fresh Indian trail at Salt Creek. A Comanche raiding party had struck Oliver Loving's ranch and killed one of his ranch hands. Major Jones, Captain Stevens and thirty four Rangers mounted up and headed in a hot pursuit.[162] The Comanche raiding party, however, was joined by a sizeable force of Kiowa warriors led by Lone Wolf and Mamanti. The Indians, numbering around one hundred and fifty, lured the Rangers into an ambush in Lost Valley. The Rangers took refuge in a brushy draw and in the ensuing skirmish four Texans and three Indians were killed.[163]

At dawn, supported by a recently arrived U.S. Army unit under Captain Baldwin, the Rangers searched the valley for the Indians only to find the Comanche and Kiowa had vanished without leaving a trail. Although Major Jones could technically claim victory, the Rangers had held the field and diverted the raiding party, in reality the Indians had outsmarted the Rangers and inflicted casualties on the hated Texans.

Overall, during their first two years in the field, the Frontier Battalion engaged in twenty-one battles with the Texas Indians. The Rangers killed at least twenty warriors and recaptured livestock valued at around five thousand dollars. The waning power of the Comanche and their allies during this era is evident by the dwindling number of raids along the frontier. Between May and October 1874, around forty Indian parties attacked Texan settlements but the next twelve months only twenty-six bands of marauders molested the borderlands. By September 1875, in the region guarded by the Frontier Battalion, no Comanche or Kiowa raiders menaced the line of Anglo civilization.[164] While Major Jones should be credited with helping to restore security and peace to the Texas frontier the 'Comanche Empire' had in fact been defeated by the twin factors of a reinvigorated federal military policy and the disappearance of the vast buffalo herds.

In July 1874, General William Tecumseh Sherman finally convinced Washington to allow the U.S. military to conduct operations against 'hostiles' based on the reservations. The Red River War (1874-75) began when approximately five thousand Comanche, Cheyenne and Kiowa abandoned the reservations and headed for the region bordered by the Red and Washita rivers.[165] The Kwahadi Comanche, the last holdouts based on the *Llano Estacado* or Staked Plains, had already announced their intentions by spearheading an inter-tribal assault on the buffalo hunting camp at Adobe Walls. While the attack was a massive failure, the hide hunters armed with .50-caliber Sharps repeating rifles held off the warriors for over three days killing fifteen Indians, the uprising proved deadly for Anglo-Americans. Indian attacks across five territories and states, including Texas, caused a swathe of destruction and cost the lives of nearly two hundred people.[166]

The U.S. responded by dispatching five powerful mounted and amply supplied military columns to converge on the Texas Panhandle. Three of the five columns were commanded by Colonel Ranald S. Mackenzie, an experienced veteran of the Comanche frontier. Mackenzie sought not to confront the Comanche or Kiowa in open battle but instead to break their ability and will to fight by burning their villages and destroying their supplies.[167] Although consistently harassed by Comanche warriors Mackenzie pressed deeper onto the plains of the Texas Panhandle in search of the elusive Comanche base camp. On September 28 1874, the Southern Column led by Mackenzie stormed a large village of Comanche, Cheyenne and Kiowa located in the Palo Duro Canyon. The soldiers razed around four hundred and fifty lodges, destroyed large quantities of buffalo meat and most devastatingly for the equestrian Comanche, shot the entire Indian horse herd, around fourteen hundred animals.[168] The Battle of Palo Duro Canyon helped break Comanche power forever, the hostile bands in the face of unrelenting military operations began to slowly straggle back to the reservations or surrender. Quanah Parker himself, the last Comanche chief, formally laid down his arms at Fort Sill in June 1875.[169]

The collapse of the southern plains Indians was also precipitated by the catastrophic disappearance of the buffalo herds. The American buffalo or bison was a key element of the economy and culture of the southern plains tribes. The vast herds provided meat, leather for clothing, sinews for bows and a variety of other goods. The excess products were used for trade purposes.

By 1900 only a few hundred buffalo remained on the Great Plains. Pioneer expeditions and the railroads had demolished the fragile ecosystem of the river valleys which the bison depended on while domestic cattle infected the herds with diseases including anthrax.[170] The Comanche themselves contributed to their decline as their vast horse herds competed with the buffalo for grazing grounds and by the 1830s the annual harvesting of over two hundred and eighty thousand animals was ecologically unsustainable in the long term.[171] The trade in buffalo hides, however, proved to be the most devastating to the bison. Hide hunters used powerful rifles to slaughter up to several million buffalo leading to the virtual extermination of the herds.[172]

The disappearance of the buffalo removed a cornerstone of the Comanche economy and food resources. The destruction of the herds helped to break the defiance of the southern plains tribes and accept the reservation and assimilation policies of the federal government. The role of the military in this extermination of the bison is worth noting, well aware of the importance of the buffalo herds to Indian resistance Colonel Richard Dodge encouraged hide hunters to kill every animal they found while General Philip Sheridan in 1875 begged the U.S. Congress to allow the destruction of the herds. The military defeat of the Comanche and their allies was facilitated to a large degree by the removal of the buffalo.

The military threat of the Comanche was essentially ended by the Red River War. Bands of Indians, however, while allegedly restricted to the Fort Sill reservations continued to engage in hunting trips into Texas often with the permission of the respective Indian agent. Texans complained bitterly about this practice as the warriors were not averse to adding Texan cattle or horses to the items on their 'hunting lists'. The military establishment defended their actions arguing that the Texan claims were exaggerated and that the inadequate supplies provided by the Department of the Interior made hunting expeditions a necessity to prevent starvation and discord.

The Texan political leadership, once again disillusioned by the apparent unwillingness of the U.S. Army to protect the settlements, ordered the Texas Rangers to resolve the problem and accomplish what the federal government could not or would not carry out. The Rangers relentlessly and overzealously pursued any Indians found 'trespassing' on Texan land leading to confrontations with military authorities. In the spring of 1879 Captain G. W. Arrington and twenty Rangers struck a party of Comanche and Kiowa, killing and scalping Sunboy, a Kiowa chief. The Rangers then located and attacked the Indian camp only to find it guarded by U.S. troops leading to a heated argument between the Ranger force and the military detachment. In June of that year Arrington was confronted by Lieutenant Colonel John W. Davidson, the post commander at Fort Elliott, who in a towering rage challenged the Ranger Captain as to whether he intended to kill Indians. Arrington replied that if they were armed he most certainly would.

The Rangers played an important role in chasing down the Native-American bands who crossed into north Texas but the practice was finally ended by the actions of a surprising ally. In 1880 the U.S. Congress, concerned by the violence and under pressure from Texan politicians, passed House Resolution 5040 prohibiting military or Indian Bureau officials from granting passes to any reservation Indian who wished to enter the Lone Star State. Texas was finally and unquestionably closed to Native Americans.

By the mid 1870s, however, a new theater of conflict had opened in West Texas. Chiricahua and Mescalero Apaches, angered by the federal reservation policy that forced the often mutually hostile groups to live on the inhospitable San Carlos Reservation, began to raid into Texas.[173]

The Rangers became embroiled in the Apache wars in October 1879, when eighteen warriors crossed into Texas near El Paso, the Apaches were en route to Mexico seeking to join the band headed by Victorio. Ranger Lieutenant George W. Baylor and and ten men headed south into Mexico after receiving the permission of the alcalde of Guadalupe who not only assented to the cross border operation but provided reinforcements. The combined Texan and Mexican force followed the Apache trail around a hundred miles into Mexico before engaging the Indians in a rocky canyon. As night fell the Apaches withdrew having lost two warriors, one was slain by Ranger Sergeant James B. Gillett.[174]

One month later, Mexican authorities invited Baylor's Rangers to participate in a 'punitive expedition' against Victorio. The Apache leader and his warriors had ambushed and wiped out two successive parties of Mexican citizens looking for Indian sign in the Candelaria Mountains.[175] While the expedition located no Apaches, the only task was to bury the dead Mexicans, the Texan-Mexican co-operation helped to stymie much of the mutual animosity in the border region. In the fall of 1880, Mexican Colonel Joaquin Terrazas invited both Texas Rangers under Baylor and the U.S. Army into Mexico to help track down Victorio. The Rangers patrolled widely across Chihuahua before Terrazza asked that all American units leave Mexico due to his concerns over the Apache scouts working for the U.S. Cavalry.[176]

At *Tres Castillos*, only a few days later, Mexican troops commanded by Terrazza, attacked an Apache camp slaughtering eighty Indians including Victorio. The death of Victorio did not spell the end of the Apache troubles in Texas. The night before the Mexican assault at *Tres Castillos* a small band of twenty Apaches including twelve warriors left the main camp and moved north into Texas. Over the next two months the small group murdered the occupants of a stagecoach in Quitman Canyon, attacked an emigrant train and ambushed two U.S. Cavalry units.[177] In January 1881 Ranger Baylor and twenty four men pursued the renegades deep into the Sierra Diablo. In the early morning of January 29, the Rangers stealthily approached the Apache campsite, as the cold light of dawn illuminated the Indians preparing their breakfast the Texans rose from hiding and used their Winchester repeating rifles to deadly effect. After the roar of gunfire had subsided eight Apaches lay dead and another three were taken captive.[178] The fight at Sierra Diablo marked the the end of the Indian wars in Texas, a long and bitter chapter in Texan history had finally come to a close.

7
The Special Force

The borderlands along the Rio Grande remained a turbulent and chaotic region plagued by banditry, livestock theft and murder. Mexican cattle thieves and desperadoes raided across the Rio Grande with virtual impunity and Anglo-Texans retaliated with characteristc violence against the ethnic *Tejanos* stimulating a bloody cycle of mutual animosity and hatred.

By the early 1870s the levels of bloodshed were spiralling out of control. In April 1872, at Howard's Well, Mexican raiders burned to death a group of American teamsters. Encinal and Live Oak Counties were harassed by large forces of bandits and throughout south Texas thousands of stolen cattle were spirited across the Rio Grande.[179] Juan Cortina resurfaced once again as a major player on the Mexican side of the border. He had survived and prospered during the whirlwind of the war with France and subsequent anarchy in northern Mexico. Cortina rose to a generalship in the Mexican Army and became Governor of Tamaulipas. By 1875 he served as *alcalde* of Matamoros and led a well organized force of bandits.[180]

On March 26 1875, approximately thirty Mexican brigands attacked Corpus Christi burning and plundering the outskirts of the city and murdering five citizens. The Texan residents responded in typical fashion by lynching a prisoner and exacting a bloody vengeance against the Mexican-American communities. The assault on Corpus

Christi, a city in Nueces County located far north of the border zone, sparked the Texan authorities into action.[181]

In 1874 Governor Coke and the Texas Legislature had established a Special Force of Rangers to protect the border and contain the lawlessness. The Special Force mirrored the Frontier Battalion in terms of organizational structure and mission. In the same fashion that the Frontier Battalion was designed to eliminate the Indian threat the task of the Special Force was to eradicate the *banditti* by whatever means were necessary.[182] Following the devastating raid on Corpus Christi, Ranger Company A commanded by Leander H. McNelly was dispatched to the Rio Grande.[183]

Captain McNelly was the perfect choice for the mission at hand, by the time of his death in 1877, he had left a legacy rivaled by few other Rangers. He was born in 1844, in Brook County Virginia, and moved to Texas in 1860. He had served the Confederate cause with distinction, as a member of the Texas Mounted Volunteers and as a guerrilla scout. Following the Civil War he had further demonstrated his courage and aptitude as a member of the Reconstruction era State Police. As pointed out by T. R. Fehrenbach, the fact that he was selected as a Ranger Captain having previously served in the despised police of the Davis administration speaks volumes regarding his ability and reputation.[184]

McNelly and his Special Force of Rangers were highly effective at combating the epidemic of banditry and cattle theft along the Nueces Strip. Between 1869 and 1874 Anglo ranchers claimed losses of approximately nine hundred thousand cattle. Following McNelly's appearance on the border the numbers dropped dramatically. By the end of 1875 instances of cattle theft were so infrequent that only a negligible number of claims were submitted to the Texas adjutant general.[185] The Ranger Captain formed a network of paid spies and informants who operated on the Mexican bank of the Rio Grande and in the *Tejano* communities. The intelligence that McNelly was able to gather on upcoming raids and the movement of the cattle thieves proved highly valuable to the Rangers.[186]

There was, however, a darker side to the success of the Special Force. McNelly and his men operated as a counter-guerrilla unit not as lawmen and as such employed an effective but brutal brand of frontier justice. The Rangers had the authority to kill any suspected cattle rustlers caught on Texan soil and were under no obligation to take prisoners.[187] Coercion, torture, excessive violence and murder were the favored tactics of the Rangers. The Mexican communities of south Texas suffered heavily at the hands of the Special Force. The Rangers terrorized the villages breaking up the *fandangos* or dances with gun shots and intimidating the residents of the border towns.[188]

The Special Force frequently resorted to torture to glean information from their prisoners. The inquisitor of choice was a Texas-Mexican rancher by the name of Jesus Sandoval known as old 'Casuse'. Ten years earlier Sandoval had caught and hung four bandits thus earning him the emnity of his countrymen south of the Rio Grande. When the Rangers captured a alleged thief or bandit spy old 'Casuse' repeatedly hung the suspect from a tree limb until the truth was revealed. Once all the necessary information had been extracted, the outlaw was often summarily executed by hanging.[189]

McNelly himself disliked the hangings but recognized the necessity he could neither afford to guard them nor simply to turn them loose.[190] The Ranger Captain's attitude in dealing with bandits was a summary yet effectual form of justice. Ranger George Durham who served with McNelly in the trans Nueces region stated that; "He didn't want prisoners. He didn't want reports...Captain said reports weren't what bandits needed. He held that a well-placed bullet from a Sharps did more for law enforcement than a hundred reports."[191]

Two episodes in 1875 best illustrate both the effectiveness and questionable nature of McNelly's methods. In June the Rangers received notice through their network of spies that Cortina had agreed to provide a large shipload of cattle to a Cuban buyer and that a cross border cattle raid was imminent. A suspected thief captured by the Rangers, when subjected to an 'interrogation' by Casuse, provided McNelly with the whereabouts of the cattle thieves.[192] As dawn broke on June 12 the Special Force caught up with the bandits trailing a herd of over two hundred stolen cattle at Palo Alto Prairie. The eighteen desperadoes, who included some of Cortina's most trusted men, formed a defensive line on a small island in the Laguna Madre. The Rangers, armed with the trusty six-shooters, broke through and pursued the raiders over six miles of brush and marshland killing all but one of their opponents. Only one Ranger, sixteen year old Berry Smith, was slain.[193]

At Palo Alto Prairie, McNelly recovered two hundred and sixteen cattle stolen from thirty four Texan ranches. The bodies of the bandits were exhibited in the public square of Brownsville as a lesson of how the Rangers would deal with future cattle thieves. The macabre display outraged the citizens of Matamoros as well as the local *Tejano* population. Cortina, allegedly threatened to cross the border and kill ten *gringos* for every Mexican murdered. The bravado never materialized into any direct action in part due to McNelly's Rangers stating that they would be pleased to "naturalize" any *Cortinistas* who crossed the Rio Grande. Unsurprisingly, over the following months incidents of stock theft stopped entirely in the vicinity of Brownsville.[194]

Five months later on the afternoon of November 17, Captain James G. Randlett of the U.S. Army intercepted a band of thieves from *Rancho Las Cuevas* crossing a large herd of stolen cattle. The soldiers opened fire killing two bandits. Randlett had been given permission by his commanding officer to pursue the thieves into Mexico but his plans were stymied by the arrival of reinforcements led by Major David R. Clendenin. The major vetoed the crossing believing that it would signify an act of war.[195] The next day McNelly and his Special Force arrived on the scene, the Rangers had received word that a herd of eighteen thousand cattle was to be delivered in Monterey and had consequently moved up the Rio Grande.[196]

On the night of November 18, the Rangers, against the express wishes of Major Clendenin, used the cover of darkness to cross the river into Mexico. At dawn, the Texans struck *Las Cucharas*, the wrong ranch, killing several Mexicans.[197] McNelly apparently was undisturbed by the deaths as in his view all Mexicans were potential bandits.[198] He was troubled, nevertheless, by losing the element of surprise. The owner of the *Las Cuevas* Ranch, Juan Flores Salinas, a noted bandit chief and general of the Mexican police led a force of around two hundred and fifty men against the invaders driving the Rangers back to the Rio Grande. McNelly boldly ordered his men to fortify an embankment on the Mexican side and the Texans held off a mounted assault led by Flores. Two Springfield bullets ended the life of the Mexican general.[199]

Large numbers of Mexican soldiers began to assemble against Rangers and a U.S. Cavalry unit of forty troopers which Captain Randlett had crossed to support the Texan defences. Lines of negotiation were opened between the two forces but McNelly refused to leave without the stolen cattle and the thieves. The *Las Cuevas* affair swiftly became an international incident with lines of communication running directly to Washington. The U.S. Cavalry detachment was withdrawn to the American bank but the Rangers stubbornly held their positions despite the demand of the U.S. Consul in Matamoros that the Texans surrender.[200]

On the afternoon of November 20, McNelly, in an audacious act of bravado, informed the Mexicans that unless they agreed to return the cattle and the bandits to Rio Grande City he would attack within the hour. The Mexican authorities surprisingly acceded to his demand and the Special Force recrossed into Texas. The next day approximately half the stolen livestock appeared on the Mexican side of the river opposite Rio Grande City. Mexican officials, however, determined to maintain national pride, insisted on a customs inspection. McNelly, infuriated by the continuing delays and percieved Mexican duplicity, ferried ten Rangers across the Rio Grande and threatened to shoot the Mexican representative if the cattle were not promptly delivered. By the afternoon the cattle herd was grazing peacefully on Texan grasses and the confrontation had drawn to a close.[201]

The incident at Las Cuevas ignited the legend of Leander McNelly in Lone Star lore. Anglo-Texans praised the Rangers for taking direct action against the Mexican crinimals regardless of the legal technicalities. The fact that McNelly's tiny band had faced down and outwitted a far larger enemy force added further luster to his deeds. It should be observed, however, that during the foolhardy expedition the Rangers had invaded a foreign nation at peace with the United States, murdered a number of innocent civilians, were almost wiped out and had created a diplomatic furore between Washington and Mexico City.[202]

Leander McNelly died on September 4 1877 at the age of thirty three. The renowned Ranger had dodged 'Yankee' and Mexican bullets but succumbed to tuberculosis in Burton, Texas, his family by his side.[203] Under his command, the Special Force of Rangers through their own brand of justice, proved successful at halting the flourishing trade in stolen livestock.[204] The chaos along the Rio Grande, however, was only ended by the ascendancy of Porfirio Diaz to the Mexican presidency. In 1876, Diaz assumed power in a coup and swiftly assumed dictatorial powers. While his legacy in Mexico is debatable, for Texas his consolidation of political power and co-operation with the U.S. military brought stability to the Rio Grande which lasted until his overthrow in 1911.[205] The end of the border troubles and the pacification of the Indian tribes did not signal an end to Ranger operations. Feuding factions and outlaws remained a poisonous thorn of instability within the Lone Star state.

8
Feudists and the Outlaw Breed

As early as 1874, the role of Texas Rangers began to shift from an irregular military corps to law enforcement. In the last decades of the eighteenth century partisan feuds and outlawry remained a major source of volatility in Texas. The Civil War left a legacy of chaos and social debris, footloose and war hardened Confederate soldiers flowed back into a state mired in financial instability while political and economic feuds between Republican and Democratic factions added to the turmoil.[206] Bandits of various ethnicities, including in their number cold blooded killers, engaged in bank robberies, horse theft and murder. Vigilante groups frustrated with the break down of the social order imposed 'lynch law' on guilty and sometimes less guilty parties.[207] The frontier itself exacerbated the problem as the sparsely populated region not only provided a refuge for fugitives from formal justice but also bred a culture of violence stemming from the inherent need for self protection and self reliance.[208]

This cauldron of burning political, economic and social disorder provided ample employment for the Rangers of the late 1800s. In August 1874, McNelly and his Special Force were dispatched to DeWitt County to deal with an outbreak of the Sutton-Taylor feud. The feud began in the late 1860s between the Sutton clan, representatives of the 'Reconstruction' establishment and the unapologetically pro-Confederate Taylor family. By 1874, the two armed factions terrorized the population and remained in a state of virtual warfare.[209] McNelly's Rangers rode into Clinton, the county seat, and remained for four months re-establishing order through a combination of protecting the courts and prisoners, scouting for renegade factions and developing a network of spies.[210] McNelly failed, however, to solve the feud and order could only have been maintained by his continual presence.[211]

The simmering quarrel erupted again in September 1876 when a physician and his son were brutally executed by a posse. Ranger Captain Lee Hall, McNelly's successor, faced a terrified populace unwilling to testify and an antagonistic sheriff whose own deputies had been implicated in the crime. Nonetheless, within three months, Hall's men had arrested seven suspects, five of whom had surrendered when the Rangers broke up a wedding celebration in dramatic fashion.[212] The accused were denied bail and conveyed to other more secure jails across the state. The Rangers had finally brought peace to DeWitt County.[213]

In the fall of 1875, Major Jones of the Frontier Battalion and twenty Rangers rode into Mason County, good cattle country intersected by the meanderings of the Llano River. The majority of the population was of German origin and Unionist in sentiment. The so called 'American' faction cherished and aggressively displayed their Confederate legacy. After suspected cattle thefts by the 'Americans' a German vigilance committee including the sheriff conducted several murders and lynchings. In response, Scott Cooley, the adopted son of one the victims, began exacting vengeance on the vigilantes. The Rangers, failed to catch the killers but their presence and patrols calmed the tensions. Cooley and his gang left the region and the sheriff also resigned his badge and departed.[214]

Almost two years later in June of 1877, Major Jones was forced to intervene in the famous Horrell-Higgins feud in Lampasas County. The troubles on this occasion were economic not political in nature. John Calhoun Pinkney Higgins, known as a hard man when dealing with criminals, and his cohorts contended that the Horrell faction were rustling their cattle. In February, in the Gem Saloon in Lampasas, Higgins' Winchester ended the life of Merritt Horrell. One month later, as the trial began in the district court, despite the presence in Lampasas of a Ranger company commanded by Captain John C. Sparks, an ambush five miles from town wounded two of Merritt's brothers.[215]

When Jones himelf arrived to take command, he learned that only four days earlier two further lives had been claimed by a gunfight in Lampasas itself. Jones responded forcefully to the challenge, at dawn on July 28, a body of Rangers led by Sergeant Nelson O. Reynolds arrested the Horrell brothers and a mere three days later captured Higgins and several of his associates. The Ranger Major pacified the feudists by forcing both sides to sign letters agreeing to end the conflict. Jones through diplomatic means at least temporaily restored peace to Lampasas County.[216] Both Sam Horrell and John Higgins lived long lives well into the twentieth century. The two other Horrell brothers, Mart and Tom, were shot to death in the Bosque County jail at Meridian, while awaiting trail for the death of a shopkeeper.[217]

In November 1877, Major Jones arrived in El Paso stepping in to a highly charged and volatile situation. The El Paso Salt War began when Charles H. Howard, acting on behalf of his father in law, attempted to assert private title to the traditionally communal Guadalupe Salt Lakes near San Elizario and force any person wishing to collect salt to pay a fee. The overwhelmingly Hispanic population of the region were infuriated by what they saw as illegal American seizure of common property. Two Mexicans who defied Howard and vowed publicly to collect salt, were brought, at Howard's instigation before a county judge. An angry armed mob of local Mexicans and *Tejanos* seized control apprehending the judge, the sheriff and Howard himself. While held prisoner, Howard was forced to relinquish ownership of the salt lakes and promise to leave the county and never return.[218] Just one week later, however, Howard did reappear, in the company of Lieutenant Louis H. Rucker and twenty U.S. cavalry ostensibly sent to guard the border against Mexican incursions. Howard, three days later, strode into Solomon Schultz's general store and gunned down Louis Cardis, a leader of the mob, before fleeing north to Mesilla, New Mexico.[219]

Over the ensuing weeks the Texas Rangers failed to distinguish themselves and left a humiliating blot on the otherwise excellent record of Major Jones. Upon his appearance in El Paso, the major began to raise a Ranger company, drawn from the local community, to keep the peace. His choice of John B. Tays as second lieutenant proved to be highly questionable, Tays, the brother of the local priest, had no law enforcement or military experience and no real skills other than integrity and willingness. Jones outraged the Hispanic community by refusing to enlist *Tejanos* in the Rangers as he felt that they could not be trusted. His decision not to arrest Howard for murder but instead allow him to voluntarily appear before a justice of the peace who subsequently released the suspect on bail further rankled the Mexican faction. Jones, however, believed he had resolved the situation and departed for Austin.[220]

In early December, Howard who had temporarily returned to Mesilla, reappeared in San Elizario with Tays and a ten man Ranger detachment. Howard was determined to intercept a Mexican caravan heading for the salt lakes. An angry crowd of around five hundred *Tejanos* and Mexicans laid siege to the Ranger headquarters. On December 17, following a five day battle, Tays surrendered on the understanding that none of the men would be killed. Howard and two other Americans, nevetheless, were seized, murdered and mutilated by the bloodthirsty mob. Tays' Rangers were disarmed and permitted to leave with town on their horses, their dignity, however, was left behind with the dead men they had pledged to protect.[221]

Governor Richard B. Hubbard, under pressure to suppress the insurrection, demanded federal action empathizing the participation of Mexican citizens. On December 20, U.S. Army troops arrived in San Elizario ending the uprising. Hubbard had also authorized Sheriff Kerber of El Paso County to raise a force of men in New Mexico to help maintain the peace. Over the next few weeks, this motley body of men, which included several known criminals, joined Tays' Rangers in perpetrating numerous atrocities on the local Texas-Mexican population. While the majority of the robberies, rapes and murders were attributed to the New Mexicans, Rangers were clearly implicated in the deaths of two prisoners shot at close range and were certainly involved in other acts of violent retribution.[222]

The conduct of the Texas Rangers during the El Paso Salt War can be judged to be a combination of incompetence, cowardice and needless brutality. The uprising was the only time when Texas Rangers have ever surrendered and allowed individuals under their protection to be executed. Major Jones himself, while not present at the clashes, was culpable of creating the poorest quality Ranger company since the inept Captain Tobin had bungled along the Rio Grande during the Cortina troubles of the 1850s.[223]

In addition to feuding factions, outlaws and criminal gangs posed a major threat to public safety and thus earned the attention of the Texas Rangers. In the mid 1870s, Kimble County, in central Texas had become a haven for fugitives and thieves. The rugged hilly terrain and cedar brakes provided excellent hideouts for the desperadoes.[224] By 1877, the criminal gangs so completely dominated the county that the process of law could no longer be executed. Judge W. A. Blackburn of the Seventeenth Judicial District wrote to Major Jones requesting a Ranger escort as the outlaws had even threatened to prevent the convening of the state district court.[225]

Jones, affronted by the deteriorating situation, mounted a swift and efficient response. In April, two companies of Rangers, maneuvering in five detachements converged on Kimble County scouring the country for known or suspected criminals. In a masterful and effective clean up operation Jones and his Rangers rounded up forty-one outlaws without a single shot being fired. The Ranger presence also enabled Judge Blackburn to summon the district court and hand down twenty-five indictments. The taming of Kimble County was an remarkable success for the Rangers. The fact that a stronghold of hardened desperadoes was pacified within a matter of days without a drop of blood being shed reflects both the ingenuity of Major Jones and the exemplary conduct of the Ranger companies involved.[226]

The 1870s also saw Rangers tangling with some of the most dangerous outlaws of the American West. On the chaparral plains between Laredo and the Nueces River, John King Fisher, a flamboyant dandified character, commanded a force of over a hundred outlaws who terrorized the region stealing property, rustling cattle and murdering those who opposed them. On June 4 1876, Leander McNelly and his Special Rangers surrounded King Fisher's headquarters on Pendencia Creek capturing the bandit chieftain along with nine of his men and retrieving eight hundred head of cattle. Arresting the desperado, however, proved to be easier than obtaining convictions. After receiving custody of the men, the Maverick County sheriff promptly released King Fisher.[227]

Following the death of McNelly, his successor, Lieutenant Lee Hall continued to pursue the elusive outlaw. Hall swiftly discovered that it was almost impossible to obtain a guilty verdict in court due to lack of substantive evidence combined with the reluctance of juries to convict such a renowned and dangerous individual. The Ranger Lieutenant instead sought to harass King Fisher through an extra legal campaign of constant indictments for a variety of crimes. After four long years of court appearances and incarcerations awaiting trial the 'king of the Nueces Strip' gave up his life of crime. Three years later in 1884 he was gunned down at the Vaudeville Theater in San Antonio.[228]

Sam Bass was born in 1851 near Mitchell, Indiana. He arrived in Texas in 1869 and worked as a farmhand and raced horses. In 1875, Bass and several comrades purchased a cattle herd on credit and engaged in a drive to the Black Hills. Bass failed to pay off the loan and invested his share in freighting, a saloon of ill repute and most notably a mine which caused him to go broke.[229] Bass and his friends turned to a life of crime, robbing trains and stage coaches. In September 1877, Bass and five companions acquired sixty thousand dollars by holding up the Union Pacific passenger train at Big Spring, Nebraska.[230]

Bass then returned to Denton County, Texas and engaged in the biggest spree of hold ups that Texas had ever witnessed. Two stage coaches and four trains were robbed within the next months stimulating public curiousity and stirring up the corporate interests. A vast array of forces, including Pinkerton detectives, bounty hunters, sheriffs, militia companies and Lee Hall's Special Force of Rangers combed Texas for the Bass gang without success.[231]

In April 1878, Governor Hubbard requested that Major Jones assume command of the pursuit. Jones, reluctant to remove Rangers from the frontier, formed a thirty man Ranger company in Dallas commanded by Lieutenant June Peak. One month later, Peak's Rangers located and clashed with Bass and his men at Salt Creek killing one bandit and capturing their horses.[232] Meanwhile Jones had ordered the mass arrest of all known accomplices of Bass and his band. James Murphy, a friend of the outlaw, agreed to join the gang as a Ranger informant in exchange for the charges against him being dismissed. In July, Jones received word from Murphy that Bass was preparing to rob the bank at Round Rock. As the Rangers prepared their ambush, Bass and two men rode into town on a final reconnaissance. Williamson county Deputy Grimes, informed that the strangers were armed, approached the outlaws but was killed in a fusillade of bullets. In the subsequent gun battle Bass was able to flee out of town but mortally wounded, he surrendered the next morning under a oak tree north of town. Two days after the gunfight, on his twenty seventh birthday, Sam Bass departed this world.[233]

The violence spawned by the Lincoln County War in New Mexico, made infamous by the legend of William H. Booney aka Billy the Kid, spilled across the Texan border in 1880. Jesse Evans was the notorious leader of 'The Boys', an outlaw band hired by the Murphy-Dolan group to oppose Billy the Kid and his posse of 'Lincoln County Regulators.' Following the decision of President Rutherford B. Hayes to allow the U.S. Army to restore order Evans and around twenty men moved to the mountains around Fort Davis. The gunfighters terrified the local authorities, but following an audacious robbery a sheriff led posse caught one gang member at Fort Stockton.[234]

Due to local fears of a potential jailbreak, Sergeant Edward A. Sieker and nine Rangers were dispatched to Fort Stockton. Arriving on June 6 the Rangers were able to prevent an attempted rescue attempt by the desperadoes. Following a tip off, Sieker and five Rangers, followed the trail of Evans and four companions from *Presidio del Norte* on the Mexican border deep into Mexico itself. A gunfight in the moutainous foothills resulted the death of one bandit and the surrender of Evans and the remaining two men. Ranger George Bingham was also killed during the battle. Jesse Evans was tried for the murder of Ranger Bingham and received a ten year sentence. In May of 1882, however, he escaped from a work detail at Huntsville Penitentiary and disappeared.[235]

John Wesley Hardin was arguably one of the most deadly gunfighters who ever lived. Hardin, born in 1853 at Bonham, Texas, killed between twenty and fifty men during his exceptionally violent life. He had been active in the Taylor faction during the DeWitt County feud but left the region in 1874 before the arrival of McNelly's Rangers. On May 26 1874, in Comanche, Texas, Hardin shot and killed Brown County Deputy Sheriff Charles Webb. It was this particular crime that placed the Rangers on the trail of the noted killer. Following the decision by the Texas legislature, in January 1875, to offer a reward of four thousand dollars to anyone who captured the outlaw, numerous bounty hunters also entered the hunt.[236]

In early 1877, Lee Hall, garnered information suggesting that Hardin had relocated to Florida. Hall enlisted Dallas police detective, John R. Duncan as a Ranger private and sent him undercover to make contact with Hardin's relatives and try to locate an address. Duncan reported back that Hardin was in Alabama using the alias John H. Swain. On August 18 1877, Duncan along with Ranger Lieutenant John B. Armstrong boarded a train in Austin and headed east to Alabama.[237] The Rangers, after arriving in the Yellowhammer State, learned that Hardin had recently travelled to Pensacola, Florida. In Florida, the Rangers recruited the asistance of the the

Escambia County Sheriff and arrested Hardin in a dramatic struggle on an Alabama bound train. The outlaw was transported first to Austin then Comanche, Texas where he was found guilty for the murder of Deputy Webb. The four thousand dollar reward was shared between the two Rangers. Hardin was pardoned in 1894 and set up a law practice in El Paso but in 1895, he was shot dead in the Acme saloon by city contable John Selman. Bizarrely perhaps, Selman was a cohort of Jesse Evans, who along with Evans had been arrested by the Rangers during their Mexican foray in 1880.[238]

During the late 1800s the Texas Rangers proved successful at adapting from an irregular military corps of citizen soldiers to agents of law enforcement. As the Indian threat receded and the international border became less turbulent, albeit temporarily, the Rangers devoted an increasing amount of time and effort suppressing 'internal' issues of feuds and outlawry. At these tasks the corps generally proved to be highly adept, with the exception of the dark episode of the El Paso Salt War, the mere presence of Rangers was often enough to calm the quarrelling factions. Rangers also demonstrated both bravery and presence of mind when dealing with notorious outlaws. In Texas, the 'bad men' of the West discovered no haven from the law, justice would be served on them, on occasion, a bullet from a six-shooter but more often a sentence handed down by a judge.

9
Tools of Big Business: the Cattle Kingdom and Industrial Growth

From their humble beginnings the Texas Rangers acted as both the guardians of the frontier and also as the defenders of Anglo-Texan economic interests. In the early years Rangers crossed the Rio Grande to retrieve stolen livestock or hunt down runaway slaves. The duties of the Texas Rangers included battling Indian warriors, Mexican raiders and outlaws of various ethnicities and through this pacification of the frontier acted as the field agents of Manifest Destiny and Anglo economic expansion. In the final decades of the 1800s, Ranger 'law enforcement' to a large degree often served the interests of the Anglo socioeconomic establishment at the expense of both *Tejano* communities and lower income white Texans. This proves to be especially true when examining their relationship with both the cattle barons and the nascent industrial businessmen.

As early as the 1690s, Spanish settlers had brought cattle into the Nueces Strip of south Texas. In the cattleman's paradise between the Nueces and the Rio Grande the Spanish longhorns flourished on the verdant grasses and abundant water. During the 1840s alone the number of Texan cattle grew from just over hundred thousand to nearly one million. By 1865, five million longhorns wandered the Texan plains.[239] Following the Mexican-American War, Anglo-American entrepeneurs and opportunists poured into south Texas dispossessing the *Tejano* landowners through both legal and quasi legal means. By the 1850s Anglo businessmen including Mifflin Kennedy, Charles Stillman and Richard King acquired enormous tracts of land ideal for raising vast herds of cattle.[240]

In 1836, Mexican *rancheros* established a cattle trail to the markets in New Orleans. This early venture was augmented in the 1840s as both Anglo arrivals and *Tejanos* drove herds to California, Lousiana and Missouri. The Civil War, notably the federal blockade of the Confederacy, stalled the emerging industry but in the post war years the growing demand for beef in the northern cities combined with the extensive cattle herds of south Texas stimulated the mass movement of Texas cattle to the railheads in Kansas and Missouri. In 1866 alone around two hundred and sixty thousand cattle took the trail to market.[241] The Cattle Kingdom had been born.

During the subsequent decades, gigantic ranches of unprecedented proportions, often backed by foreign investors, dotted the Lone Star State. The XIT operation owned land in nine Texas counties and ran cattle along a two hundred mile range, while the JA ranch of Charles Goodnight and John G. Adair, located in the Palo Duro canyon, comprised of seven hundred thousand acres.[242] A number of future Texas Rangers including James B. Gillett worked as cowboys on the trail drives and ranches of Texan cattlemen. As the cattle industry developed the corps frequently acted in the interests of the powerful syndicates at the expense of the small farmers and ranchers whether Anglo or Hispanic.[243]

The King Ranch, owned by Richard King, comprised of four divisions totalling eight hundred and twenty five thousand acres in the Nueces Strip.[244] King, a legendary Texas figure, enjoyed especially cordial relations with the Texas Rangers. A close investigation of the *Las Cuevas* Affair of 1875 (see Chapter 7) reveals the tight affiliation between the King Ranch and the Rangers. Prior to the raid the

Rangers had enjoyed the hospitality of the ranch and following the return of the stolen cattle Captain McNelly himself and four Rangers drove the sixty-five beeves bearing the King brand to the sprawling Santa Gertudris division. King and his family gave a feast to thank the Special Force and his daughters even baked two cakes to honor the exploits of 'The McNelly Rangers'.[245] King himself, also demonstrated his gratitude by equipping the Special Force with thirty brand new Winchester repeating rifles and abundant ammunition.[246]

The close ties between the King family and the Rangers resurfaced in 1902 during an incident that outraged the *Tejano* community of south Texas. The de la Cerda family were a wealthy ranching family whose land bordered the King Ranch and who opposed the further expansion of their Anglo neighbor.[247] It is also highly probable, however, that members of the family also mavericked cattle from the King herd. In May, Sergeant A. Y. Baker and two Rangers, while engaged in a nocturnal patrol for thieves, discovered Ramon de la Cerda placing his own brand on a King steer. Both men shot at the same time, de la Cerda's round killed Baker's horse but the Ranger's bullet struck the the thief above his right eye slaying him instantly. The official inquest, conducted by Justice of the Peace Estevan Garcia, concluded that the Ranger had acted in self-defense. An unofficial inquest, however, raised friction by claiming that de la Cerda had been tied and dragged before his death.[248]

Amid heightened tensions, Rangers Baker and Emmet Roebuck along with a King Ranch employee were ambushed while en route to Brownsville. The attack slew Roebuck and left Baker badly wounded. Nineteen year old Alfredo da la Cerda, who had made threats against Baker's life was arrested then released on bond. One month later, in a Brownsville store, Baker shot and killed the young *Tejano*.[249] Baker claimed that de la Cerda was preparing to draw and he was therefore acting in self-defence.[250] This version of events was accepted by the Brownsville court who acquitted the Ranger of murder. Local Mexican residents, nevertheless, asserted that the young man was unarmed and that Baker shot him in cold blood after stalking him as if hunting a wild animal.[251] The true version of events may never be known but it clear is that during the de la Cerda affair the Rangers acted on behalf of the King Ranch and were recognized as doing so by the local Mexican community.

The role of the Rangers during the so called Fence Cutting War of the mid 1880s offers further evidence that the corps had become the law enforcement tool favored and utilized by the large cattle syndicates. In 1874, barbed wire, was successfully patented by Joseph Glidden in Illinois. By the 1880s, wealthy Texas cattle barons, impressed by the usefulness and relative affordability of the new invention, had enclosed vast swathes of Texas with barbed wire. To give one example, by 1885, the XIT ranch had surround virtually all its three million acres with the new fencing.[252]

While a boon to enormous operations, small farmers and stockmen resented the fencing off of the open range. The larger ranch owners habitually seized, often illegally, the best land and water resources and subsequently fenced in their claims with barbed wire. The sharp twisting wires also crippled cattle and even led to death through screw-worm infection.[253] A number of homesteaders and small ranchers also resisted the fencing on moral grounds asserting that the wire destroyed the traditional open range and the access to communal grassland and water.[254] Sparked by the drought of 1883, small operators, arguably joined by cattle rustlers and other petty criminals, formed night riding bands of armed men, who cut the offending structures, 'liberated' stock and threatened fence builders. Adopting names such as the 'Knights of the Knippers' or 'The Land League', the cutters terrorized local communities and created a atmosphere a fear and animosity.[255]

In January 1884, Texas Governor John Ireland presented a special session of the legislature with a proposal to make fence-cutting a felony. The lawmakers agreed and approved a fund of fifty thousand dollars to combat the nippers.[256] From March 1884 the Rangers were tasked with the duty of restoring order by rooting out the offenders and ending the practice of fence-cutting. Governor Ireland, dipping into the fund provided, also hired Pinkerton and Farrell detectives to work with the Rangers during the operation.

In typical fashion, the Rangers adopted an aggressive but utimately successful approach in dealing with fence snippers. Ranger detachments engaged in several violent confrontations with armed bands of nippers. In July 1884, a Ranger detachment exchanged fire with several men on G. B. Greer's ranch slaying one perpetrator. Two years on property belonging to L. P. Baugh, four Rangers accompanied by Baugh's men ambushed and killed two suspects.[257] Ranger Ira Aten moved aggressively beyond the boundaries of the legal process by designing a "dynamite boom", a home made contraption intended to detonate when the wire was snipped.[258] Although ordered to remove his booby traps, Aten had demonstrated his devices to local ranchers and the threat of the dynamite bombs greatly reduced instances of nipping in the region.[259] It is clear that during the Fence Cutting War the primary mission of the Texas Rangers was to protect the ranches of the Anglo Texan elite and specifically to eradicate the practice of fence cutting by small ranchers and farmers.

In a similar fashion, as a nascent industrial system developed in Texas, the Rangers, as the representative arm of the state, acted to safeguard the interests of large capitalist enterprises. By 1890, the growing industrial base included over five thousand factories employing over thirty five thousand workers. In 1869, Texas only possessed around five hundred miles of railroad track, over the next twenty years the rail network increased exponentially to eight thousand five hundred miles. The massive railroad construction was mirrored by extensive coal mining operations especially in north Texas.[260]

The low pay and poor working conditions, especially in the mines, helped to stimulate unionization and strikes. The 1880s saw escalating number of strikes, sixty four in 1886 alone, many of which were orchestrated by The Knights of Labor. The KOL, formed in 1869, was a nationwide union with approximately seven hundred and fifty thousand members by the mid 1880s. The huge organization had dominated the labor arena in Texas since 1882 with approximately thirty thousand members scattered across the Lone Star State.[261] The increased labor unrest and appearance of the KOL concerned the 'kings of industry' and their allies in the political establishment.

The large mining and railroad corporations enjoyed close relations with the state government and as a result the Rangers, despite an alleged responsibility of impartiality, were frequently required to act as strikebreakers and support corporate goals over the aspirations of the workforce. In 1886, the KOL conducted a massive strike against the Missouri Pacific rail network owned by Jay Gould. During the Great Southwest Strike, over two hundred thousand workers, angry over diminishing wages and layoffs, went on strike across five states including Texas. At Fort Worth the strikers were confronted by hired thugs and Pinkerton detectives intent on breaking up the strike. The Texan authorities also acted swiftly, Governor Ireland dispatched two hundred and seventy seven Texas National Guardsmen and three Ranger companies to the scene. The Rangers played a minor but crucial role in ensuring the failure of the strike. Ranger units patrolled the railroad yards to protect property and ensure that strikebreakers could operate the trains.

In September 1888, the coal mines on the border of Erath and Palo Pinto counties came into the possession of the Texas and Pacific Coal Company headed by Robert D. Hunter. The new owner, determined to both revive the mining operation and remain in total control of the business, alienated the already striking workers by turning the company town of Thurber into a virtual fiefdom and refusing to allow any unionization of his workers. In December, nearly eight-five percent of the workforce was on strike shutting down the mines. Sheriff J. J. Humphries, acting on behalf of the TPCC, requested a Ranger presence in Thurber. Captain Sam A. McMurry and nine Rangers were dispatched and arrived in Thurber around one week later.[262]

The Rangers, despite officially remaining neutral in the matter, in reality McMurry and his men were firmly allied with Hunter and the TPCC. The Rangers enacted a number of repressive measures designed to intimidate the striking miners while protecting those still at work. When Hunter organized the importatation of over one hundred strikebreakers, McMurry ensured the safe passage of the 'scabs' from Dallas to Thurber, effectively breaking the strike by June 1889. During the troubles at Thurber, it is clear that McMurry and his Rangers were not impartial mediators in the labor dispute. The Rangers not only shared the corporate distaste of socialism and unions as unsurprisingly received fulsome praise from the TPCC management for their actions. Even more tellingly perhaps, the Ranger unit while in Thurber, collected their provisions from the company store and even wrote reports on TPCC letterhead.[263]

The year of 1894, saw the Rangers embroiled in further labor disputes. In March, Hunter and his TPCC had reduced wages in the coal mines which in turn stimulated worker organization and threats of violence. On June 8, Captain Bill McDonald, arrived in Thurber, the presence of the Rangers calmed the volatile sitaution. McDonald demonstrating a degree of impartiality, met with the miners, most of whom simply wanted to work, and was able to back down the minority of workers who favored a strike. The Pullman Strike, which began in June 1894 in Chicago, reached Texas when Eugene V. Debs, leader of the American Railway Union, threw the weight of his organization behind the strikers. The strike was eventually broken by a combination of court rulings and federal troops. Nevertheless, in Texas, Ranger companies under Captains' McDonald and John R. Hughes were forced to patrol the vast rail network stretching from the Red River to the Gulf of Mexico and engaged in several minor fracas.[264]

In 1903, the Rangers were once again called to maintain order in Thurber. Up to this point, the TPCC had successfully resisted any attempts to unionize the mineworkers at Thurber. In the summer of 1903, however, the United Mine Workers of America, fresh from a number of labor victories, infiltrated the company town and attempted to stir up union sentiment. On September 5th Captain John R. Rogers and a small group of Rangers reached Thurber. Rogers, held strong anti-union views, but recognized that the TPCC, in order to endure as a viable business, might be forced to accept unionization.

The decision over five hundred miners to defect from the TPCC and the subsequent costly failure to acquire strikebreakers ended the impasse with a deal to accept union recognition. The Rangers who had been requested by the TPCC, on this occasion adopted a restrained approach, and were praised by both management and workers for preventing disorder and keeping the peace.[265]

At the dawn of the 20th century, the duties of the Texas Rangers clearly included service as a tool of the primarily Anglo-Texan political and economic system. The corps, through force if need be, were expected to suppress any threats to the economic stability and future of the Lone Star State. This alignment of the Rangers with Anglo business would be further demonstrated nearly sixty years later by their repression of striking farm workers in the Rio Grande Valley (see Chapter 14). It would also embroil the corps in the most shameful episode of Ranger history, the brutal suppression of the Plan de San Diego.

10
Bandidos, Sediciosos and the Plan de San Diego

The Anglo colonization of the south Texas border region, especially along the Rio Grande, had established a socioeconomic system based on race designed to ensure that control of the economy and political system remained in the hands of white Americans. The *Tejanos* despite outnumbering the Anglo-Texans became second class citizens in their own established communities. In the words of Benjamin Heber Johnson, the Texas-Mexicans became "a conquered people subjected to the rule of their conquerors."[266] Anglo racism combined with land theft and the brutal actions of McNelly's Special Force created a climate of racial tension and sproradic violence. Following the overthrow of Mexican dictator Porfirio Diaz in 1911, Mexico tore itself apart in spirals of revolutionary bloodshed leading to further chaos and violence in the Rio Grande borderlands.[267]

The San Ambrosia Affair neatly encapsulates the sentiment in both the Anglo and *Tejano* communities during the late 1800s. In May of 1885, Ranger Sergeant Ben Lindsey accompanied by six men was scouting San Ambrosia Creek near Laredo looking for escaped convicts. The Ranger patrol encountered two Mexicans who immediately turned and fled. In the subsequent scuffle both Mexicans were wounded and Ranger Frank Sieker was shot through the heart.

When the Rangers continued their pursuit they were confronted by an armed posse headed by the deputy sheriff of Webb County. After a hot debate the Rangers agreed to proceed to Laredo with the deputy and the two prisoners. The sheriff, Dario Gonzales, a relative of the prisoners, promptly arrested the Rangers who would remain in jail for nearly a month. The two captives, however, were released and vanished into Mexico.[268]

From the viewpoint of the Texas Rangers, the patrol came upon two suspicious Mexicans, who attempted to flee at the mere sight of the lawmen and fatally gunned down a Ranger. Faced by an armed mob of the suspects' friends, the Rangers agreed to compromise only to be arrested and jailed by a vengeful *Tejano* sheriff who allowed the murderers of policeman to go free. To the Mexican community, however, two innocent men were chased by the *rinches*, known for shooting ethnic Mexicans in cold blood, they justifiably defended themselves and the sheriff rightly ensured they could not be convicted.[269]

In 1891, Catarino Garza led a rebellion to protest against both the Diaz regime in Mexico and the subjugation of *Tejanos* and Mexicans in the United States. Garza, born in Matamoros, Mexico, was a Texas resident who worked as a newspaper editor. In 1888, after accusing a U.S. Customs Inspector of murdering an ethnic Mexican, Garza was arrested by the Texas Rangers. The following month Garza himself was shot and wounded by the customs inspector sparking mass protests among the Mexican community. Three years later, Garza leading nearly one thousand men declared a revolution.[270] The *Garzistas* behaved as both patriots when battling the armies of the dictatorial Diaz and but also as brigands looting and plundering the Texan ranches.[271]

The U.S. government spurred by the urgent diplomatic protests from the Diaz regime dispatched cavalry to apprehend the revolutionary leader. Two Ranger Companies commanded by Captains' John A. Brooks and J. S. McNeel also took to the field. The Garza Revolution proved to be a total failure, Garza left Texas in 1892 for Central America and his followers faded away. The Rangers could take little credit, however, for the campaign. The companies made a mere handful of arrests and failed to catch either Garza himself or the killers of two Rangers who died during the conflict.

The spring of 1899 saw an outbreak of smallpox in the border town of Laredo. State regulations required that all infected individuals be isolated and all other citizens receive an inocculation. The substantive ethnic Mexican community, suspicious of Anglo authorities, refused to accept these measures especially the seclusion of friends and relatives deemed infected. A number of *Tejanos* threatened armed resistance against any attempt to implement the laws. In March, Captain John H. Rogers was dispatched to Laredo with small group of Rangers to keep order and ensure compliance with the health regulations. At the house of Agipito Herrera, a gun fight broke out between the Rangers and local Mexicans resulting in the death of Herrera and the wounding of Captain Rogers and ten townspeople. The innoculations only continued following the arrival of a force of U.S. soldiers, sent from Fort McIntosh to keep the peace.[272]

The life of Gregorio Cortez, immortalized in numerou Mexican *corridos* or folk ballads, is often cited as demonstrative of *Tejano* attitudes towards Anglo Texans and especially the Rangers. Cortez was born in Mexico in 1875, and later moved north of the border as a child.[273] Among historians, it is disputed whether Cortez was an upstanding citizen or a renowned horsethief.[274] What is not debatable, however, is that on June 12 1901, sheriff W. T. Morris of Karnes County, a ex Ranger, attempted to arrest Cortez and in the ensuing gunfight received fatal wounds. Two days later a bungled attack on the house where Cortez was hiding, left a second sheriff dead.[275]

During the course of the next ten days, Cortez eluded hundreds of pursuers including sheriffs and Texas Rangers in a chase that lasted across five hundred miles of chaparral country in south Texas.[276] The fugitive was finally captured by Ranger Captain Rogers eight miles from the Rio Grande after a tip off from a *vaquero*. For many *Tejanos*, Cortez became a folk hero and symbol of defiance against the hated *rinches*.[277] Cortez himself was sentenced to life in prison but received a pardon from Texas Governor Oscar Branch Colquitt in 1913.[278]

It should be noted, though, that in spite of residual ethnic tensions an acculturation of Anglos and Mexicans did occur through intermarriage and alliances between elites. The political machine of south Texas represented this fusion of cultures. While Anglo elites were typically elected to higher offices, *Tejanos* in exchange for mobilizing the Hispanic vote received patronage positions or obtained other benefits. Despite residual tensions between the communities as represented by periodic violent clashes this cultural synthesis brought a degree of stability to the borderlands.[279]

The early 1900s, however, saw dramatic changes in the Rio Grande valley. The railroad reached Brownsville in 1904 helping to create a market oriented economy tightly linked to the rest of America. As real estate prices rose, previously wealthy *Tejanos*, unable to pay increasingly higher property taxes, lost their lands. Anglo-American farmers also poured into the fertile region seeking a subservient Mexican labor force and challenged the political machine which they viewed as corrupt.[280] Many Texas-Mexicans angry at these new changes in their communities sought inspiration from the 'peasant armies' of the Mexican Revolution, seen as destroying the corrupt establishment leading directly to the Plan de San Diego.[281]

In January 1915, Basilio Ramos, a Mexican citizen who had spent a number of years in the U.S., crossed the Rio Grande bearing a copy of a manifesto which if successful would have shattered American control over the southwest. The Plan de San Diego appealed for a 'Liberating Army for Races and Peoples' to regain control of Arizona, California, Colorado, New Mexico and Texas. Once liberated these states would either be annexed to Mexico or form an independent republic. The Plan de San Diego also called for the execution of all prisoners and Anglo men over the age of sixteen.[282] Ramos himself was arrested and the plot revealed leading to adding fuel to Anglo-Texan fears of a potential race war. In July, Hispanic raiders, known as *sediciosos* or seditionists, led by Luis de la Rosa and Aniceto Pizana began a campaign that murdered dozens of Anglo-American farmers and ranchers as well as engaging in stock theft and attacks on passenger trains. Elite *Tejanos* were also targeted by the insurgents and many were robbed or killed.[283]

In response to the insurrection, Texas Governor James E. Ferguson ordered Captain Henry Lee Ransom to south Texas to 'clean up' the chaos along the border by whatever means necessary.[284] The Texas Ranger led counterinsurgency comprised of a campaign of violent repression and terror against the *Tejano* communities. Suspects were frequently summarily 'evaporated' with a bullet from a Colt 45 and mass lynchings were not uncommon.[285] Following a *sedicioso* raid on the Norias Division of the King Ranch, two Rangers and an unidentified third man posed for a photographer while on horseback with their lariats bound around the legs of dead Mexican 'bandits'. The photograph which was turned into a picture postcard further tainted the Ranger image.[286] The Rangers also indiscriminately harassed Hispanics and even launched deliberate campaigns to relocate entire communities across the international border.[287] It has been estimated that up to five thousand *Tejanos* may have been killed by during this bloody period.[288]

By June 1916, the 'bandit war' was over, U.S. regulars commanded by Major General Frederick Funston controlled the border and the *sedicioso* attacks had ended. The Texas Rangers, however, continued to enthusiastically 'evaporate' potential bandits.[289] Ironically, the unsuccessful revolt only served to heighten the plight of *Tejanos* along the border. The Anglo farmers used the rebellion as an excuse to disenfranchise the Hispanic vote, impose segregation and develop a caste system with the *Tejanos* at the bottom of a new social order.[290]

The Big Bend region of west Texas is a rugged region of canyons, mountains and grassy plateaux. During the early decades of the twentieth century, the Texan cattle ranchers were plagued by Mexican bandits and revolutionaries who preyed on their herds. Ranger Captain J. Monroe Fox and fifteen Rangers, headquartered at Marfa, lacking in both numbers and competence failed to secure the region.[291] The Rangers' increasingly relied on the U.S. army to guard the border, their only noteworthy act in policing the Big Bend was to add yet another dark stain to their already blemished record. On January 28 1918, at the mountain village of Porvenir, a combined force of Rangers and ranchers executed seventeen Mexicans including two teenagers.[292]

Following American entry into World War One the Rangers were appointed as draft officers receiving fifty dollars for every 'draft dodger' arrested. Rangers also meted out justice to those deemed 'disloyal'. Inevitably, Mexican-Americans, whether citizens or not, were frequently targeted by Ranger units.[293] The constant harassment helped to create a mass exodus of *Tejanos* across the Rio Grande into Mexico.[294]

The actions of the Texas Rangers during the Mexican Revolutionary era form the most shameful episode in their history. The bloody repression of the Plan de San Diego along with other atrocities committed against ethnic Mexicans would taint the Ranger image for decades to come. In 1919, in response to Ranger brutalities, J.T. Canales, a Texas-Mexican state congressman from Brownsville, called for an investigation of the Rangers that severely discredited the corps. On March 31, the Texas legislature passed a bill reducing the number of Rangers to seventy-six and removing their function as the primary state police force.[295]

11

The Roaring Twenties

The 1920s, the Jazz Age, as termed by American writer F. Scott Fitzgerald, represented both an era of excess characterized by rebellious music and sexual freedom but also traditionalist reactions to the new social norms as reflected in the growth of religious fundamentalism, nativist sentiment and racial prejudice. The United States in the postwar years was a nation torn between contradictory visions of its political and social future often drawn along lines which pitted cosmopolitan urbanites against insular rural communities determined to maintain what they viewed as the American way of life.[296]

In Texas, the Rangers confronted immense new challenges which tested their ability to function as a viable tool of law enforcement. The dramatic development of the oil industry created boomtowns which soon became epicenters of vice and corruption, the implementation of prohibition laws proved to be both unpopular and unenforceable while increased racial clashes and the influence of the second Ku Klux Klan hampered the due process of law. The rise of 'iconic' gangsters during the 'public enemy era' of the early 1930s exposed the weakness of the Ranger corps when confronted by criminals equipped with modern automobiles and weaponry even as the polititization of the Ranger force led to questions over the future of the organization.

The Texas Oil Boom began with the discovery of the Spindletop Gusher in January 1901. By the 1920s, a mass of boomtowns, both permanent and transitory, had sprouted up across North Texas. The towns swiftly degenerated into hotspots of criminality and chaos. Illegal liquor and gambling operations sprung up almost overnight while prostitutes freely plyed their trade amongst the oil field workers without restraint. Town and county offical including the police either accepted bribes or were active participants in the criminal enterprises. The sheer volume of illicit activity overwhelmed the ability of the honest local peace officers to enforce the law. Throughout the 1920s, a key component of the Ranger agenda would be establishing order and ending the corruption in the Texan boomtowns.[297]

On October 25 1917, the Texas and Pacific Coal Company discovered oil in Eastland County transforming the small community of Ranger into a burgeoning oil town. Vice and criminality, however, accompanied the fincancial boom, the notorious Commercial Hotel owned by Alfred "Kid" Jordan and Cleve Barnes was a particular showpiece of misconduct notably illegal gambling. By 1921, the numerous grievances concerning the chaos in Ranger convinced Adjutant General Thomas D. Barton to travel to the oil town and see for himself the allegedly chaos and iniquity. Barton discovered that Ranger was indeed infested with criminality and the Commercial Hotel was the centerpiece of the vice and corruption.[298]

On February 11, Captain Roy W. Aldrich and three Rangers raided the establishment arresting an impressive ninety patrons. After questioning the crowd the Rangers released three individuals, the remaining eighty seven gamblers were saved from jail when Barnes and Jordan offered to cover the fines and bail for each one of their patrons. The two owners kept to their word and duly paid around eighteen hundred dollars in fines. The Rangers despite the clear evidence of criminal activity failed to convict either Barnes or Jordan who were cleared of all charges by a local jury.[299] Both Governor Pat Neff and Adjutant General Barton realized that any future trials would be futile without the assistance of the local law enforcement, who were firmly in the pocket of the corrupt factions, and seeing no point in leaving the Rangers in town, on April 1 they pulled the Rangers out of the very town named in their honor.[300]

Governor Neff and the Texas Rangers enjoyed greater success in Mexia, a small community located on the boundary of Freestone and Limestone Counties. In August of 1921, towering gushers signaled the presence of oil in the area, almost overnight, the tranquil cotton region with around twenty-five hundred inhabitants was transformed into an anarchic, violent, crime ridden community of over fifty-five thousand oil field workers and parasitic thugs controlled by crooked lawmen and corrupt businessmen. The two largest and most notorious emporiums of sin were the Chicken Farm and the Winter Garden, at both establishments patrons gambled and drank under the watchful gaze of armed guards while the local authorities, well aware of what was going on, turned a blind eye.[301]

By December 1921, Governor Neff was so besieged by complaints that Adjutant General Barton dispatched an undercover Ranger to investigate. The subsequent report so shocked the the Adjutant General that he insisted on a second investigation by the Ranger this time in the company of a federal prohibition agent. When the second report proved to be to be even worse, Governor Neff turned to the Texas Rangers.[302] On January 7 1922, twenty Rangers armed with the latest Thompson Model 21 submachine guns and accompanied by six federal agents launched a formidable two pronged assault on Mexia. One team commanded by Captain Frank Hamer raided the Winter Garden while a second squad under the leadership of Captain Thomas R. Hickman hit the Chicken Farm. The Rangers arrested twenty-two suspects as well as impounding gambling equipment and liqour. The evidence of collusion with local law enforcement quickly became clear, both district and county judges along with lawmen including the sheriffs' of both Freestone and Limestone counties either withheld cooperation or gave low levels of assistance.[303] Amazingly, the Rangers discovered that a Limestone County Deputy not only lived only two hundred yards from the Chicken Farm but had sold the exact acreage where the establishment now stood. The deputy, however, clearly a sensible man, had retained the mineral rights.[304]

On January 11, Governor Neff, frustrated by the lack of collaboration by the local authorities, declared martial law in areas of both counties. Brigadier General Jacob F. Wolters along with around fifty National Guardsmen from the 56th Cavalry and 141st Infantry arrived in Mexia, Wolters ironically even used the Winter Garden as accomodation for his troops.[305] The presence of both the National Guardsmen and the Rangers had a positive impact on Mexia. Three thousand ruffians swiftly left town, many of those that remained were given orders to be gone by sundown. Local residents became active in regaining control of the town and before being reorganized even the recalcritant local authorities suddenly became more obliging.[306]

By the end of February, Mexia and the vicinity and been cleansed of organized crime and corruption. On March 1, the governor ended martial law. The combined force of Rangers and soldiers had made six hundred and two arrests, seized twenty-seven stills, destroyed over two thousand gallons of liquor and more than two hundred barrels of corn mash. In addition, the Rangers retrieved fifty three stolen automobiles and confiscated narcotics valued at four thousand dollars.[307] Most significantly, however, Mexia remained peaceful and free of vice or corruption. Former Ranger Alfred Mace became chief of a completely new police department and other key county or city offices were occupied by honest citizens.[308]

Borger, located in Hutchinson County, part of the Texas Panhandle, would prove to be far harder to tame. The town was founded on the bank of the South Canadian River in March 1926 by Asa P. "Ace" Borger and his business partner John R. Miller. Within three months the population grew to forty-five thousand and the booming oil town was tightly controlled by the two partners in collaboration with the Oklahoma crime syndicate of "Two-Gun Dick" Herwig. Prostitution, gambling and illegal liquor joints flourished and while other forms of criminality including widespread theft of machinery were rampant.[309]

In August 1926, Dallas J. Matthews, the adjutant general to Governor Miriam A. "Ma" Ferguson, dispatched Rangers J. B. Wheatley and H. D. Glasscock to investigate conditions in Borger. The Rangers quickly noted the presence of organized crime but were unable to act on their observations as the "business community" objected to their presence and due to their complaints Governor Ferguson withdrew the two men from the oil town. On October 1, however, a fifteen year old girl was shot and killed by thieves in Borger. Ten days later four Rangers led by Captain Roy Nichols arrived in Borger where they joined forces with five federal prohibition agents including former Ranger Manuel T. "Lone Wolf" Gonzaullas. The task force closed twenty businesses and arrested fifty individuals who were taken to jail in Amarillo. The remaining undesirable elements were ordered to leave town and by the end of the month following the election of John R. Miller of as mayor and his promise of an honest and efficient police force, the Rangers left Borger.[310]

By the spring of 1927, however, Borger was once again dominated by a criminal element whose activities included hold ups, bootlegging and numerous forms of vice. Conditions in the oil town bordered on anarchy. Over the course of March and April gangsters murdered a city policeman and two sheriffs deputies. Governor Daniel J. Moody ordered the Rangers to restore order and on April 7, Captains' Frank Hamer and Tom Hickman accompanied by eight privates arrived in Borger. During a three week operation the Rangers broke up a massive illicit enterprise involving both local officials and criminal gangs. The bootlegging traffic was cleaned up and over two hundred slot machines were destroyed. It was also estimated that around twelve hundred prostitutes left town. In addition, a number of public officials including the police chief and and Mayor Miller were forced to step down.[311] Ominously, however, significant elements of the broken criminal conspiracy remained in town including the corrupt sheriff, Joseph Ownbey.[312]

As early as June 1927, the pastors of the Baptist and Methodist churches expressed concerns about the resurgent power of the corrupt faction within the town.[313] By 1928, despite the presence of a vigorous reform group, the town was firmly under the control of a corrupt mayor, Glen Pace, his police chief and the ubiquitous Sheriff

Ownbey. In April 1929, the district attorney John A. Holmes asked the governor to authorize a permanent Ranger presence in Borger. Two months later seven Rangers commanded by Captain Hickman swept through town arresting thirty-five men on a by now familiar mission. The Rangers could not remain long however, as duties elsewhere required them to move on. Following their withdrawal the criminal factions reasserted their rule over the town.[314]

On September 13, Holmes was gunned down in his garage. The murder was almost certainly committed by the underworld in Borger possibly even by corrupt law enforcement officers. Governor Moody, facing a deluge of public outrage, acted swiftly, ordering Hamer and Hickman accompanied by three other Rangers to Borger. Following the receipt of a damning report from Captain Hamer the governor dispatched five more Rangers including Sergeant Gonzaullas, who had returned to the corps, to assist in the clean up. On September 28, after a series of meetings with key players, Governor Moody declared martial law in Borger and once again appointed General Wolters to command the mission.[315]

The combined Ranger and National Guard operation finally cleansed Borger of the stains of vice and corruption. Known mobsters were placed behind bars, sundown orders were enforced and the gambling joints were closed down. Over three hundred offenders were arrested. General Wolters refused to lift martial law until the mayor, city commission and all law enforcement officers resigned their posts and suitable replacements were found.[316] Once the conditions were met Governor Moody withdrew the military from Borger although the Rangers remained until the new police departments could function in an effective fashion. On October 29, the governor ended martial law. Two Rangers, however, stayed in Borger for a number of months as a deterrent to any lingering elements of the criminal community.[317] Although the murderers of district attorney Holmes were never brought to trial for the crime, the Rangers and National Guard had finally pacified the rowdy oil town.[318]

On October 3 1930, Columbus Marion "Dad" Joiner discovered a promising oil well in Rusk County, East Texas. Joiner had drilled into one the of largest oil fields ever discovered comprising of six hundred square miles in four Texas counties.[319] The small farm towns of East Texas were rapidly swamped by wildcatters and oil men accompanied by the usual assortment of bootleggers, con men, gamblers, prostitutes and robbers. In fact, the swarming criminal element in East Texas far exceeded levels previously experienced in Ranger, Mexia and even Borger.[320]

By this point in time, however, the Rangers had become adept at taming the oil towns through tried and trusted measures. Following a request for state aid from Gregg County Sheriff Martin Hays, Captain Hickman posted Sergeant "Lone Wolf" Gonzaullas and two privates to the town of Kilgore in February 1931. During their first month in town the Rangers forced around five hundred undesirables to leave the area. In March, they were reinforced by Captain Mace and six more Rangers. Within a twenty-four hour period the eleven Rangers had closed fifteen illegal establishments and made over five hundred arrests.[321] As Kilgore did not even have a jail Gonzaullas requisitioned the First Baptist church and handcuffed prisoners to a trotline attached to the pulpit.[322]

With Kilgore pacified the Rangers then proceeded to clean up Gladewater and Henderson the two other boomtowns of the vast oil patch. Throughout the spring months of 1931, the "Lone Wolf" and his men enforced the law in the piney woods of East Texas. The gamblers, prostitutes and other unlawful characters were not tolerated and received no quarter. Sergeant Gonzaullas opted for an extraconstitutional but effective test to determine the honesty of a suspect - check their hands. A man with dirty and calloused hands was likely to be a hard working citizen whereas an individual with smooth skinned hands was most probably a criminal whether a gambler, pimp or outlaw. The smooth skinned characters were swiftly hauled to the trotline.[323] Under the watchful eyes of the Rangers the East Texas boomtowns were repeatedly swept clean of violators and the crinimal fraternity.

The massive oil field, however, provided a new problem for the Texas Rangers, the illegal pumping of oil. All the producers in the East Texas strike drew their wells from the same oil pool and therefore raced to pump as much of the 'black gold' as fast as they possibly could. The vast amounts of oil being pumped forced down prices and threatened the entire depression era oil market. Although the Texas Railroad Commission attempted to regulate output through proportionally calculated caps on production well operators challenged the restrictions in the courts while others simply ignored them and boldly continued to pump.[324]

On August 16 1931, in an attempt to restore order and save the oil industry from total collapse, Governor Bill Sterling declared martial law in Gregg, Rusk, Smith and Upshur counties. General Wolters was once again called to take command. Twelve hundred National Guardmens aided by fourteen Rangers closed down the entire oil field.[325] On September 2, production was allowed to resume provided operators respected the per-well limit set out by the Railroad Commission. The regulations, however, remained impossible to enforce, producers used an array of techniques to avoid the laws and many continued to defiantly exceed the limit set. The quest of the Rangers and guardsmen to prevent the pumping of 'hot oil' achieved few successes and as early as October production far exceeded the maximum levels allowed by the commission.[326]

On January 16 1919, the Eighteenth Amendment was ratified when Nebraska became the thirty-sixth state to accept it. The amendment forbade the manufacture, sale and transportation of intoxicating liquors. The federal law was the result was the result of decades of effort by temperance organizations such as the Anti-Saloon League and represented the reforming zeal and moral righteousness of elements within the Progressive movement.[327] In Texas, the Eighteenth Amendment forced the Ranger corps to act as statewide agents of Prohibition. In enforcing the law the Rangers were impeded by the long and porous Mexican border, a long seacoast, the proximity of Cuba to Texan ports, notably Galveston, as well as public hostility to a federal law that many Texans neither wanted or respected.[328]

The Rio Grande border with Mexico stretching from the South Texas chaparral country to the Big Bend had been a hotbed of smuggling activities for decades. Nationwide Prohibition laws led to a massive increase in the activities of the *tequileros*, Mexican liquor traffickers. In Mexico, a gallon of liquor could be procured for as little as two dollars a gallon then sold in the United States for up to ten dollars a quart.[329] Heavily armed bands of smugglers crossed into Texas on horseback handing the liquor on to criminals in fast cars who then distributed the contraband to cities as far as away as St. Louis, Missouri.[330]

The responsibilty for the three hundred and fifty mile South Texas border between Brownsville and Laredo fell onto the shoulders of Captain Will Wright. A fifty-three year old Ranger veteran, Wright personified integrity and professionalism. Wright usually accompanied by around six Rangers and one or two federal customs agents scouted the chaparral country looking for the signs of *tequilero* activity. Locating and chasing down the well armed smugglers was tough and dangerous work frequently resulting in a gunfight. In 1921 alone the Rangers captured or destroyed ten thousand quarts of illicit liquor. During the month of November, Wright and his men engaged in three gun battles over a five day period arresting six smugglers and confiscating four thousand quarts of whiskey.[331] On one notable occasion, the *tequileros* had also left behind two freshly cooked goats, which the hungry Rangers swiftly requisitioned to state use.[332]

The rugged mountains and canyons of the Big Bend Country also presented major obstacles to the lawmen. A number of Rangers posted in the region were competent and able men, notably Arch and Ray "Pinochle" Miller who patrolled the Rio Grande east of the Chisos Mountains. Although the Rangers would occasionally capture smugglers they were not highly effective and failed to catch the infamous Chico Cano who had been bedeviling lawmen for over a decade. The lack of success of the Big Bend Rangers can be attributed in part to their egotistical and posing captain, a political appointee by the name of Jerry Gray. The six-shooter mentality also prevailed in the Big Bend country in the Rangers' dealing with Mexicans whether innocent or guilty.[333]

The smuggling of illicit liquor, however, was a comparatively minor problem compared to the vast number of illegal moonshine stills that had rapidly materialized across the state. While the majority of Texans were so called 'drys' who approved of prohibition, the vast number of 'wets' provided a rich business for the moonshiners. With the exception of arid West Texas, huge numbers of stills appeared in almost every county across the state. Some local law enforcement officers appealed to Austin for Rangers while others either ignored the problem or profited from the traffic in the 'white lightning'.[334]

The community of Glen Rose, in Somervell County, was known to state officials as the 'mountain moonshine rendezvous'. Located approximately fifty miles southwest of Fort Worth in craggy forested hills with plenty of springs, the locale was ideal for distilling moonshine and hiding the tell tale stills. The moonshiners of Somervell County supplied liquor to cities all across the Lone Star State including Dallas, Fort Worth, Waco and Wichita Falls. The local community including the sheriff profited from the enterprise and resented any outside interference.[335]

Governor Pat Neff, a Baptist, who possessed a deep seated personal conviction in the righteousness of prohibition, dispatched an undercover officer to Somervell County in July 1923. The agent, Richard Watson, within one month obtained enough evidence of illegal moonshining to warrant a raid. On August 25, Rangers Marvin 'Red' Burton and R.D. Shumate led a posse of local lawmen into Glen Rose. In two days the Rangers arrested fifty men, killed the leader of a moonshining syndicate in a gunfight and demolished twenty three stills. The raid was a formidable setback for the county's distillers but despite Neff's best intentions, slowly and steadily Glen Rose stealthily moved back into the lucrative moonshining industry. Richard Watson, while testifying in Cleburne, where the trials were held, was shot dead one night.[336]

In September 1925, Captain Roy Nichols and several Rangers were present in Marshall, located in Gregg County, to prevent the potential lynching of three African-Americans who had murdered a white man in neighboring Panola County. Nichols, however, not only thwarted the attempted lynching but also engaged in an energetic campaign to root out the moonshiners in that part of East Texas. The Rangers destroyed four sills, arrested over one hundred and forty suspects and captured ten thousand quarts of liquor. On December 29, two Rangers accompanied by four local lawmen attempted to arrest the operators of a still northwest of Marshall. The moonshiners, allegedly the biggest bootleggers in East Texas, chose to fight it out with the result that one criminal died and the rest were seized by the Rangers.

San Antonio, with a population of two hundred thousand, was predominantly Mexican-American and hosted a large military base at Fort Sam Houston. The residents of the Alamo city brazenly ignored the prohibition laws and enjoyed the vast amounts of both locally distilled moonshine and illicit liquor flowing north from Mexico. The city administration and the police saw no need to enforce the federal laws and typically turned a blind eye. Governor Neff, however, was deeply offended by this flagrant violation of the 18th Amendment and on July 24 1923 Adjutant General Thomas D. Barton accompanied by Captain Hamer and three Rangers raided several joints including the Pastime Club where they arrested twenty-six people.[337]

Governor Neff swiftly organized an emergency Ranger unit to enforce the law in San Antonio. In September 1923, Company E, comprising of ten men led by Captain Berk C. Baldwin took up residence in the oldest city in Texas. In the months that followed, Baldwin and his Rangers actively pursued not only moonshiners and bootleggers but fell on gambling joints and other law breakers as well. In one notable incident the Rangers burst into an illegal cockfight apprehending one hundred and fifty suspects including policemen and deputy sheriffs. Neff, ignoring the loud protests from the San Antonio mayor John W. Tobin, local judges and law enforcement agencies, kept the Ranger force in San Antonio until the end of his tenure as governor. Company E only departed the Alamo city in February 1925 following the election of Miriam 'Ma' Ferguson.[338]

Although, Baldwin and his men never succeeded in entirely pacifying the party loving citizens of San Antonio the Rangers did achieve a number of impressive statistics. Company E, captured three hundred stills, one hundred and ten thousand gallons of illegal alcohol as well as closing over forty gambling joints and a number of cockfighting arenas. Governor Neff could lay claim to three hundred and sixteen convictions all stemming from violations of the federal prohibition law.[339] Implementing prohibition laws had transformed the Rangers, albeit temporarily, from citizen soldiers who battled Indians, Mexicans and outlaws to vice cops who attempted to enforce an unpopular law on an often unwilling citizenry. The Rangers during prohibition faced an impossible and thankless task. Following the repeal of the Eighteenth Amendment in 1933, few Rangers lamented its passing.

The 1920s was in many ways a decade of excess marked by a new social morality in which young people, especially in the larger cities, experimented with new forms of entertainment, recreation and sexuality. The 'modern' social norms, however, combined with the political radicalism, labor strikes and race riots sparked a traditionalist backlash connected Anglo Saxon racism, Nativism and Protestantism.

At the infamous Sacco and Vanzetti trial, two anarchist Italian immigrants, Nicola Sacco and Bartolomeo Vanzetti were accused of stealing sixteen thousand dollars and murdering a paymaster and a guard. The evidence was overwhelming and the two defendants were executed in 1927. The presiding judge, however, was clearly biased, privately describing the men as "anarchist bastards."[340] The so-called Scopes "monkey trial" of 1925 was also reflective of public sentiment. John T. Scopes, a high school science teacher was placed on trial in Dayton, Tennessee for violating a state law that forbade the teaching of evolution. Although Scopes was found guilty, nobody denied he had taught evolution, the trial was historically significant as a public duel between fundamentalist Christianity and modernism. It is worth noting that in Texas, Governor "Ma" Ferguson directly outlawed any school textbook that contained Darwinist thought.[341]

The turbulent post war era, also saw the rise of the Second Ku Klux Klan. Founded by William J. Simmons near Atlanta in 1915, the invisible empire, based on the Reconstruction era vigilante group, only accepted native born Anglo-Saxon Protestants as members and was dedicated to a bigoted traditionalist vision of the American way of life. African-Americans, Catholics, Jews and immigrants were the targets of the hooded and robed terrorists.[342] It should be noted, however, that the Klan also claimed to stand for law and order, albeit its own warped version, and opposed both crime and fraud in government. Thousands of Klansmen who had never seen a Catholic or a foreigner viewed the organization as a tool to fight back against criminal activities and corruption.[343] The second KKK enjoyed a membership as high as four million during the 1920s and held significant sway in local politics. The Klan, however, was never powerful enough to seriously challenge the political power structure and its willingness to use violence alienated most Americans.[344]

In Texas, the first KKK chapter, the Sam Houston Klan Number 1, was formed in Houston on October 9 1920. The 'King Kleagle' of Texas, George B. Kimbro, then began a vigorous recruiting campaign across the Lone Star State.[345] By 1922, the Second Klan had more than one hundred chapters in Texas, with up to ninety thousand, mostly proletarian, members.[346] Flaming crosses lit up the starry skies while hooded night riders terrified communities administering 'justice', including floggings and lynchings, to bootleggers, moonshiners, prostitutes and individuals of 'low morality' as well as African-Americans or Hispanics who pushed the boundaries of the racial caste system within the state.[347]

It is probable that a number of Texas Rangers quietly supported the agenda of the hooded order and a few may have even held membership. During the 1920s, peace officers, including sheriffs and policemen throughout Texas, joined the organization and on occasion donned the white hood and participated in the barbarity. Even lawmen who did not become members frequently and judiciously ignored the Klan's violence in their jurisdiction. Governor Neff, although no Klansman, shared a similar code of morality, and he both refused to criticize the KKK and never dispatched the Rangers against the order. Although opposed to the brutal vigilante violence adopted by Klan supporters, many Rangers were undoubtedly sympathetic to the organization and were relieved not to be forced into a direct encounter with the 'robed knights'.[348] It should be noted, however, that in 1922, the Anti-Klan League demanded an investigation regarding KKK membership within the Rangers. After a formal inquiry including interviews with all serving Rangers, Adjutant General Thomas D. Barton reported back that there were no Klansmen within the Ranger Corps.[349]

The Klan of the 1920s did not introduce white supremacy to the Lone Star State. Segregation, the so called Jim Crow laws and racial deference had been embedded in Texan politics and culture since the 1890s. The racist nature of the social order was solidly entrenched and unquestioned by Texans. Any challenge to Anglo-Texan supremacy, especially sexual relations between a black man and a white woman, was met with savage brutality whether in the form of lynchings or mob violence. While the Texas Rangers of the 1920s were white Texans and undoubtedly supported Anglo supremacy, the organization also stood for law and order. Rangers unlike local law enforcement officers proved to be both willing and able to prevent mob action against African-Americans. The mere presence of a Ranger was often, though always, enough to prevent a race riot.[350]

In July 1919, Longview, a small town of around seventeen thousand people in Gregg County, erupted into violence. A black man who allegedly made sexual advances on a white women was whipped then lynched. On July 10, groups of African-Americans began to form to counter Anglo violence against their community. Shots were fired as the two mobs clashed and the homes of prominent black leaders were burned down. At the request of the sheriff and county judge, Governor William P. Hobby dispatched eight Rangers commanded by Captain William M. Hanson along with one hundred National Guardsmen. Following the murder of a black doctor, Hobby declared martial law and sent another one hundred and fifty guardsmen to Longview. While the military pacified the town, the Rangers investigated the events and subsequently arrested twenty-six whites and twenty-one blacks. On July 18, the governor ended martial law and local authorities astutely dropped the charges against all the suspects thus defusing racial tensions.[351]

On February 26 1924, in Lufkin, located in Angelina County, a African-American man, Booker T. McMillan, shot and murdered a white male. McMillan was promptly arrested by Sheriff R. V. Watts and placed in the county jail. An incensed crowd of local white residents swiftly gathered and surrounding the jail demanded a lynching. The mob only dispersed after the sheriff and his deputies opened fire wounding three men. Governor Neff initially posted a military presence in Lufkin and then ordered Adjutant General Barton, Ranger Captains' Nichols and Aldrich along with three other Rangers to replace the guardsmen. Under the watchful eye of the Ranger detail the trial took place in an orderly atmosphere and the team only departed following the safe arrival of McMillan at the Huntsville penitentiary.[352]

The Sherman Riot of May 1930 was arguably one of the most appalling and vicious incidents in Texan history. It also represents a rare occasion when the Rangers failed to protect the life of a prisoner in their custody. On May 3, a forty-one year old black field hand named George Hughes brutally raped his employer's wife near Sherman in Grayson County. Hughes was swiftly arrested and confessed to the crime. As early as May 5, a rowdy and ugly crowd began to gather in Sherman determined to administer their own form of justice. In the hope of avoiding mob action the trial was scheduled for May 9 and at the request of District Judge R.M. Carter, Governor Moody dispatched Captain Frank Hamer and three Rangers to support the sheriff and his deputies.[353]

On the morning of the trial, with the court in progress an angry mob attempted to storm the courthouse and seize the defendant.

Time and time again a wave of infuriated citizens charged the stairs towards the courtroom only to be repelled by the Rangers armed with shotguns, rifles and tear gas. The crowd then changed tactic, a can of gasoline was flung into the basement and the seventy-one year old courthouse caught alight. Hughes, had earlier, for his own safety been locked in a huge steel and concrete vault in the county clerks office. Hamer, unable to locate, anyone with the combination and fearing for the safety of his men as the fire spread was forced to abandon the prisoner.[354] While a large number of the four thousand strong mob then besieged the Rangers and National Guard reinforcements in the jail others retrieved the body of Hughes which was hung from a cottonwood tree in a black section of the city and burned by a bonfire lit beneath him. The crowd then proceeded to loot and burn black businesses and homes. It was not until 4am the next day that a force of two hundred National Guardsmen and Ranger reinforcements led by Captain Tom Hickman regained control of Sherman. Out of the thousands of participants in the riot only one man was ever brought to trial. He was convicted in June 1931 and served two years in the Huntsville Penitentiary.[355]

While Captain Hamer could hardly be condemned for his actions, he had done all that he could under the circumstances, when a repeat tragedy threatened to occur a mere two months later the Rangers adopted a more aggressive approach. On July 11, a black man, Jesse Lee Washington, beat to death a white Texan woman, Mrs. Henry Vaughan in the town of Shamrock situated in Wheeler County. Following the suspect's arrest in nearby Collingsworth County and subsequent confession, an infuriated mob threatened to demolish the black district of Shamrock.[356]

In response to a request from Sheriff W. K. McLemore of Wheeler County, on July 13, Governor Moody sent four Rangers including Manuel T. 'Lone Wolf' Gonzaullas to enforce the law and protect the prisoner. Upon their arrival, the well armed Rangers informed all interested parties that not only Washington but all other African-Americans would be protected regardless of the cost. On July 16, Sheriff McKinney with Ranger assistance engaged in an elaborate ruse to fool the mob when delivering his prisoner to the Gray County jail in Pampa. The next day the sheriff and Rangers once again thwarted the angry crowds by safely transporting Washington first to his arraignment in Shamrock then returning him to jail in Pampa. Four Rangers remained in Pampa to guard the prisoner until his trial. At his trial Washington was sentenced to the electric chair, his eventual fate was in little doubt, the question was whether he would executed legally according to state law or be murdered at the hands of a vengeful mob.[357]

The 1920s represented an era of prosperity for many Texans and as a result labor disputes were infrequent. Nevertheless, many workers remained underpaid and labored in poor working conditions. Inevitably, this led to unionization and strikes. As on previous occasions the Rangers were frequently required to act as strikebreakers by enforcing the laws of state and ensuring an uninterrupted flow of commerce as desired by the business community. Galveston and Denison provide two examples of the key role played by the Ranger corps in suppressing strikes and keeping open the conduits of trade.

In 1920, Galveston was the busiest cotton port in the whole country. On March 19, sixteen hundred coastwise longshoremen (dockworkers who unloaded coastal as opposed to ocean going ships) belonging to the International Longshoremen's Association joined a nationwide strike for higher wages. The striking dockworkers demanded a wage increase from sixty to eighty cents and hour to achieve parity with the longshoremen who handled the oceangoing freight. Race was also a factor, the coastwise workers were predominantly of Afro-Caribbean origin while the deep-sea workers were primarily white locals. On May 10, an attempt to bring in non-union strike breakers to the island city led to outbreaks of violence including gunfire across the docks.[358]

Adjutant-General W. D. Cope, in response to a request for Ranger assistance, dispatched Captain Aldrich and three Rangers to Galveston. Aldrich reported back that the city was a potential powder keg of violence. Cope himself then travelled to the city at the behest of Governor Hobby who had been appealed to by the business community. On June 7, based on Cope's report, and more than aware that a bumper cotton crop as well as hundreds of tons of other merchandise remained at the wharves, the governor declared martial law. Once again General Wolters took command of a thousand National Guardsmen to impose law and order. By June 10, strikebreakers were able to load the first ship with a cargo or cotton and rice.[359]

Hobby, however, decided to seize the opportunity to clean up the island city a notorious hotbed of gambling, prostitution and bootlegged liquor. The Rangers and guardsmen, more than aware that alcohol further fueled the tensions leading to more violence, enthusiatically implemented the prohibition laws. On the other hand, the lack of local assistance led Hobby to suspend the entire Galveston police department and and removed any law enforcement powers from the city authorities. The governor though, after meeting with a citizens committee on September 18 did agree to end martial law as soon as possible and hand full authority to the Rangers. Captain Joe B. Brooks commanded a force of over twenty Rangers which patrolled the streets of Galveston and formally took control on October 7 when Hobby ended martial law. By December, the strike and been defeated and Galveston had been tamed, at least temporarily. During their four month visit, the Rangers had made over fifteen hundred arrests and when they deaparted, Mayor H.O. Sappington made no secret of his desire to see the Rangers remain in the city.[360]

Two years later, Governor Neff faced his own unpleasant and nettlesome confrontation between labor and management. On July 1 1922, during a dispute over pay cuts, four hundred thousand railroad workers nationwide walked off the job against the wishes of Union officials.[361] In Denison, Texas, the largest freight depot south of Chicago, fourteen hundred workers joined the strike, effectively bringing to a standstill the Denison railyards of the Missouri, Kansas and Texas Railroad as well as the Texas Pacific Railroad. The strikers drew up picket lines, damaged company property and intimidated other employees. On July 11, the striking workers, with the connivance of local law enforcement, kidnapped twenty-four strikebreakers, took them to the Red River bridge and after brutally flogging them banished the scabs into Oklahoma.[362]

On July 15, the governor ordered Adjutant General Barton and Captain Hickman to Denison to investigate the situation. Neff himself, in disguise, also visited the city in order to form his own opinion of the crisis. On July 23, the governor ordered forty-four Rangers, virtually the entire force to Denison to maintain order. The federal government, however, prompted by the concerns of the railroad companies, believed that hundreds more armed and well trained men were needed. After a thinly veiled threat by a U.S. Army Colonel that federal troops from Sam Houston would be dispatched to Denison unless the governor summoned the National Guard, Neff grudgingly declared martial law on July 24. The Rangers aided by nearly five hundred National Guardsmen rapidly established order and kept the peace. Denison remained under martial law until October 22.[363]

Governor Neff, justifiably concerned about the economic implications if the strike spread to other Texan railroad cities invoked the Open Port Law on July 26. The law, passed under the Hobby administration, banned any action which interfered with free trade anywhere across the state.[364] Rangers were posted to fifteen railheads across Texas including Captain Hamer in the Panhandle and Captain Hickman in Denison and Sherman. A contingent of emergency Rangers was also formed to supplement and aid the regular force. The fact that this force, as many as four hundred and fifty men, were paid by the railroad conglomerates, neatly demonstrates the close ties between big business and law enforcement during this period. The Rangers ran the trains, guarded against sabotage and secured the tracks until the Open Port Law was cancelled in January 1923. At both Galveston and Denison, the determination of the respective governors to crush the strikes helped to endure major victories over the labor movement and were serious setbacks for the unions. In the eyes of the workers, however, the Rangers once again appeared to the tools of big business and the political establishment.[365]

The 1920s bore witness to an explosion in crime especially bank robberies often committed by so-called celebrity gangsters. Outlaws such as Pretty Boy Floyd, Machine Gun Kelly and most famously John Dillinger, making use of the new federal and state highways, sped across the South and Midwest in powerful automobiles holding up banks or stores and murdering those who attempted to stop them. This new class of heavily armed bandits posed fresh challenges for law enforcement agencies nationwide including the Bureau of Investigation headed by J. Edgar Hoover. The eruption of bank robberies across Texas also placed question marks on the effectiveness and relevance of the Texas Rangers.[366]

In February 1925, the Rangers scored a major success in the arrest of the Story gang. In the town of Denton, north of Dallas, local police arrested N. A. Story on suspicion of auto theft. Within a few minutes his heavily armed comrades appeared in the town square provoking a major gun battle in the small community. The gang then withdrew to a cottage belonging to one of their associates. Ranger Captain Hickman, unarmed and accompanied by the attorney for the Story family entered the cottage and in a protracted negotiation achieved the surrender of the gunmen. Hickman, however, believed that the gang were involved in more than merely car theft. In a subsequent investigation the Rangers discovered common links in a number of unsolved bank robberies including the use of acetylene torches, numerous weapons and powerful automobiles. Hickman deduced that the gang used Denton County as a base of operations and on August 24, the captain supported by both Rangers and local police raided the Story ranch arresting six men including Yancy Story the brother of the original suspect.[367]

On September 8 1926, Ranger Hickman brought to justice another violent band of thieves who had been plaguing the Lone Star State. Hickman had begun to increasingly search for common modus operandi among the robberies as well as placing undercover agents in the criminal fraternity. He noted that one particular gang had been using women to reconnoiter the banks and take possession of the stolen loot. The Ranger Captain also observed that this particular group preferred to hit the banks at noon when there were fewer customers.[368] After receiving a tip that the Red River Bank in Clarksville could be the next target of the gang Hickman accompanied by an ex Ranger, Stewart Stanley, kept the bank under surveillance from Hickman's car. After observing two male suspects enter the bank and emerge with a suitcase Hickman and Stewart with guns leveled, confronted the pair and ordered them to surrender. The robbers foolishly opened fire on Hickman, a noted marksman, and within a few seconds both men were dead. The Ranger captain had recovered over thirty-three thousand dollars and personally received a reward of two thousand three hundred dollars. The Bexar County District Attorney also heartily commended the 'Hickman method' of preventing bank robberies.[369]

By late 1927, bank robberies were becoming a daily occurrence across Texas. On December 23 of that month the most dramatic bank heist in state history occurred in the railroad town of Cisco in Eastland County. Four armed men, one bizarrely dressed in a bright Santa Claus outfit, stole over twelve thousand dollars in cash and one hundred and fifty thousand dollars worth of nonnegotiable security bonds. The gang then engaged in a protracted shoot out with police and enraged locals mortally wounding Chief of Police G. E. 'Bit' Bedford and one of his deputies. As the robbers attempted to change vehicles during the subsequent high speed car chase one of the criminals was mortally hit by a bullet and the cash and securities were abandoned. Captain Hickman assisted by Sergeant Gonzaullas then took command of one of the biggest manhunts in Texan history. The Rangers armed with Thompson machine guns used bloodhounds and even an biplane, the first time a Ranger had ever used aircraft to search a suspect, to pursue the fleeing gangsters. The Santa Claus robber was shot and captured by an Eastland County sheriff's posse on the December 27 and three days later exhausted, near starving and wounded the two remaining robbers were arrested in the town of Graham.[370]

On May 23 1934, the 'celebrity gangsters' Bonnie and Clyde were gunned down by a five man posse, including former Ranger Frank Hamer, deep in the piney woods of Bienville Parish, Louisiana.[371] Bonnie Parker and Clyde Barrow, despite their now legendary status, rarely made headlines during their lives due to a national press focused on the exploits of John Dillinger. In Texas, however, the couple became notorious criminal icons due to their love of guns, fast automobiles and their brief but exceptionally violent criminal careers.[372] Raised in Dallas, the outlaw pair roamed half a dozen states committing numerous robberies and the Barrow gang was responsible for twelve homicides. In January 1934, the unsavory pair, busted four of their accomplices from the Eastland Prison Farm resulting in the death of a prison guard.[373]

Following the brazen prison breakout, Ranger Captain Estill Hamer led a team that kept the 'heat' on the criminal couple but the Rangers would ultimately fail to track down the outlaws. In fact, it was ex Ranger Frank Hamer, the brother of Estill, who would ultimately play a key role in ending their murderous spree. On February 11, Texas prison director Lee Simmons, embarrassed and furious over the escape from Eastland, hired Hamer to track down the killers. The search intensified after Barrow and his compadre Henry Methvin shot down two Highway Patrolmen near Grapevine, in Denton County, north of Dallas.[374] Unbehown to the felonious couple, Methvin had in February agreed to betray them in exchange for a pardon from Texas Governor Miriam Ferguson. After several weeks of waiting and planning, a team commanded by Bienville Parish Sheriff Henderson Jordan and including Hamer, former Ranger B. M. 'Manny' Gault, two Dallas County Sheriff's Deputies and a Bienville deputy sheriff lay in wait for the crooks on a rural gravel road near Gibsland, Louisiana. As the murderous pair approached, the lawmen fearing that Clyde might once again shoot his way to freedom, opened fire on the tan Ford V-8. In the ensuing shootout both Bonnie and Clyde were killed.[375] The bullet ravaged vehicle was discovered to contain a veritable arsenal of weaponry including three Browning automatic rifles, two sawed off shotguns, one revolver and nine automatic pistols.[376]

The spree of bank robberies, forty-three between 1924-27 and fifteen in the first nine months of 1927, also led to unforeseen and tragic consequences.[377] The Texas Bankers Association, frustrated with the inability of law enforcement to end the crime wave and equally unimpressed by the failure of the courts to convict and hand down severe sentences to the crooks, took drastic measures of its own. In each of the fifteen hundred member banks in Texas a large sign was placed stating clearly and unequivocably "Reward Five thousand dollars for dead bank robbers not one cent for live ones."[378] Association president W. M. Massie stated that the aim was "to make bank robbery unhealthy in Texas." [379] The reward may or may not have deterred some would be thieves but what is certain is that the bank robberies continued apace.

The Texas Bankers Association, in placing the reward, did however create more problems for the Texas Rangers. By tapping into the avariciousness of the Texan public the bankers had complicated the task of law enforcement. Following an alleged heist, posses of armed men swarmed chaotically in search of the criminals seriously impeding the efforts of the local police and Rangers. In the view of Captain Hickman, during the hunt for the the fugitives who held up the Cisco bank in December 1927, the Rangers faced serious difficulties in locating the bandits due to the crowds of bounty hunters and possemen.[380] The lure of mammon also led to more sinister results. Captain Frank Hamer, noting a apparent increase in bank robbers being killed at night by local law enforcement, investigated the matter and discovered that officers in West Texas were luring unsuspecting drunks to the banks then after gunning down the supposed robbers the policemen would collect the five thousand dollar reward. Hamer, after the bankers showed little enthusiasm in altering or removing the reward, turned to the press. On March 12 1928, in the State Capitol in Austin, the Ranger captain handed a written and signed statement to reporters documenting what he termed "a perfect murder machine". While no bankers were ever indicted the media campaign forced the association to modify the reward.[381]

The crime and violence of the 'public enemy era' helped to expose the growing inadequacy of the Ranger corps as a modern law enforcement agency. Rangers carrying Winchester rifles and Colt six-shooters were hardly a match for criminals toting the latest weaponry including automatic rifles and submachine guns. While the celebrity gangsters utilized the fastest and most powerful automobiles on the market the Rangers possessed no official vehicles and either furnished their own or took the railroad. In West Texas the Rangers provided their own horses for police duties and still made their rounds on horseback.[382] Lawmen in Detroit had the honor of using the nation's first police radio system and other forces followed in fairly swift succession. In Texas, however, modernity was slow to arrive, the Rangers possessed no radio system and following the 1929 murder of a Mason County Sheriff were forced to use a San Antonio radio station to publicly broadcast the pertinent information to other law enforcement agencies.[383] New scientific and technological methods including ballistics, fingerprinting and forensics were far behind the level used by other state police.[384] As observed by Robert Cox; "The Ranger's reputation for toughness continued to be the force's most effective weapon."[385]

The Ranger corps was also hamstrung by Texan politics. When serving competent and honest governors committed to fighting crime and ensuring justice the Texas Rangers remained both relevant and effective. Under Pat Neff (1921-25) the Rangers engaged in so called 'battles of the peace' against bootleggers, criminal syndicates in the oil towns and in so doing became increasingly efficient and professional. While Neff was perhaps soft on the hooded order of the KKK he nonetheless cared about ending racist violence and unlawful lynchings.[386] Dan Moody (1927-31) restored the authority of the Rangers over the often corrupt local law enforcement and continued to battle both the rowdiness of the oil patch and racial riots as well as tackling the plague of bank robberies across the state.[387] His successor, Ross Sterling (1931-33), sought a efficient, trustworthy and well respected Ranger corps and in achieving this goal he elevated the force to their highest pinnacle since the frontier era.[388]

Under unscrupulous and self serving political leaders the Rangers suffered in terms of leadership, respect and capability. William P. Hobby (1917-21), after ascending to the governorship was determined to secure election in his own right and used the Rangers as one of many political tools. Hobby expected loyalty from Ranger captains and require all ranks to actively promote his candidature.[389]

'Ma' and 'Pa' Ferguson, however, arguably represented the worst excesses of corruption and politicization of Texas politics directly impacting the effectiveness of the Rangers. James E. 'Pa' Ferguson, took office in 1915 but was impeached in July 1917 on ten counts including misappropriation of public funds and receiving 'loan' of one hundred and fifty-six thousand dollars from the Texas Brewers' Association. 'Pa' Ferguson was removed from office and banned from ever holding an electoral office in Texas.[390] In the 1924 gubernatorial election, his wife Miriam A. 'Ma' Ferguson entered on the ballot as a figurehead for her husband after his name was removed on the orders of a state judge. Following her victory in the election, 'Fergusonism' reigned in the state capitol. Political corruption, and in all probability, financial incentives dominated the agenda. Most damagingly for the Texas Rangers 'Ma' Ferguson reduced the force from fifty one to twenty eight, withheld Rangers from localities where they were not requested and made political appointments.[391] The governor also pardoned around two thousand convicts some of whom had not even reached the penitentiary leading to further accusations of corruption.[392] Although beaten by Dan Moody in 1926, 'Ma' Ferguson regained the governorship in 1933 defeating the incumbent Ross Sterling.[393] The third Ferguson administration not only proved to be as fraudulent as ever but had an axe to grind against the Texas Rangers who had openly supported Governor Sterling. On inauguration day, January 18th, 'Ma' Ferguson humiliated the corps by formally dismissing the entire force of forty-four men and revoked all Special Ranger commissions. Their replacements were political appointees or individuals who could demonstrate Ferguson credentials.[394]

The devastating economic downturn of the Great Depression, led Texas, along with many other states to reduce expenditures through a restructuring and trimming of state government. A joint committee of the legislature formed to investigate the issue, hired Griffenhagen and Associates, a firm specializing in public administration and fiscal policy, based in Chicago, Illinois.[395] Griffenhagen and Associates produced a two thousand page report, *The Government of the State of Texas*, separated into thirteen individual volumes relating to various aspects of government.[396]

Part three, which was provided on January 10 1933, dealt with law enforcement in the Lone Star State. The study heavily criticized the entire system of policing and justice including a shrievalty reliant on local politics and fees, the legal technicalities yoking and encumbering the courts and in the case of the Rangers critiqued the legislature for a lack of support through funds and legislation. The Griffenhagen specialists, however, did not view the Rangers as a key part of their recommendations. The report advocated the creation of a Department of Public Safety (DPS) which would comprise of a Bureau of State Police and a Bureau of the Texas Rangers. In this department the former highway patrol would be transformed into a state police force with full authority while the Rangers would be restricted to minor operations in the border country in the south and west. The Fergusons, who had returned to the statehouse in 1933 chose not to act on most of the recommendations and simply disregardeded the volume on law enforcement.[397] The Griffenhagen Report would nevertheless be a central influence on the eventual creation of a state police and reorganization of the Rangers under in 1935.[398]

By 1935, the Rangers had served Texas for over a century. From their humble beginnings as an irregular body of mounted horsemen, over the following decades, when operating under captains such as John "Coffee" Hays, "Rip" Ford and Ben McCulloch, the corps, attained iconic status as guardians of Texas achieving notable victories over both Native tribes and Mexican forces. The Rangers, however, notably Captain Leander H. McNelly and his Special Force, became renowned for both incredible courage but also a darker legacy of brutality and violence. An apparent collusion with the Anglo politico economic establishment and the actions of the Texas Rangers during the bloody repression of the Plan de San Diego would further taint the Ranger image. During the 1920s, the Texas Rangers, weakened by the Canales hearings and the politization of the force faced new issues, booming oil towns, enforcing prohibition, a resurgent Ku Klux Klan and modern gangsters possessing the latest in weaponry and automobiles. These challenges exposed fundamental weaknesses in the ability of the Rangers to function as a viable tool of law enforcement and led to questions over the future of the organization. The fate of the Ranger corps would lie in the hands of the newly elected Democratic Governor James V. Allred.

Early 'Rangers' assemble to protect
the frontier and confront Comanche raiders.
"Courtesy of Texas State Library and Archives Commission."

Captain John 'Coffee' Hays.
"Courtesy of Texas State Library and Archives Commission."

Captain Samuel H. Walker.
"Courtesy of Texas State Library and Archives Commission."

Major John B. Jones.
"Courtesy of Texas State Library and Archives Commission."

The Frontier Battalion in 1896.
"*Courtesy of Texas State Library and Archives Commission.*"

The oil boomtown of Desdemona in 1919.
"Courtesy of Texas State Library and Archives Commission."

Captain Manuel T. 'Lone Wolf' Gonzaullas.
"*Courtesy of Texas State Library and Archives Commission.*"

Department of Public Safety Director Homer Garrison Jr.
"Courtesy of Texas State Library and Archives Commission."

During the Mansfield High School desegregation crisis of 1956, Ranger Sergeant E. J. Banks speaks with the a group of students. *"Courtesy of Texas State Library and Archives Commission."*

Captain Alfred Y. Allee.
"Courtesy of Texas State Library and Archives Commission."

1935-PRESENT DAY

12

The Department of Public Safety: A New Era Begins

On January 15 1935, James V. Allred was inaugurated as the 33rd Governor of Texas. An ardent New Dealer and fervent supporter of President Franklin D. Roosevelt, the former attorney general swept into office buoyed by popular support for federal relief programs.[399] The ascension of Governor Allred to the Texas Governors Mansion in Austin marked the end of the days of 'Fergusonism' an epoch marked by political corruption and cronyism. It also signalled the beginning of a new era in the history of the Texas Rangers.

While serving as attorney general, Allred observed the weaknesses of the criminal justice system within the Lone Star State. As early as spring 1934, during his campaign to win the Democratic primary, the then gubernatorial candidate stressed the need to establish a modern professional statewide police force to enforce the law. To achieve this goal, Allred assembled a task force led by National Guard officer and Dallas lawyer Albert Sidney Johnston. The team drew their conclusions from the Griffenhagen Report as well as in depth studies of state police agencies in Illinois, Michigan, New York and Pennsylvania. Former Ranger Captain Tom Hickman, who had embarked on a three month study trip to ten states, provided both ideas as well as copies of useful bills and statutes. By July 1934, six months before taking office

Allred possessed a draft bill ready to submit to the legislature.[400]

One week after taking office, on January 23, Allred ordered adjutant general Carl Nesbitt to dismiss all but three of the Ranger corps and begin active recruitment of their replacements. In addition, Nesbitt retracted all Special Ranger commisions handed out by the Ferguson administration. It was discovered that among those deemed deemed worthy of a Special commission were gambling house security guards, a dentist and most intriguingly of all a wrestling referee. The very next day a senator from DeKalb, John W. E. H. Beck, entered Allred's bill, now Senate Bill 146, for consideration by the Texas State Senate. Following its passage through the senate, State Representative Alfred Petsch introduced the bill to the House of Representatives. After several months of political debating and shenanigans the legislature finally approved a revised version of Senator Beck's bill for a new statewide law enforcement agency. The failure to attain the the support of two thirds of the House of Representatives meant that the law would only come into effect following a ninety day period.[401]

On August 10 1935, Governor Allred's vision finally became a reality, the new Department of Public Safety was born. The DPS was comprised of both the old Highway Patrol and the Texas Rangers. The department was administered by a Public Safety Comission consisting of a three person board who would supervise a director and assistant director. A DPS Headquarters Division was to be located in Austin including a crime laboratory and a communications system. The renamed Texas Highway Patrol was to be increased to one hundred and forty officers who were now empowered with full statewide law enforcement authority. In the past the patrol officers only possessed the authority to implement traffic regulations. It was implicit in the new law that the Highway Patrol was now the official state police.[402]

The Ranger corps, now officially titled the Texas Rangers for the first time in history, were trimmed down to three companies including a Headquarters Company, comprising a total of thirty-six men. The captain of the Headquarters Company held the position of Senior Captain and reported to the director of DPS. The new law implied that the Rangers, while too cherished in Texan lore to be disbanded, should primarily operate along the border and the Texas Highway Patrol should conduct the police investigations. Three hundred Special Rangers were also sanctioned under the new law but they were subject to surety bonding, DPS supervision and possessed severely curtailed legal powers.[403]

As the DPS reported to the Public Safety Commission and was no longer under the authority of Adjutant General's Department neither the Rangers nor the patrolmen needed to gain political support in order to remain lawmen. A merit system was established in order to ascertain an individual's suitability for both acceptance into as a law enforcement officer and subsequent promotions. A intense training program was also established for both existing and new officers. Ability, not political cronyism, would from now on determine the career path at DPS leading to an increased level of competence and professionalism.[404]

The Department of Public Safety, as with so many newly formed organizations, did suffer a number of teething problems. On August 11, against the wishes of Governor Allred, the Public Safety Commission appointed Tom Hickman as Senior Ranger Captain. Hickman was an obvious choice, as well as being the most experienced Ranger he had contributed significantly to the concept of the DPS. The famous Ranger, however, proved to be a dismal choice as Senior Captain. Hickman refused to move to Austin, travelled widely without providing any way to contact him, failed to assert any authority over the other Ranger companies and his relationship with DPS director Louis G. Phares was distinctly icy.

Governor Allred had already opposed Hickman's appointment based on his apparent inability to close down an exclusive gambling joint named the Top o' the Hill Terrace. Allegedly, the club's owner, Fred Browning, was a friend of Hickman's. The Senior Captain also drew up five Ranger districts of which his personal jurisdiction encompassed the principal gambling districts of Corpus Christi, Dallas-Fort Worth, Galveston, Houston and San Antonio. Furthermore, Hickman ordered that no clubs could be raided without his permission.[405]

In October, Allred explicitly instructed Hickman to raid the Top o' the Hill Terrace and a date was set for November 2. Supposedly, only Allred, his secretary Ed Clark, Hickman and Phares knew of the planned raid. When Hickman and two Highway Patrolmen entered the club no evidence of gambling could be found. Hickman's behavior during the raid could at best be described as highly unusual. The Senior Captain only spent around five minutes in the establishment and earlier insisted on driving his own personal car not the state car with fake plates that had been provided. Patrons in the club were apparently informed that a Ranger visit would take place at 11:30pm and following the raid gambling once again resumed.[406]

Four days later, at the instigation of the governor, Captain J. W. McCormick and Ranger Sid Kelso led a second raid capturing gambling equipment valued at eight thousand dollars and arresting Browning and four of his employees. The Public Safety Commission after meeting with Director Phares demanded Hickman's resignation and following his refusal to resign the commission fired the celebrity Ranger on November 12. The very same day James McCormick was promoted to Senior Captain. Hickman, however, refused to go quietly and his friends in the legislature initiated a three man legislative investigating committee to examine the charges against DPS. The politically motivated investigation, however, ended after Governor Allred, who rightly suspected his enemies of conspiring against him, burst in on the second meeting, testified as to his account of the events and provided a written report explaining the thirteen reasons why Hickman had been discharged from service.[407]

The choice of Louis G. Phares as Director of DPS would also lead to controversy. Phares, the fifty-five chief of the old Highway Patrol and former Ranger, was initially appointed head of the newly formed Texas Highway Patrol by the Public Safety Commission in August 1935, then swiftly promoted later the same month to acting director of DPS. Phares was an effective but stubborn administrator who sought to professionalize DPS including the Texas Rangers. One example of his approach was DPS General Order Number 1 which instructed every Ranger to submit to headquarters written reports every week detailing their daily activities. Phares, perhaps realizing the difficulties inherent in this order later directed the Rangers to present their reports to their respective company captain.[408]

While a number of Rangers may have been aggravated by the increase in paperwork a more serious issue was Phares' apparent desire to turn the corps into a modified version of the Highway Patrol. Phares viewed the Rangers as S-Men, he opposed the traditional Ranger image of a rugged individual sporting a cowboy hat and six-shooter who used intimidation and physical toughness to enforce the law. Instead the newly appointed acting director sought to mold the Rangers into a force of polite plainclothes information gatherers similar to FBI G-Men. When infiltrating gambling houses Phares even toyed with the idea of dressing Rangers as women complete with dresses, wigs and even makeup. Needless to say, his vision of the corps was the antithesis of Ranger sentiment and led to antagonism and discontent in the ranks.[409]

The Sheriffs' Association of Texas also opposed the appointment of Phares believing that he not only sowed dissension between the patrolmen and Rangers but had a history of failing to co-operate with local law enforcement. On April 7, the Public Safety Comission voted two to one to hire Phares as director on a permanent basis. A large number of Texas sheriffs openly protested his appointment and presented their own candidate, Sheriff J. B. Arnold of Bee County. The outspoken sheriff of Bexar County, Albert West Jr. stated that the sheriffs did not trust or respect Phares and would not work with him. Realizing that it would be untenable to keep Phares as director given his relationship with both the Rangers and sheriffs the commission asked for and received his resignation on May 9 and reappointed him as head of the Highway Patrol. Phares did not last long in his new position, three years later, on April 1 1938, Phares was dismissed allegedly due to incompatibility and lack of co-operation.[410]

When considering potential replacements the Public Safety Commission swiftly realized that selecting either a former Ranger or patrolman could arouse further tensions. The commissioners opted against choosing a sheriff as they clearly lacked the appropriate qualifications or experience as well as noting the more political nature of the shrievalty. The commission thus settled on forty-eight year old war veteran and Lieutenant Colonel of the National Guard Horace H. Carmichael.[411]

Carmichael, who had also served as assistant adjutant general to successive gubnatorial administrations, proved to be a successful director of DPS. Carmichael through the mediation of the Public Safety Commission persuaded Captain McCormick to yield the title of senior captain to the DPS director and instead lead a new company based out of Wichita Falls. Carmichael viewed himself as an honorary Ranger and was determine to restore the effectiveness and lustre of the famous force. He sought to merge the traditional Ranger approach to justice with a new understanding of update scientifice techniques and an ability to gather evidence as opposed to merely adminsistering summary justice. As noted by Robert M. Utley; "To Carmichael belongs the credit of launching the modern Texas Rangers toward their ultimate status as the elite law enforcement arm of the state of Texas."[412]

In the fall of 1938, tragedy struck however, forcing yet another change of command at DPS. On the September 24, Director Carmichael died a of heart attack while driving in Austin and his assistant director, Homer Garrison Jr. became acting director of the department. Three days later the appointment was made permanent by the Public Safety Commission. The new director had been a captain in the Highway Patrol earning praise for his work in the training program and had been borrowed by the State of New Mexico to aid the establishment of their own state police.[413]

Garrison was competent, intelligent, politically savvy and highly personable. He would remain as DPS Director for nearly thirty years until his death in 1968. Under his leadership the Rangers became well trained, well equipped and highly professional lawmen. Garrison improved the crime laboratory, initiated training programs and successfully convinced the state legislature to increase both funding and the size of the corps. The new director earned not only the respect of the Rangers but gained accolades across the nation and abroad. Garrison, became the personification of the DPS in the same way that J. Edgar Hoover came to symbolize the Federal Bureau of Investigation (FBI). Equally importantly, the Rangers came to venerate the chararcter and personality of the DPS chief, a man who despite his heavy responsibilities left his office door open and encouraged all his personnel to drop by and chat whenever they felt the need.[414]

The formation of the DPS also brought other changes to the Ranger corps. On a stylistic level the Rangers remained free to choose their own clothing and unlike the Highway Patrol were not required to wear a uniform in the line of duty. Ranger units operating in the South Texas chaparral or arid West Texas typically dressed in the same fashion as their predecessors; broad brimmed hats, cowboy boots and dungarees comprised were commonplace. The so called 'City Rangers' who primarily operated in the urban areas of East Texas tended to discard the western style of their colleagues in favor of business suits and other urban outfits. The success of the Rangers when investigating mobsters and other metropolitical criminals relied to a large extend on their ability to resemble the local citizenry. When working in city environments Rangers only donned western clothing when they wished to appear noticeable and prominent. Nevertheless, at ceremonial events all Rangers continued to sport high heeled boots, cowboy hats and holsters as well as white dress shirts and tan suits.[415]

In terms of weaponry, the Rangers, since the 1870s, traditionally carried the Colt 45 'Peacemaker' and Winchester '73 rifle. As noted earlier, however, these weapons left Ranger units outgunned when confronting modern gangsters or bank robbers armed with the latest armaments. Following the formation of DPS the corps gradually phased out the Colt 45 in favor of the Colt Model 1911.45, a semiautomatic pistol comprising of a seven round magazine or Smith & Wesson double action revolvers.[416] The Winchester was replaced by the .30-06 semiautomatic rifle. By the 1970s Rangers were armed with .357 Magnum revolvers and 12 gauge automatic shotguns as well as being able to obtain a number of other special issue weapons including sub-machine guns and scoped rifles.[417]

Horses, the stereotypical form of Ranger transportation since the 1820s also proved to be somewhat obsolete by the mid 1900s. While useful in rugged terrain along the border or in rural West Texas they could hardly compete with modern criminals travelling in high powered automobiles. Even cattle rustlers and border smugglers tended to use motorized vehicles making it is essential for the Ranger corps to have access to the fastest and most reliable transportation available. By the early 1970s, the force was provided with the most advanced law enforcement vehicles available including Dodges and Plymouths with four-barrel carburettors and heavy duty springs.[418] The Rangers also possessed armored cars, helicopters, an airplane, a twenty-one foot fast boat and a tank.[419]

The Headquarters Division at Austin was intended to become the nucleus of a contemporary, progressive and efficient law enforcement organization. It comprised of four separate sections; a Bureau of Communications, a Bureau of Education, a Bureau of Identification and Records as well as a Bureau of Intelligence.[420] Regarding communications, Homer Garrison himself was also determined to improve the the communication system at DPS. By December 1940, the DPS possessed a radio facility providing the ability to broadcast key information over the airwaves. The station, however, was barely powerful enough to cover Travis County and in addition officers operating in the field could neither talk to each other nor headquarters.[421] Slowly but surely the director was able to construct a radio network that kept Rangers and Highway Patrolmen in contact with each other, their captains and other lawmen.[422] By the 1970s the Rangers were equipped with the latest radio technology comprising of eight separate channels and a secret surveillance channel frequency.[423]

The Headquarters Division also comprised of sections specializing in intelligence, education as well as identification and records. The Bureau of Education focused on providing training for all new DPS recruits and offered specialized courses for local lawmen. Identification and Records, like communications, began with humble beginnings.

Led by Chief C. G. McGraw, the department suffered from a lack of techonology and even space, initially sharing offices with the Bureau of Intelligence. The fingerprint program began with a mere fifteen hundred prints supplied by the Beaumont Police Department. Under the astute command of McGraw, however, within twelve months the bureau was not only obtaining prints from over two hundred sources but was developing the aptidude to analyze and identify individual correspondence whether handwritten or typed.[424]

In September 1935, acting DPS Director Phares appointed the legendary Ranger Manuel T. "Lone Wolf" Gonzaullas to head the new Bureau of Intelligence.[425] Gonzaullas brought to his new position a vast array of skills in both criminal science and investigations. His areas of expertise included the analysis of documents, ballistics, microscopic testing, moulage casting and the use of ultraviolet light.[426] In January 1937, Gonzaullas accompanied by Director Carmichael embarked on a two month tour of crime laboratories in both the U.S. and Canada to ensure that the Texan facilities possessed the most up to date forensic methods and technology.[427] By 1940, the capacity and resources of the DPS Bureau of Intelligence superseded the capabilities of even the FBI.[428]

The establishment and development of the DPS fundamentally altered and improved the Ranger Service freeing the corps from political involvement and providing tools to both modernize and professionalize a respected and treasured part of Texan history. Reporting solely to the DPS director. the Rangers were no long required to rally political support or be subject to the whims of a gubnatorial administration. A successful career in the Ranger service could now be achieved on merit alone. Furthermore, the increased training combined with the vast improvements in communications, scientific analysis and weaponry helped to create a highly professional and efficient police agency. The old time guardians of the frontier had been transformed into an force of elite lawmen The formation of DPS truly opened up a new chapter in the history of the Texas Rangers.

13
Challenges: Old and New

During the first decades of its existence the newly formed Department of Public Safety faced a host of challenges. Criminals, both small timers and gangsters linked to organized crime continued to plague the Lone Star State. Racial tensions and labor unrest became increasingly dangerous catalysts in Texan life. The storm clouds of war hovering over Asia and Europe during the thirties not only caused the tragedy at Pearl Harbor embroiling the United States in a costly global conflict but also brought new difficulties for the Ranger Service. The mid 1900s, however, also saw a flowering of the Ranger legend, both in Texas and across the world.

In December 1934, before the DPS came into existence and even before the inauguration of Governor Allred, the new administration faced a challenging task. San Augustine, Texas, deep in the piney woods on the Louisiana border was a relic of the Old South. The ruling families were white Anglo-Saxon Protestants many of whom could trace their ancestry in the area to before the Civil War. African-Americans comprised one third of the population and not only were segregated but remained 'belonging' to particular family. The town had become dominated by the Burlesons and McClanahans, two violent families with ties to criminal syndicates. Just prior to Christmas 1934, a shootout in a hardware store claimed the lives of four men. Outgoing Governor Miriam Ferguson dipatched three 'Ferguson

Rangers' who unsurprisingly responded to type and achieved nothing during their stay in town. Twenty-eight Special Rangers, recommended by the corrupt sheriff and the gangsters themselves, merely worsened the situation and cowed the local citizenry.[429]

In the last week in January 1935, Captain J. W. McCormick, Private Leo Bishop and two other Rangers arrived in San Augustine on the instructions of Governor Allred. After serving discharge papers of the Ferguson men and the Special Rangers the four lawmen swiftly engaged in tough psychological warfare against the criminal clans. The Rangers insulted, menaced and on occasion beat up the nastiest of the culprits. Ranger Bishop confronted Charlie McClanahan, widely believed to be the responsible for the majority of the violence, stating that he would gun him down if he ever saw him on the street again. McClanahan promptly fled to Louisiana and most of the other thugs swiftly left San Augustine.[430] The Rangers then engineered the forced resignation of the sheriff who was quickly replaced by an honest lawman. By mid March, the Rangers had achieved a pattern of indictments and convictions breaking the power of the felonious clans. On March 22, the grateful citizens of San Augustine held a mass celebration in their honor and presented McCormick, Bishop and Ranger Hines with a pair of silver mounted .38 Colt six-shooters as a gift from the city.[431]

The Old West crime of cattle rustling remained a problem in the mid 1930s. The 'modern' stock thieves favored fast trucks on paved roads making the stolen beeves harder to track. The last months of 1935 saw an explosion in the theft of livestock leading Ranger Captains Bill McMurrey at Hebbronville and Red Hawkins based in San Angelo to engage in a co-ordinated operation with local lawmen, cowboys and ranchers to combat the trade. Rangers patrolled the highways, searched stock trucks for proof of ownership and even stood guard in grazing pastures in an unrewarding attempt to end the problem.[432]

By 1941, with the price of a single steer at one hundred dollars the incentive for modern stock rustlers was high and Texas cattlemen were suffering heavy losses in the range country. In the summer of that year, Homer Garrison ordered Ranger Sergeant Ernest Best to tackle the issue. Best launched a three pronged assault against the cattle rustlers: Rangers on horseback were dispatched to rural camps to check for stolen beeves, roadblocks were placed on the principal highways and trucks transporting livestock were checked for ownership papers. Finally, Best set up a methodical and regular system of monitoring auctions and other locations where cattle could be sold. Garrison called the operation a great success and the newly elected Governor Coke Stevenson, himself a rancher, was highly impressed by the efficiency of the Ranger program.[433]

In November 1936, the Rangers were called to investigate the disappearance of Luther Blanton, a south Texas farmer, and his son. On November 18, the Blantons, whose land bordered on the King Ranch, left their farm and illegally crossed onto the King property to shoot ducks on a nearby lagoon. The owners of the King Ranch were known to be tough on trespassing especially illegal hunting and the two men were never seen again. The inability of the investigating Rangers to solve the case combined with the well known fact that Rangers had traditionally always enjoyed the hospitality of the King family led to media attention and negative publicity.[434]

The Rangers proved to be more adept when handling the murder of Marion County Sheriff J. A. Brown. On March 10 1937, the sheriff was shot and killed in Jefferson, a riverboat town in East Texas. The Ranger investigation, led by Captain H. B. Purvis, swiftly arrested a suspect, an alleged thief named Charlie Brooks, and located the murder weapon, a .12-gauge shotgun. The expeditious and effective Ranger response helped to smooth out any lingering concerns or tensions that Texas sheriffs may have had regarding the establishment of the DPS.[435]

In January 1943, Robert Lacy, a convicted murderer and frequent prison breaker, escaped once again accompanied by fellow inmate Cleo Andrews. "Lone Wolf" Gonzaullas, who had returned to the Rangers three years earlier, supervised the manhunt. Following a tip off from an informant, Gonzaullas and two Rangers, along with two sheriffs and a number of other local police officers, trapped the felons in a stolen vehicle in the town of Gladewater, Texas. Instead of surrendering, however, the convicts chose to shoot it out with the lawmen. Lacy died in the ensuing of bullets and Gonzaullas assumed that Andrews had met with the same fate. The convict, however, was still alive and when the Ranger Captain approached the vehicle and opened the door Andrews fired at point blank range wounding the lawman. The "Lone Wolf", although injured, promptly delivered justice from the barrel of his revolver.[436]

On the morning of Sunday December 7 1941, the Empire of Japan launched a surprise attack on the American naval base of Pearl Harbor in Hawaii. The assault, a tactical victory for the Japanese, sunk or destroyed a total of nineteen ships, obliterated one hundred and eight aircraft and killed over two thousand four hundred Americans. The attack on Pearl Harbor was a defining moment in world history, the Japanese had silenced American isolationists and awoken a sleeping giant. The following day, December 8, the U.S. Congress passed a resolution calling for war against the Empire of Japan. Germany and Italy, the other Axis Powers and members of the Tripartite Pact declared war on the U.S. three days later. The United States was once again embroiled in a global conflict.[437]

Even before the tragedy of Pearl Harbor the majority of Texans had supported intervention against both Germany and Japan. In fact, Texans, displayed greater hostility towards Nazi Germany and imperial Japan than any other Americans. Polls from both Fortune and Gallup decisively demonstrated that Texan belligerence against totalitarianism was far higher than any other American region including the South and Anglophile New York. Long before Pearl Harbor a large number of Texans had crossed the northern border to enlist in the Canadian forces.[438] Ranger Captain Frank Hamer, after reading reports of the German invasion of Poland in September 1939, even wrote to King George VI of England offering the services of forty-nine Rangers to help defeat Hitler. The idea was shot down, however, by

President Franklin D. Roosevelt who wrote to Texas Governor Coke R. Stevenson and reminded him of U.S. policy of neutrality in the conflict.[439] Throughout the war a disproportionate number of Texans served in the armed forces. Audie Murphy, a Texan cotton farmer who later became a movie star, was awarded more combat medals than any other soldier in the U.S. Army while the Navy's most decorated man was another Texan by the name of Sam Dealey.[440]

The advent of World War brought new challenges and responsibilities for the Texas Rangers. Following Pearl Harbor and the weakening of the Pacific Fleet the U.S. military considered a Japanese landing in Mexico a real possibility. If such an attack occurred Texas could form the first line of defence against Japanese aggression. Ranger W. E. Naylor was tasked with criscrossing the state demonstrating to local law enforcement the various aspects of 'war preparedness' including how to recognize enemy aircraft and deal with gas attacks. Naylor and a number of other DPS officers were taught how to construct molotov cocktails and engage in guerrilla warfare by a British lieutenant colonel at Camp Bullis near San Antonio.[441]

Protecting the oil refineries and other high risk security concerns was an ongoing issue for the Rangers throughout the war. Surveillance of so called 'Fifth Columnists', German, Italian or Japanese Americans who worked against the U.S. from within, was also a time consuming problem for the Rangers. In Galveston, on February 27 1942, Rangers in co-ordination with the FBI and local law enforcement arrested forty-four individuals suspected of aiding the enemy. Among the evidence gathered by the Rangers were firearms, gunpowder, radios, maps of several Texan ports and an aerial photograph of a carbon plant.[442]

The Rangers also played a significant role in rounding up the one hundred and forty-two German prisoners of war who escaped from camps across the state. Over two hundred U.S. military deserters or soldiers being held for disciplinary reasons also broke out and frequently committed robberies or other crimes. On a lighter note, in November 1942, Ranger Company E, based in San Angelo set out to guard the frontier the old fashioned way, riding the river on horseback. Needless to say, the unit discovered no Japanese soldiers although they did engage in a little deer hunting and were able to capture a Mexican mule which has evidently illegally crossed the Rio Grande into the Lone Star State.[443]

In addition to their wartime duties, the Ranger force had to contend with the usual crimes of bank heists and cattle theft. Escapees from state prison farms also soared due to a lack of personnel as large numbers of prison guards left the Department of Corrections to serve in the military. In October 1942, the Rangers were called to Bastrop County in search of a missing girl. A highway patrolman discovered the child, unconscious and sexually assaulted in a ravine north of Bastrop. Nearby, were deep tire tracks and after questioning witnesses the Rangers learned that a military vehicle had been seen in the area. The investigation moved to Camp Swift army base east of Bastrop. The military police quickly discovered a suspect, Private George S. Knapp, who had checked out a similar vehicle and whose locker contained bloody clothing. The private had stolen a car and was now AWOL. The suspect, however, was arrested by an Austin policemen and when back on the base confessed under Ranger interrogation to committing the murder. Knapp was convicted in a military trial and hung in March 1943.[444]

The war also served to demonstrate the global reach of the Ranger legend. During the Dieppe raid in 1942, a rumor rapidly spread through Europe that the Texas Rangers had landed along with the Allied Forces. According to the Associated Press, this caused great exhilaration among French officials and diplomats. The citizens of the Third Reich were, needless to say, less enthused by the possibility of Texas Rangers arriving in their midst and the consternation was so great that Dr. Joseph Goebbels, the propaganda minister, was forced to issue a radio broadcast reassuring the German people that no Rangers had landed at Dieppe.[445]

The end of World War II signalled the defeat of Nazi Germany and imperial Japan and the emergence of the United States as a genuine superpower. In Texas, the Rangers were relieved of the additional wartime responsibilities but crime, nevertheless, continued unabated. In 1946, the city of Texarkana, located in the northeast of the state, suffered a series of brutal attacks and murders which eventually brought an entire Ranger company to the region. On February 22 a masked and armed man attacked a young couple beating the boy unconscious and sexually assaulting the girl. The couple survived, but in March his next two victims were found shot to death. Following the double homicide, Ranger Jim Geer arrived in Texarkana to assist the Bowie County Sheriff's Department. After the killer struck again, on April 14, Captain Gonzaullas along with Ranger Company B, a party of Highway Patrolmen and four DPS crime techincians left for Texarkana. The Rangers, however, were able to neither prevent a further double killing, across the state lines in Arkanas but only ten miles from the city, nor could the combined efforts of local and state lawmen catch the murderer. Gonzaullas, did however, provoke a confrontation with the Texarkana, Arkansas police chief when showing a reporter around the crime scene.[446]

Gambling, though still prohibited by state law, was generally tolerated by Texan law enforcement as both city officials and the urban electorate tended to favor non intervention in the illicit business. Rangers, who frequently viewed raids as a disruption from fighting real crime, only intervened when requested. The infamous Top o' the Hill gambling emporium, had continued to flourish throughout the thirties and forties and finally incurred the ire of a Fort Worth clergyman who demanded that the Rangers take action. On August 11 1947, "Lone Wolf" Gonzaullas accompanied by two Rangers and a Special Investigator struck the notorious establishment arresting Browning, his staff and fifty patrons as well as destroying all the expensive gambling machines. Needless to say, aided by the leniency of the Fort Worth officials, the Top o' the Hill reopened soon after and remained in business until Browning died in 1953. In a quirk of fate, when the building reopened one year later it had paradoxically become a Baptist theological seminary.[447]

World War II had provided a much needed boost to the American economy. The War Production Board, established in 1942, set astounding production goals stimulating a soaring economy, surplus in jobs and the development of the American West.[448] In the post war era, the economic boom continued, factories and other businesses switched from military production to the manfacturing of a vast range of comsumer goods. The American industrial sector had emerged virtually unscathed from the war while the manufacturing sectors of competitor nations including England, Japan and the Soviet Union had been utterly destroyed leaving the U.S. in prime position to dominate international trade.[449] Texas, like many other states, possessed a thriving economy along with rising affluence and for many families an excess of capital.

The new found prosperity, nevertheless, brought a new challenge for the Texas Rangers. The Mafia, the embodiment of Italian organized crime, appeared to be intent on spreading its tentacles into Texas. Homer Garrison, however, was determined to keep the mob out of the Lone Star State. In July 1949, Carlos Villone, a known underworld character with a long record, was blasted to death with a shotgun while driving home in Houston. Ranger John Klevenhagen, upon investigating the crime discovered that the Mafia had demanded a chunk of the new casino that Villone was constructing. When Villone refused, the mobsters hired a Houston grocer by the name of Diego Carlino to undertake the contract hit.[450]

In 1952, Carlino was on trial again, this time for the murder of a gambler and club owner named Vincent Vallone. Once again, Carlino hired the the skilled and ostentatious Houston attorney Percy Foreman to defend him. When the jury passed a verdict of not guilty, an infuriated Ranger Klevenhagen accompanied by Harris County Sheriff Buster Kern confronted and assaulted the flashy attorney in the San Angelo courthouse. Both lawmen pleased guilty to simple assault and were fined five dollars. DPS director Garrison did not appear to be unduly concerned about the fracas and apparently took no action against Klevenhagen.[451]

For the most part, the character and direct actions of the Rangers had more effect at dissuading mobsters than any actual police work. A classic example of Ranger deterrence is the case of Mickey Cohen. Cohen, a Californian mafioso had developed an interest in expanding his operations into Texas. His intentions, however, had come to the attention of the DPS and specifically the "Lone Wolf" Gonzaullas. On August 30 1950, Cohen and two associates flew from Los Angeles to Odessa before checking in at the Kemp Hotel in Wichita Falls. The mobster, however, would not get the long night of sleep he had likely been anticipating after his journey from the west coast. At 3am that night, Cohen was visited by Ranger Captains Gonzaullas and Richard R. Crowder who without a warrant kicked down the hotel room door, seized the mobster and his companions and unceremoniously deposited the trio in the Wichita County jail. The crooks were then taken to Fort Worth and placed on a flight back to California. While extrajudicial in nature the Ranger approach was highly effective, Mickey Cohen never returned to Texas.[452]

Since the turn of the century political control of the South Texas counties had remained in the hands of powerful bosses or 'patrons'. The 'patron' system was based on paternalism and reciprocity. In exchange of electoral votes, the county boss, generally Anglo-Texan but on occasion Hispanic, would distribute cash, jobs and other perks to their supporters. A boss held almost complete power over the economy, politics, land and people. By the 1930s, the most powerful 'patron' was Archie Parr, the so-called 'Duke of Duval' who held absolute dominance over Duval County located west of Corpus Christi. Upon his death in 1942, his son, George Parr took over as a virtual dictator.[453] In 1948, Parr was responsible for the contentious election of Lyndon Johnson to the U.S. Senate when he 'discovered' over two hundred uncounted votes in Jim Wells County.[454]

By 1949, Parr faced opposition from the Freedom Party, founded by *Tejano* war veterans and even supported by a number of Anglo-Texans. The threat of violence hung over the local elections in 1952, exacerbated by the determination of the Parr family to remove State

District Judge Sam Reams. The judge, who had been defeated by a Parr candidate in 1950, remained in his seat after the the state canvassing board refused to certify the result due to clear evidence of irregularities. In April 1952, Reams further aggravated the Parrs by launching a grand jury investigation into the electoral fraud. To ensure a peaceful election and protect the grand jury Company D Captain A. Y. Allee dispatched Rangers Joe Bridge and Charlie Miller to San Diego, the seat of Duval County. Nevertheless, the Parr candidates triumphed with ease and Reams himself was unseated.[455]

The Rangers were soon to return to Duval County. On September 8 1952, a hired assassin shot and killed Jacob Floyd Jr. outside his home in Alice, Texas. The intended target had been his father, Jake Floyd, an attorney and enemy of the Parr family. The Rangers were not the only agency interested in the Parrs, the Department of Justice, the Internal Revenue Service and the Post Office Department all sent teams of agents to investigate tax irregularities and postal fraud. On January 16 1954, at a political rally in San Diego, the 'Duke' threatened Manuel Marroquin, a reporter for a Spanish language anti-Parr newspaper, with a pistol. Marroquin, with Ranger support, filed against Parr on the charge of illegal gun carrying. On January 18, when the case came on the Jim Wells County courthouse docket, Parr posted bond. While waiting to do so, however, the boss and his nephew, Archie Parr, the Duval County Sheriff encountered Captain Allee and Ranger Bridge. Harsh words were spoken and during the subsequent brawl Allee struck the elder Parr across his ear, dragged him into the courtroom and ordered him to cease his violent repression.[456]

The 'Duke' pushed for indictments against the two Rangers for assault with intent to murder and hired the remowned New York attorney Arthur Garfield Hays to lead the prosecution. In March, the judge dismissed the charges against Ranger Bridge but Captain Allee was forced to face trial. In a stunning development, however, after questioning Allee on the stand, Hays praised the honesty of the Ranger Captain and on the following day, April 20, Hays stepped down as lawyer for the prosecution and Parr subsequently dropped all charges.[457]

Over the following years the federal investigators with the help of Texas Rangers amassed solid cases against the Parr machine. On July 17 1957, the district court found Parr and ten accomplices guilty of mail fraud. The by now infamous Houston attorney, Percy Foreman handled the appeals process and although the conviction was upheld by the Fifth Circuit Court of Appeals it was reversed by the Supreme Court on the technicality that state law required that tax notices were sent out. The justices, however, acknowledged that the defendants were clearly guilty of massive fraud and embezzlement. The Parr dynasty had been challenged but for now were able to continue their reign of corruption and violence.[458]

Charles Brogdon, aka the 'See More Kid', was born in San Antonio in 1933. The product of a dyfunctional childhood, Brogdon slipped into a life of crime at an early age while living in the town of Mission in the Rio Grande Valley. After having suffered the horrors of an orphanage and reform school, Brogdon, who had a way with horses, worked for several ranches often departing on the back of a stolen horse. By 1953, Brogdon was based out of the Texas Hill Country where he lived in the wilderness breaking into cabins for supplies when needed. This inevitably attracted the attention of local law enforcement who by the spring of that year sought the fugitive for over forty burglaries, horsetheft and a stolen jeep. Brogdon, however, proved highly elusive and rubbed salt into the wound by leaving taunting notes for the police including "The See More Kid sees more and does less."[459]

The local lawmen, frustrated by their inability to catch Brogdon, asked for Ranger assistance. Ranger L. Hardy Purvis, an old hand, took up the task and readied a task force including a horseback posse and a pack of coondogs. Learning that Brogdon was a regular visitor to Camp Mystic, a summer resort for wealthy Texan girls, Purvis made his move, releasing the dogs on Brogdon's trail. The 'See More Kid', knowing the ways of dogs, eluded his pursuers once again. Purvis, undeterred, waited for the next sighting which occurred near Wallace Canyon. On this occasion, the old Ranger brought a Piper Cub search plane, manhunting hounds from Huntsville as well as a mounted posse. The lawmen confronted Brogdon in a cabin but the outlaw was able to flee into the woods. Brogdon lost the posse after leaping into a oak tree from the rim of the canyon but the hounds were unrelenting until he shot all four dogs. Purvis continued to follow the trail of burglarized cabins and mocking notes before the bandit was finally apprehended in a Rocksprings hotel after a tip off from a twelve year old boy.[460]

The Maximum Security Unit at Rusk State Hospital, which contained only inmates diagnosed as criminally insane, was a spartan compound in which the convicts suffered from a brutal and degrading regime. In April 1955, eight-one black inmates, led by Ben Wileyrevolted against the disgraceful system in place at Rusk. The mob armed with a number of weapons, including ice picks, beat up several 'bouncers', inmates tasked with maintaining order, and seized three hostages. The editor and publisher of the *Rusk Cherokean* newspaper, Emmett Whitehead, bravely entered the Maximum Security Unit and interviewed Wiley. The convict, pleased to have a forum to vent his grievances, announced that the rioters sought better activities and counseling as well as the same rights as the white inmates. He also threatened to murder the hostages if lawmen stormed the compound or his demands were not met.[461]

DPS director Homer Garrison ordered Ranger Captain Bob Crowder, based in Dallas, to hurry to Rusk as fast as possible. Crowder, noted for his fast driving, took ninety minutes to cover the one hundred and twenty miles from Dallas to Rusk in his 1955 Oldsmobile. Just before the Ranger's arrival, Riley announced that he would talk to a Ranger Captain if he was able to represent the state. Crowder, carrying two .45s and backed up by a highway patrolman with a sniper rifle, coolly walked over to the Maximum Security Unit and spoke with Riley on the doorstep. Crowder listened to the list of complaints but stated that the rioters actions were not helping their cause. The Ranger, however, promised Riley a hearing with the head of the hospital then demanded that all the rioters release the hostages, discard their weapons and surrender. Wiley and his band of inmates promptly complied with the instructions. Due to the authoritative nature and quick thinking of the Ranger Captain the riot had ended with no further violence.[462]

One month later on May 14, near Thornton in central Texas, N. J. Tynes a local farmer with a history of mental illness stalked and shot his friend Johnny Ray Bentley while he was ploughing his cornfield. Later that night, Limestone County Sheriff Harry Dunlap with two deputies, approached the Tynes farmhouse but were driven back by rifle fire. Early the next morning, the sheriff, his deputies, two highway patrolmen and Ranger J. H. Rogers surrounded the property with the intention of flushing Tynes out by use of tear gas. Although Rogers was able to fire a canister of gas into the property, Sheriff Dunlap, spying the farmer lurching on the back porch from the effects of the gas, stepped into the open and ordered Tynes to surrender. Tynes promptly seized his gun and shot the sheriff dead before disappearing back into the house. Gunfire resumed as the lawmen launched a barrage of shots but failed to hit the killer.[463]

Ranger Captain Clint Peoples, en route to a law enforcement seminar in Oklahoma City, heard the news on the police radio and immediately drove to Thornton and took charge of the siege. As Rogers had already called for an armored car, Peoples simply cordoned off the area, summoned an ambulance and issued orders that Tynes was to be captured alive. While the lawmen awaited the armored vehicle two patrolmen, using a metal table top as a shield, were able to retrieve the body of Sheriff Dunlap. The armored car, requisitioned from Fort Hood, arrived that afternoon and was promptly put to use. Peoples together with Fall County Sheriff Grady Pamplin and an army driver drove towards the house once again intending to use tear gas to force Tynes from the residence. Having systematically fired numerous canisters into the house, the car approached the back porch when Peoples accidentally dropped a canister into the vehicle. As the lawmen rose for air, Tynes appeared with his rifle and shot at the two officers, Peoples fired the gas gun hitting the farmer in his left arm.

As Tynes fled into the house Rangers' Rogers and Bob Crowder burst through the front door. In the ensuing struggle, Rogers shot Tynes in the shoulder as he lunged at the lawman headbutting him in the stomach. The stand off was finally over, Peoples had captured Tynes alive but the murderer died in hospital the next day.[464]

In July 1956, a deputy sheriff in Somerville, Texas, was murdered by a man suffering from serious mental problems. Ranger Johnny Klevenhagen, based out of Houston, took charge of the manhunt. Klevenhagen, on horseback and assisted by bloodhounds, tracked the killer down in Yegua Creek bottom. The suspect, well hidden in brush, promptly began shooting at the police officers. Klevehagen, however, galloped his horse forward and introducing himself, stated that if the man was to surrender he would not be harmed. The murderer emerged, but holding a pistol in each hand opened fire at the mounted Ranger. Klevenhagen, after controlling his bucking horse, dismounted and promptly ended the gunfight with two volleys of buckshot from his 12-gauge.[465]

Gene Paul Norris was a sadistic Oklahoma criminal with gang ties and a substantive record including numerous murders. In March 1957, Norris and William Carl 'Silent Bill' Humphrey arrived in Fort Worth with a plan to rob the payroll of a branch of the Fort Worth National Bank located at Carswell Air Force Base. The crooks had been supplied with a floor plan and the address of a cashier by James E. Papworth who had served jail time with a previous manager of the branch who had been convicted of embezzlement. On the morning of the payroll delivery, scheduled for April 30, the two men planned to murder the cashier, a Mrs. Barles and her young son, then use her car complete with a base sticker and bank keys to gain entrance to the branch. The gangsters then planned to seize the payroll and then return to the Barles residence and escape in their own vehicle.[466]

Norris, however, also had a second mission in mind. In 1937, his brother had been sent to prison for ninety-nine years on the testimony of John Brannan. On April 17, Norris and Humphrey broke into the Brannan home in Houston and brutally murdered Brannan and his wife by repeatedly smashing their heads with hammers. The violent killings attracted the attention of Ranger Captain Klevenhagen who obtained arrest warrants for the two men as well as locating evidence tying the two crooks to recent robberies. The FBI, who had been tipped off by Papworth, knew all about the planned Fort Worth heist. Federal agents met with the Rangers and local law enforcement in Fort Worth and developed a plan of action.[467]

The FBI bugged the Houston motel room where the two villains were staying and when Norris and Humphrey returned to Fort Worth on April 27 they were tailed by federal agents. Through a continued surveillance link the lawmen were able to ascertain that the gangsters were planning a dry run of escape routes and it was decided to capture them in their vehicle. The planned ambush failed when the crooks spotted the car containing Sergeant Arthur Hill and two other Rangers. The subsequent high speed chase ended on a caliche based country road in Parker County. Humphrey, who was driving the 1957 green Chevrolet owned by Norris, crashed into a ditch whereupon both men sprang from the vehicle opening fire on Rangers' Klevenhagen and Banks in the pursuit car, while running towards Walnut Creek. As the crooks attempted to cross the swollen creek the Rangers opened fire and within seconds two of the most dangerous gangsters in Texan history had themselves become history.[468]

Since the 1920s, gambling and other illicit activities had flourished in the port city of Galveston. For decades the island city's politics and gaming industry had been controlled by two Italian immigrant bootleggers Salvatore and Rosario Maceo. The island possessed an enormous red light district and numerous casinos and gambling emporiums, notably the Balinese Room, located on a long pier jutting into Galveston Bay. The city officials were controlled by the Maceo's who also benefitted from the support of the local population whose businesses prospered due to the illegal trade. The Maceo's had both died by 1957 but their nephews Anthony and Victor Fertitta maintained the lucrative family business.[469]

In 1957, however, newly appointed Attorney General Will Wilson, who as district attorney had led the clean up of Dallas, decided to finally end the illicit gambling business in Galveston. Wilson requested the help of the Rangers in achieving his mission. The first raid, on the Balinese Room, took place on June 6 but proved to be an embarrassing failure due to an informant tipping off the Fertittas. Nevertheless, by June 10, Wilson was able to ask for injunctions against forty-seven establishments engaged in gambling or prostitution. Five days later, on June 15, Captain Klevenhagen launched a raid on Fort Travis, an abandoned coastal artillery defence, and in the old concrete bunkers and barracks the Rangers discovered and destroyed approximately three hundred and fifty thousand dollars worth of gambling equipment and accessories. As the transportation of gambling machines across state lines had recently become a federal crime, it would have been hard for the Fertittas to acquire repalcements, Klevenhagen's raid essentially put the the Galveston gambling trade out of business.[470]

The Rangers, however, maintained a conspicious presence on the island city for three more years. A nightly routine developed in which two Rangers conspiciously dressed in Western clothes and sporting six-shooters along with their badges would enter and remain in any club suspected of continuing illicit activity. By 1960, the gambling trade was finished in the island city once known as a mecca of sin and vice. While the determination and tenacity of the Ranger units was crucial taming in Galveston, the growth of Las Vegas, Nevada as the new paradise for legal gambling ensured that the Rangers would rarely be called upon to deal with the problem of illicit gambling.[471]

On June 28 1959, the Sam Houston Museum, located in the town of Huntsville, was broken into by two robbers who stole thirty-one antique guns including five which had been owned by Houston himself. The Chief of Police in Huntsville and the Walker County Sheriff requested the aid of the Rangers in recovering the treasured artefacts which were so indelibly linked to Texan history. Rangers' Ed Gooding and Mart Jones, compiled a detailed list of the missing firearms and passed it out to antique stores and gun dealers across Texas and the southwest. Captain Jay Banks of Ranger Company B was contacted by a Dallas antique dealers who had noted the vehicle registration of two young men who attempted to sell him some old guns. The owner of the vehicle turned out to be a preacher whose son drove the car. Banks, upon learning that the son and a friend were in Daingerfield, Morris County, contacted the local sheriff who swiftly arrested the pair on July 1. The young men admitted to the crime and guided the Rangers to the weapons which had been hidden along the Sulphur River.[472]

Throughout the mid 1900s race remained an an explosive catalyst in Texan life. White supremacy, exhibited through segregation and imposed caste, reigned throughout the Lone Star State. Any challenge to the system, whether perceived or real, could lead to horrific violence. Sexual intercourse between a black man and a white woman, whether consensual or forced, was an especially emotive issue for Anglo-Texan society.

In October 1935, in the town of Columbus, west of Houston, two African-American teenagers were arrested for and allegedly confessed to the rape and murder of an honor graduate from Columbus High School. On the 22nd, Colorado County Sheriff Frank Hoegemeyer transported the duo to jail in Houston for their own safety. Ranger E. M. Davenport helped escorted the prisoners to ensure their security. On November 14, without asking for Ranger backup, Sheriff Hoegemeyer and his deputy, collected the two boys and began the drive to Columbus where they were supposed to face trial. En route, the sheriff was forced to surrender his prisoners to a mob who dragged them to the scene of their crime and promptly lynched them. The hanging was praised by both county's attorney and judge and it is highly likely that the sheriff knew of the plan hence his failure to request Ranger support.[473]

The Texas Rangers could hardly be blamed for the lynching. After all when Ranger Davenport had been present no harm had come to either prisoner and it is most probable that had a Ranger transported the two boys back to Columbus they would have avoided their gruesome fate. The ability of the Rangers, despite their own racial prejudices, to protect black prisoners from white vigilantes was frequently demonstrated. In June 1936, Rangers descended on the town of El Campo, in rural and highly racist Wharton County. Nine African-Americans, five men and four women had been accused of murder. When a mob of white citizens numbering around three hundred attempted to seize and lynch the suspects the Rangers ensured the safety of the prisoners. One month later, in Franklin, also located in a sparsely populated region suffering from bigotry, a mere four Rangers, albeit armed with machine guns and tear gas, were able to protect a black man who was on trial for the rape of a thirteen year old girl.[474]

The Rangers, on the other hand, as products of a racist society and segregation were not immune from the prevailing attitudes of the time. In 1940, Ranger Captain Gonzaullas was dispatched to Dallas to investigate the bombing of a black home in a primarily Anglo-Texan neighborhood. He concluded that the Dallas Police Department were able to take care of the situation. A year the 'Lone Wolf' returned, U.S. Attorney General had received numerous complaints from the black community in Dallas concerning a series of racially motivated events and expected Governor Coke Stevenson to take action. Gonzaullas, while acknowledging that a number of incidents had occurred again expressed confidence in the abilities of the local law enforcement.[475]

A decade later, a spate of bombings rocked south Dallas. Black properties in formerly all white districts were being targeted for dynamiting by a group of unknown individuals. Gonzaullas was once again placed in charge of investigating the bombings which had begun in February 1950. By June of that year, the Ranger Captain had made little progress and once again affirmed his confidence in the Dallas police. The 'Lone Wolf' also downplayed the situation stating that it was merely a manifestation of the racial tensions affecting all American cities at the time.[476] On July 11 1951, another blast hit south Dallas and this time Captain Crowder, who had replaced Gonzaullas following his retirement, acting on information received from a tip off, was able to arrest two suspects and subsequently unraveled the case leading to thirteen indictments by September of that year.[477]

The port city of Beaumont had a legacy of racial violence. On June 15 1943, following the purported rape of two white women by a black assailant three thousand workers from the Pennsylvania Shipyard headed towards the police station. After being informed that one of the women was unable to pinpoint her attacker the white mob now numbering up to four thousand and armed with a variety of weapons including guns stormed through the black neighborhoods looting homes and stores and burning buildings. Two people, one black and one white died during the rioting. The next day following a declaration of martial law, Rangers Highway Patrolmen and National Guardsmen restored order to the city. The Rangers, notably, Captain Hardy Purvis and Ranger Company A, played a key role in the following investigation and along with other agencies made over three hundred arrests.[478]

On May 17 1954, the U.S. Supreme Court, in a unanimous decision on the case *Brown v. Board of Education of Topeka, Kansas*, ruled that the doctrine of 'Separate but Equal' had no place in the field of education. The landmark ruling sparked antagonism and hostility across the southern states but especially in Virginia as well as the Deep South. Citizens' Councils were formed by middle and upper class whites to ensure racial boundaries remained in place. U.S. Senator Harry F. Byrd of Virginia called for "Massive Resistance" against the decision while one hundred and one members of congress signed the 1956 'Southern Manifesto' labeling the court decision a misuse of judicial power. Two and a half years later, in December 1956, in six southern states not one black child shared a school with white children.[479]

In Texas, the decision caused uproar, but little violence compared to other states of the former Confederacy. Although polls showed that although Anglo-Texans overwhelmingly opposed the federal goverernment's support of Civil Rights, the 'modern Texas' of the 1950s had no taste for the civil disorder that plagued the Deep South. On occasion, however, isolated flare ups did occurr most notably at Mansfield in 1956.[480]

When the Fifth Circuit Court of Appeals in New Orleans ruled in favor of the federal lawsuit filed by National Association for the Advancement of Colored People (NAACP) Mansfield erupted into chaos. The court ordered the desegration of the school district and the enrolment of twelve black students in Mansfield High School. The ruling was to take effect for the 1956-57 school year. As the dates for registration, August 30-31 and September 4, approached, tensions began to rise. Flaming crosses lit up the black section of town and two effigies of African-Americans were hung outside the school while another sporting a sign stating: "This Negro Tried To Enter a White School, wouldn't this be a horrible way to die." decorated Main Street.[481]

On August 30, a mob of several hundred white citizens gathered in front of the school trading insults with Tarrant County Sheriff Harlon Wright and his deputies. Wisely, perhaps, none of the black students attempted to register at the high school. Although the NAACP's attorney leading the case, L. Clifford Davis, wired both Governor Allan Shrivers and Homer Garrison asked for state law enforcement, he was rebuffed by both men who argued that legally they could only send Rangers if requested by the sheriff.

The following day the crowd gathered again, stopping cars outside town and running a Dallas camera crew out of town. Shrivers finally acted, ordering Rangers to Mansfield and to cooperate with local law enforcement to keep the peace. Sergeant Jay Banks and Ranger Ernest Daniel arrived in town before noon, but once again no potential black scholar sought to register. On September 4, the final day of registration, Captain Bob Crowder and five Rangers with weapons and riot gear stood ready to prevent trouble from the several hundred strong crowd. In the face of such vitriolic white hostility, however, the black students supported by the NAACP chose not to enroll and instead continued to attend the African-American school in Fort Worth.[482]

The attempted desegregation at Mansfield directly impacted events of the national stage. A year later in Arkansas, National Guardsmen, confronted by a violent mob, refused to escort black students into Little Rock's Central High School. On this occasion, however, President Dwight D. Eisenhower both dispatched the regular army to enforce federal laws and federalized the National Guard. The role played by the Rangers at Mansfield is highly indicative of both the attitudes of the Texan state government and the corps itself regarding Civil Rights and desegregation. Governor Shrivers publicly blamed the NAACP for causing this crisis and instead of ordering the Rangers to enforce the court order commanded them to arrest anyone, black or white, whose actions were disturbing the peace. Allegedly, the governor also instructed Captain Crowder not to escort the black students into the school. At Mansfield, as well as a subsequent crisis in Texarkana, the Rangers made it clear that their role was to maintain order not act as agents of Civil Rights. If African-American students sought to register the Rangers would attempt to prevent violence erupting but they would not escort anybody in or out of the school.[483]

The increase in industrialization of the mid 1900s stimulated the rise of powerful unions which subsequently led to labor unrest. The was especially true during the massive militarization of the war years and the economic boom post World War II. Texas, far more conservative than many other states, viewed unions with great suspicion. Labor leaders were considered to be troublemakers and even racketeers. During the war, labor unions were deemed to be unpatriotic and as the Cold War heated up were labeled as agents of Communism. In the often violent battles between big corporations and the unions the Ranger corps found itself in an uneviable position. By protecting strikebreakers and preventing violence on the picket lines the Rangers were depicted once again as the agents of big corporations yet when property was damaged or destroyed the company managers portrayed the force as union sympathizers.[484]

On October 11 1935, a mere two months after the formation of the DPS, longshoremen struck once again, closing down ports all along the gulf coast of Texas. A flashpoint developed in Corpus Christi where violence loomed between unionized workers and the strikebreakers. The city council asked Governor Allred for Ranger support and several days later five Rangers including A. Y. Allee arrived in the harbor city. The Rangers proved to be highly effective at containing violence but their actions did not endear them to the striking longshoremen. In addition to guarding the scabs and protecting a convoy of supplies the Rangers were not afraid to threaten the labor leaders. After an outbreak of violence injured a strikebreaker in early November, union organizer Gilbert Mers received a verbal message from Ranger Allee stating that if any further violence was to occur in Corpus Christi Mers would end up on a cold slab.[485]

Early in 1941, a strike at the Rogers-Wade Furniture Factory in Paris, Texas, kept a captain and three Rangers occupied for several months. Unionized workers not only went out on strike but pickets roughed up strikebreakers and those employees who chose to work. Captain Gonzaullas and three Rangers including Bob Crowder were dispatched to Paris to ensure peace and uphold the law. Assuming a stance of neutrality, the Rangers allowed peaceful picketing but prevented further acts of violence against the strikebreakers. Nevertheless, the Rangers were derided by the union workers who accused the corps of supporting the management at the expense of worker rights. The Rangers stayed in Paris for eleven weeks, even remaining for around ten days after the factory owners and the union had reached an acceptable settlement.[486]

The tense relationship between unionized strikers and the Texas Rangers is typified by an encounter between acting Captain Allee and a union official by the name of Arthur Hajecate. In September 1947, Gulf Coast oil workers went on strike and allegedly severely damaged a number of wells and pipelines. The Rangers were called out to ensure peace and stability. The chaparral country of South Texas and its oil wells fell under the jurisdiction of Company D led by Ranger Allee. Allee was known to be a tough, old style Ranger, who while well respected by his men possessed a aggressive temper when provoked. During the course of the strike, at a heated moment, Hajecate seized Allee from behind and spun the Ranger around, before the union man could finish his sentence, Allee hit him so hard that it sucked the oxygen from his lungs, before calmly stating that if Hajecate had something to say it would be wise not to touch him first.[487]

In 1947, the Texan legislature, concerned by an escalation of labor disturbances and union walkouts nationwide, passed a number of laws designed to restrict the power of organized labor within the Lone Star State. It became unlawful for unions to force workers to take up membership, pay dues or participate in boycotts, picketing and secondary strikes. Mass picketing would not be tolerated nor would the presence of pickets on private property or public utilities. When picketing a certain distance had to be maintained between pickets. The legislation also forbade the right of public employees to strike and applied antitrust laws to the unions. While the regulations ensured a lack of legalized violence that plagued a number of other states they infuriated labor leaders and led to an rise of union activism in Texan politics.[488]

The infamous Lone Star Steel Strike of 1957 reinforced the opinion of many Rangers that they had no business becoming involved in labor disputes as they would merely gain the emnity of both parties. On September 21, nearly three thousand members of the United Steel Workers union, against the wishes of union officers, engaged in a massive wildcat strike in a massive demonstration of discontent against the company grievance procedures. Lone Star Steel, based in Daingerfield, was owned a by Dallas investor named E. B. Germany who was known to despise unions and the cause of organized labor. Germany stated that he would never compromise and promptly arranged for replacement workers to take over from the strikers. Sensing trouble, DPS sent a combined force of Rangers and Highway Patrolmen, commanded by Ranger Sergeant Arthur Hill, to Daingerfield.[489]

In spite of the presence of the state lawmen, the situation swiftly escalated out of control. The strikers, infuriated by the stance taken by Germany, resorted to numerous acts of sabotage and violence. The protestors burned buildings, damaged vehicles, intimidated people, killed livestock and even exploded dynamite bombs. The police task force, despite working long hours attempting to restore order, was unable to prevent many of the acts of wanton destruction. The striking workers, however, made a crucial mistake when mistakenly destroying the gas pipe to the town of Pittsburg. Needless to say, this error turned public opinion firmly against the strike. On November 3, the strike ended with no concessions granted by Lone Star Steel. The Rangers took heat from both company management appalled by their inability to prevent property damage but also from the unions who inevitably viewed their efforts to keep the peace as demonstrative of Ranger support for Lone Star Steel.[490]

The Rangers had always been iconic figures in Texan lore, at least for Anglos, but beginning in the 1930s the corps also attracted the interests of academics which both solidified the Ranger myth and also exposed their activities to greater scrutiny. *The Texas Rangers: A Century of Frontier Defence*, written by Walter Prescott Webb, was first published in 1935. Webb, a traditionalist hisitorian, viewed the Rangers as heroic defenders of Texas liberty and justice. He emphasized the valiant nature of the Rangers while staunchly defending the Rangers' record against charges of incompetence or brutality. For Webb, Texas was a battleground between three races of which the Anglo Texans were inherently superior. Mexicans, according to Webb, were volatile, ignorant, cruel, and cowardly while the Comanche were primitive and ferocious savages, incompatible with civilized Anglo Saxon culture. Although the book was a well-researched and absorbing historical narrative, the border patriotism and Anglo-Texan nationalism of the author produced a glorification of the Rangers which detracted from an otherwise excellent work.[491]

Twenty-three years later, in 1958, the Univeity of Texas Press published a far more critical analysis of the Rangers which contested the truthfulness of the Ranger legend. *"With His Pistol in His Hand": A border ballad and its hero*, by Americo Paredes explores the legend of a Mexican agricultural worker who killed a Texas sheriff in self-defense and became a fugitive and folk hero glorified in 'El Corrido de Gregorio Cortez'. The author weaves into the work an analysis of the border country and the relationship between Anglo-Texans and the Hispanic population. The Texas Rangers, or *'rinches'*, as they are referred to by the *Tejano* community feature prominently in the book. Paredes argues that in reality the Texas Rangers were far from the heroic fearless men of Anglo Texan myth. He states that it was well known fact along the border that Rangers would ambush and shoot innocent unarmed Mexicans, carry a rusty pistol to place near a Mexican body to claim self-defence and typically embroider their fights with supposed *bandidos*, above all, inflating the number of opponents they faced and vanquished. While Paredes utilized an impressive source base, his approach was compromised by a clear pro-*Tejano* bias and a certain antipathy toward Anglo-Texans.[492]

Between 1935 and 1960, the newly formed Department of Public Safety faced a host of challenges both old and new. The 'Old West' crimes of bank robberies and cattle theft continued unabated albeit with modern weaponry and transportation. Rangers to draw the unpopular task of enforcing anti-gambling laws as well as combating a vast array of more serious crimes ranging from theft, murder and the quelling of riots. The outbreak of World War II brought additional duties for the Ranger force including the protection of high risk industries, surveillance of 'Fifth Columnists' and recapturing escaped POWS. In the booming post war economy Rangers were called upon to dissuade mafia expansion into the Lone Star State. Racial tensions remained an explosive issue especially following the growth of the Civil Rights movement while increasing labor unrest cast the lawmen as the protectors of big business while gaining the emnity of both management and the unions. The twin issues of white political dominance and the rights of workers would unite in the 1960s placing the Rangers in the middle of several highly publicized crises that would severely tarnish their reputation both in Texas and nationwide.

14

Los Cincos Candidatos, La Huelga and the Swinging Sixties

The 1960s and early 70s were an era of upheaval and turbulence as a new youthful generation revolted against the rigid traditionalist society of the post war era. The "sixties" have become synomymous with the Civil Rights struggle, the New Left and social rebellion. Many young Americans of the so called baby boomer generation became disillusioned with the 'modern life' and the actions of the U.S. government. This new cynical yet idealist generation, in many cases turned to activism to achieve their goals. The appeal of the New Left, typified by organizations such as the Students for a Democratic Society (SDS) and the free-speech movement, spread to colleges all across the nation. The escalation of the war in Vietnam stimulated a massive anti-war movement. In 1967, a demonstration in Central Park, New York City, drew up to five hundred thousand protesters. The alleged complacent corporate consumerism of American life drew many youngsters into a counterculture characterized by drugs, rock and roll and a rejection of materialism.[493]

The Civil Rights movement also gained momentum throughout the 1960s. On August 28 1963, Martin Luther King addressed a crowd of over two hundred thousand blacks and whites. His celebrated 'I Have a Dream' speech looked forward with hope to an era of racial equality and harmony. The 1964 Civil Rights Act prohibited racial segregation in public facilities while the Voting Rights Act of the following year guaranteed all citizens the right to vote.[494] Activists from other minority groups such as gays, Native-Americans and Hispanics began to agitate for more rights including greater tolerance, political rights and economic oppoertunities. A key figure in the Hispanic-American political movement was the inspirational Cesar Chavez who in 1962 formed the United Farm Workers (UFW) to protect the interests of Mexican American agricultural workers.[495]

The political and social radicalism of the era was challenged by conservative backlash among traditionalists causing deep divisions in American society and leading in many cases to violence and tragedy. In the summer of 1964, three Student Nonviolent Coordinating Committee (SNCC) activists working on voter registration were murdered by the KKK near Philadelphia, Mississippi. Dozens of other volunteers were shot and hundreds arrested by local authorities. Four years later, in April 1968, Martin Luther King, who more than any other African-American leader epitomized the struggle for Civil Rights, was killed by a white supremacist assassin. In the late sixties, many cities exploded into flames as African-American youths rioted against economic and social discrimination. The Black Panther movement was vociferously militant and anti-white leading to public panic before disintegrating into internal violence.[496]

As the conflict in South East Asia continued to drain the nation's blood and treasure the anti-war movement polarized American society. Following the invasion of Cambodia, protesters at Kent State University in Ohio burned down the Reserve Officers' Training Corps building on the campus. The Ohio National Guardsmen, called in to restore order, opened fire when attacked by the rioters killing four bystanders. In national polls, a majority of the public supported the actions of the National Guardsmen. In New York City, anti-war protesters who gathered to demonstrate against the shootings and the invasion of Cambodia clashed with and were dispersed by a crowd of construction workers. The Gay Rights movement also led to violence in June 1969 when a police raid on a homosexual bar in New York caused a riot that lasted for several days.[497]

For many Texans, the social upheaval of the 1960s was both disrupting and unsettling. The counterculture, the widespread use of drugs and the anti-war protests clashed with the conservative morality and patriotism that a majority Texans respected and followed in their own lives. The Civil Rights agenda of equality and desegregation was also viewed with suspicion by Anglo Texans. Racism certainly played a role but so did the fear of civic disorder and turmoil as traditional caste boundaries were challenged by a new generation determined to assert their economic and political rights as U.S. citizens. The Texas Rangers, both as symbols of Anglo supremacy and agents of law enforcement, were caught up in the maelstrom and as a result suffered from extensive criticism and vilification which reached levels akin to the aftermath of the bandit troubles fifty years before.

Among the palm trees and balmy weather of subtropical South Texas a storm was brewing that would challenge the unquestioned Anglo domination of that region of *ebonal* and *brasada* with its fertile alluvial soils. Since the early 1900s, the southern counties had been characterized by Anglo domination of the economy and political structures. The benign climate encouraged the development of massive agricultural enterprises including the Texas citrus industry. The primarily Anglo businesses relied on a poorly paid Hispanic underclass many of whom were recent immigrants from south of the Rio Grande. Conditions in the rural areas were described by outsiders as 'feudal' while the towns were marked by rigid residential segregation and a structured caste system based on racial discrimination.[498]

In 1929, the League of United Latin American Citizens (LULAC) had been founded in Corpus Christi, Texas, to fight discrimination and ensure that Hispanics to received their rights as American citizens. Following service in World War II, Mexican-American veterans in 1948 formed the American G. I. Forum of Texas. Both organizations were primarily middle-class and sought acceptance into mainstream American society. The 1960s, however, saw the growth of increasingly militant activists who sought to energize the entire Latino population to combat economic inequality and political subordination. This new generation of activists embraced the pejorative term '*Chicano*' to assert a political consciousness and ethnic identity.[499] A leading figure in this movement was Jose Angel Gutierrez, the son of a doctor who had ridden with Pancho Villa. Gutierrez, raised in Crystal City, deplored the discrimination practiced against his people and had a vision of reconquering *Aztlan*, the original Aztec homeland, which he believed was based in the American Southwest. Unlike his ancestors, however, Gutierrez sought to achieve his victories in labor disputes and at the ballot box.[500]

Crystal City, the county seat of Zavala County, was located in the heart of the Texas Winter Garden agricultural region. The area produced eighty percent of the U.S. spinach crop leading Crystal City to become known as the "Spinach Capital of the World". Like the rest of South Texas the large economic interests and local government were controlled by Anglos. Mexican-Americans, who comprised eighty-five percent of the population worked for low wages in the fields or packing plants. The Del Monte Corporation operated a cannery that employed a large, primarily Mexican-American and unionized workforce.[501] The *Tejano* population also suffered the humiliation of residential and social segregation. One notable example was the use of the municipal swimming pool. The pool was cleaned on Thursdays and only Anglos were permitted to use the facility for the next three days, Mexican usage was only permitted once the water was already dirty.[502]

In October 1962, the Political Association of Spanish Speaking Organizations (PASO) joined forces with Teamster leaders within the (AFL-CIO) in a Hispanic voter registration drive with the goal of challenge Anglo-Texan control of the city council.[503] In the seven months preceding the city elections, scheduled to be held in April 1963, union and PASO organizers, including PASO state executive secretary Albert Fuentes, descended on Crystal City to help mobilize and register Mexican-American electoral votes. In February, a group of Hispanic residents formed the Citizens Committee for Better Government and approved a plan to run five candidates, *Los Cinco Candidatos*, for positions on the city council. Fuentes and other official, however, faced obfuscation and outright defiance from city officials and many members of the white community. Henry Munoz and Carlos Moore, two organizers for the Teamsters Union were even summarily ejected from a local hotel.[504]

The Anglo community became increasingly concerned by the electoral awakening of the *Tejano* population and city officials requested Rangers to keep the peace. They specifically called for the comforting presence of Captain Allee based out of Carrizo Springs. It should be noted that the Ranger Captain's cousin, Tom Allee, was a Zavala county commissioner. The Rangers, specifically Captain Allee, were heavily criticized by the PASO and union officials who alleged the Rangers threatened organizers, broke up political rallies and assaulted *Tejanos* in an attempt to maintain white supremacy. Jose Angel Gutierrez claimed that after speaking at a rally he and some friends were roughed up by the Ranger Captain and several other unidentified Rangers. Nevertheless, the Ranger presence ensured a semblance of order and prevented riots or other incidents of mob violence.[505]

On Election Day, *Tejano* voters were separated from Anglos and were forced to line up on the side of the street where there was no shade. The California Packing Company at first refused to let its workers vote then offered double wages for those employees who chose not to engage in their civic responsibilities. The now primarily *Tejano* voters were not to be cowed and approximately ninety-seven percent of the electorate turned out and submitted a ballot. The Rangers and local police displayed themselves prominently and kept tight control of the crowds discouraging any potential violence. When the final votes were tallied *Los Cinco Candidatos* had won places on the city council.

The Ranger role in the drama, however, had not yet fully played out. After the results had been announced, Captain Allee promptly drove to the house of the new elected mayor, Juan Cornejo, and lectured him on his official responsibilities. The Ranger then closed down a celebratory party at the nearby Veterans' Bar. At the first formal council meeting, a Laredo newpaper reporter observed Zavala County Sheriff C. L. Sweeten barge into Mayor Cornejo. At the following meeting, on April 29, Captain Allee and several other Rangers were in attendance. Following a verbal altercation, Allee, accompanied by Sheriff Sweeten, Tom Allee and the city manager, dragged Cornejo into a side room. What happened in the room appears to be ambigious, according to Cornejo, Allee slapped him and smashed his head repeatedly into a wall. According to the other witnesses, Allee merely registered his verbal displeasure with the new mayor.[506]

On May 6, Chris Dixie, a Houston labor attorney, acting for Cornejo, filed a federal lawsuit against Ranger Allee, asking for a restraining order and fifteen thousand dollars in damages. The lawsuit, however, was eventually rejected by the courts and both DPS Director Homer Garrison and Texas Governor John Connally expressed their support for the Rangers in Crystal City and highlighted the success the officers had achieved in keeping the peace. Regarding *Los Cinco Candidatos*, two were removed from office as they did not fulfill the criteria of property ownership, the remaining three, including Cornejo, served their terms but achieved little of note due to infighting and the hostility of the Anglo business and political community.[507]

A second more dangerous political crisis, at least in terms of public perception of the Rangers, erupted three years later in Starr County. Rio Grande City, the county seat, was situated in the southern tip of Texas just a few miles form the Mexican border. Agriculture was the bulwark of the local economy. Irrigation had transformed the Rio Grande Valley into a growers paradise producing crops of citrus, melons and various vegetables. The economic success of the farmers, however, rested on the cheap stoop labor provided by Latino workers, both *Tejano* and Mexican migrants.[508] For wages as low as forty-five cents an hour workers cultivated and picked the harvest for up to sixteen hours daily, in many cases, even without the most basis sanitary facilities.[509] Nevertheless, with Mexico located just across the Rio Grande there was no shortage of eager workers despite the poor conditions and low wages.

In the spring of 1966, a California labor organizer named Eugene Nelson arrived in the valley. Nelson was an associate of the famous *Chicano* labor leader Cesar Chavez and had participated in the successful strike against California grape growers the previous year. In south Texas, Nelson was able to form the workers into the Independent Workers Association which would soon join the National Farm Workers Association led by Chavez.[510] On June 1st 1966, the workers struck eight corporate growers with the main target being La Casita Farms, a sixteen hundred acre enterprise located near Rio Grande City.[511] The primary goal of the strikers was to raise their hourly wage to the federal minimum of $1.25. The early strikes proved to be unsuccessful in part due to migrant workers from south of the border who continued to work for the lower wages paid by the Texas cultivators.[512]

In an attempt to publicize the plight of the agricultural laborers Nelson called for a march on Austin to demand that the legislature include farmworkers in the minimum wage law. *La Marcha* began on July 4 when approximately one hundred workers and two thousand supporters started their trek north to the state capitol. Governor John Connally refused to meet the marchers or support the minimum wage for agricultural workers but U.S. Senator Ralph Yarborough and other Texan liberals met with the protesters and spoke supportively of their actions. Arguably more importantly, the marching workers with their slogan *Viva La Huelga* (Long live the Strike), attracted media attention on both a state and national level elevating the local issue to nationwide notoriety. Bolstered by the apparent success of La Marcha, labor activists continued to strike and agitate throughout the fall of 1966.[513]

The Rangers were first dispatched to the Rio Grande Valley in November 1966 following a suspicious fire that damaged a Missouri Pacific Railroad trestle. Starr County authorities, along with the railroad, requested Ranger assistance in solving the crime. Although the Rangers arrested several strikers it could never be proven who was responsible for the fire. The strike, however, heated up in the spring of 1967. A record melon crop was approaching harvest time and when the growers hired Mexican workers to replace the unionized workers labor organizers countered by stating that they would ensure that the melons did not leave the valley.[514]

On May 11, DPS director Homer Garrison ordered Captain Allee and eight Rangers to investigate the situation. The actions of the Rangers in Starr County have been subject to, in the words of Ranger Joaquin Jackson, "an unfortunate disconnect between reality and perception."[515] The bitter history between Rangers and Hispanics in south Texas combined with the accounts of a number of historians as well as activists has led the Rangers to have been portrayed as strikebreakers who sided with the growers and coerced the strikers both verbally and physically. In fact first of all, Texas is a 'right to work' state meaning that under state law workers cannot be forced to join a union and labor organizers cannot interfere in an employee's right to work. The Rangers were not present in Starr County to intimidate the workers but instead to stop union men from illegally preventing laborers from engaging in their basic rights under the law. Equally important to note, is that when the Rangers protected the produce trains it was not the non-union melons that they were guarding but ensuring the public right of way. Threats had been made to sabotage the train service and an attempted arson had already taken place on a major railroad bridge.[516]

Two events in particular aroused liberal indignation and inspired furious criticism of the Rangers and their methods. Both incidents once again involved the actions of Ranger Captain Allee. On May 26, Rangers arrested ten picketers for trying to prevent the passage of a freight train bearing produce. That evening, Reverend Ed Krueger of the Texas Council of Churches and his wife arrived on the scene. Krueger was involved in the labor action and made no secret of his sympathy for the strikers. According to Ranger Jackson, who was present on the scene, Krueger behaved like a petulant child pestering the Rangers and demanding to be arrested. The reverend's plan was to have his wife photograph the incident to generate publicity.[517] Eventually, Captain Allee arrested and possibly accosted Krueger at which point his wife produced the hidden camera although it was promptly seized by Ranger Jack Van Cleve and the film exposed. Nevertheless, the arrest was sensationalized by the press which universally accepted Krueger's account as fact and ignored the Ranger version of the affair.[518]

On June 1, Captain Allee and Ranger Tol Dawson obtained an arrest warrant for one Magdaleno Dimas. Dimas was a convicted killer and borderlands thug who had been utilized by the *Huelgistas* to intimidate the workers and potential Mexican strikebreakers. Earlier that day Dimas and an accomplice Benito Rodriguez had threatened the life of the foreman of La Casita Farms and had previously been seen with a rifle in his hand.[519] Following the arrest Dimas spent four days in hospital and the bruising and lacerations noted by three different doctors suggested that he had been badly beaten. Rodriguez also suffered a number of injuries. Allee, however, testified in court that he only lightly touched Dimas and the two men while attempted to escape tumbled into each and hit an open door. This second episode perhaps arouses a little more skepticism of the Ranger account of events yet it should be remembered that Dimas was a hardened criminal with a history of violence and murder.[520]

By June 1967, the strike had collapsed, the completion of the melon harvest and a temporary injunction by a state district judge prohibited picketing at La Casitas Farms. Union funds were depleted by the arrests and susequent fines while the wages for farmworkers had risen to the desired $1.25 an hour.[521] The damage to the reputation of the Texas Rangers, however, was far from finished. A class action lawsuit was filed by the farmworkers, specifically by one Francisco Medrano and including Dimas and Rodriguez, against Rangers' Allee, Dawson, Van Cleve and Jerome Preiss as well as a number of local law enforcement officers.[522]

According to the lawsuit, known as *Medrano v. Allee*, the Rangers had deprived the workers of their rights as laid out under the first and fourteenth amendments and questioned the constitutionality of six Texas statutes. In 1974, the case reached the U.S. Supreme Court whose majority opinion declared that law enforcement officers had engaged in systematic intimidation and used their authority under existing laws in an unconstitutional fashion. In should be noted, however, that three justices dissented from the majority ruling. In addition, the question of offending statutes was deemed moot due to the laws being earlier altered or repealed. In the end, the prolonged legal ruling essentially only gave the Rangers little more than a reproof but the publicity led to a brief campaign to abolish the corps which became an issue in the gubernatorial race between liberal Frances "Sissy" Farenthold and conservative candidate Dolph Briscoe. Following Briscoe's electoral victory in 1972, however, the issue receded into virtual obscurity.[523]

In 1969, the Rangers were recalled to Crystal City to preserve the peace during a dispute between *Chicano* students and the school board. On December 9, hundreds of *Tejano* students at the junior high school and high school refused to attend class and by the second week fifteen hundred children were particpating in the boycott. The initial spark that fanned the flames was the fact that the homecoming queen was selected by the alumni association but could only be eligible if a parent had attended the high school. This stipulation automatically ruled out most of the Hispanic students. The root causes of the boycott, however, were deeper seated, including Anglo domination of student organizations, lack of academic counselling for Hispanics and insulting comments from faculty members directed at Mexican-American students. Rangers, including Captain Allee, attended the meetings in the town plaza, ostensibly to prevent trouble but allegedly also took notes and conducted surveillance on persons of interest. The walkout ended amicably however, after mediation by the U.S. Justice Department, the school board opened negotiations with the students and gave in to most of their demands. On the morning of January 6 the boycotting students returned to class.[524]

Eleven days later, on January 17, Jose Angel Gutierrez and three hundred Chicanos, formed a political organization known as *Partido Nacional de La Raza Unida* or National United Peoples Party. In the local elections of April 1970, *La Raza Unida* put forward candidates in Carrizo Springs, Cotulla and Crystal City winning two mayoralties as well as control of two city councils and two school boards. On June 10, the Crystal City council passed a resolution declaring the city off limits to both Rangers and the Highway Patrol. DPS Director Wilson Speir acknowledged his receipt of a copy of the resolution but was entirely aware that in reality the DPS had the legal authority to operate wherever it wished within the state of Texas.[525]

Gutierrez, however, had loftier ambitions for *La Raza Unida*. Zavala County authorities, including Sheriff Sweeten, remained firmly in the hands of the old establishment and represented a clear indication of Anglo political hegemony. The Chicano activist aimed to end the *ancien regime* and *La Raza Unida* filed candidates for the upcoming county election in November 1972.

On Election Day, November 7, Ranger Joaquin Jackson was dispatched to Crystal City to ensure that the heightened political tension did not turn to violence and chaos. A volatile situation erupted at Precinct 5. Under the Texas Election Code, two poll watchers per candidate were permitted to be present at the precinct. With their thirty candidates, *La Raza Unida* were legally permitted to place sixty observers in Precinct 5 but wisely chose to delegate four people to the duty. The Anglo election judge, however, ordered them removed due to an supposed lack of space. The prospect of rioting loomed as the still seated observers were carried out of the building by clerks and sheriff's deputies while Gutierrez backed up by bodyguards and young Chicanos, many armed with pistols, attempted to push them back inside.

Jackson, the sole Ranger in Crystal City, used his physical presence backed up by common sense to broker a compromise. The Ranger leaned heavily on the election judge and threatened to withdraw all law enforcement offices unless the official relented. Faced by the Ranger Jackson's uncomprising stance the judge agreed to two poll observers, a stance acceptable to Gutierrez and his supporters. When the final tally was released *La Raza Unida* had crushed the Democratic candidates including Sheriff Sweeten.[526]

Two years later in 1974, Gutierrez himself was elected county judge. The reign of *La Raza Unida* would nevertheless prove to be shortlived. After eight months in office, a group of activists rebelled against Gutierrez and demanded a Ranger inquiry into alleged corruption. Ranger Jackson, in charge of the investigation, uncovered evidence of fraud and thievery and arrested a number of officials. The party remained plagued by corruption, factionalism and scandals including the arrest of the state leader on drug charges. By the end of 1978, *La Raza Unida* had collapsed.[527]

On September 30 1970, Captain A. Y. Allee retired after after thirty-nine year career in the Texas Rangers. Allee, during the sixties, represented perhaps the best and worst of of the stereotypes that were held of the Ranger corps. The cigar smoking Allee was born in September 1905 in Encinal, Texas. He joined the Rangers in 1933 after serving as a lawman in Bee County. After a brief two year spell back as chief deputy officer in Bee County between 1933-35 he returned to the Rangers and remained in the corps until his retirement.[528]

Allee, whose father and grandfather had been Rangers, was a genuine leader who inspired loyalty from his men and was fearless in the line of duty.[529] He was, however, a controversial figure with a quick temper who was named as defendant in several lawsuits though never convicted.[530] Allee came from a generation of Texans who still viewed Mexico as the enemy and therefore Anglos not *Tejanos* should remain the authority in Texas, which needless to say, colored his dealings with the Hispanic population.[531] To call him a racist though, would be misleading. In the fifties, Allee had stood up for the *Tejanos* of Duval County against the corrupt Parr regime and perhaps most tellingly, in 1969 when Arturo Rodriguez Jr. became the first Mexican-American Ranger he claimed that it was due to the recommendation by Captain Allee.[532] By the 1960s, the world that he operated in and understood was changing and Allee was ill-equipped to deal with the new realities. For liberals and many Mexican-Americans he came to personnify all that was wrong with an outdated Ranger force. Allee is best described in the words of Ranger Joaquin H. Jackson; "he adhered to a code too simplistic to guide us in modern times, but he lived or died by it. This was honor as he understood it."[533]

The labor unrest of the sixties was not confined to Hispanic workers in south Texas. On October 27 1968, around two thousand unionized workers at the Lone Star Steel plant struck in protest against the working conditions. E. B. Germany who had owned the company during the 1957 strike had moved on but his successor George Wilson proved to be equally intransigent and refused to compromise and swore to continue production. The strike would prove to be the most violent in Texan history involving over two hundred physical assaults including stabbings, numerous drive by shootings, the use of dynamite bombs and even the killing of a strikebreaker.[534]

The Rangers, probably unwillingly, were again embroiled in a labor dispute. DPS officers were requested by the Morris County Sheriff early in the dispute as his office had only two deputies and could not deal with the escalating violence. Captain Bob Crowder was placed in command of the DPS personnel which comprised of up to twenty-six Rangers and forty-six highway patrol officers. Although the Rangers enjoyed some successes including arresting thirty suspects for the murder of the company scab and the removal of a bomb planted in a mess hall, neither the state nor local law enforcement were able to adequately contain the violence. The whole Ranger experience during the strike was disillusioning and frustrating. The DPS officers become the targets of both sides and consequently had bottles, bricks and verbal epithets heaped upon them, Bob Crowder was even shot at. To add insult to injury, none of the individuals arrested were ever placed on trial due to the obvious difficulty of obtaining convictions. When, after seven months, in May 1969, the union voted to return to work thus ending the dispute, the Texas Rangers, almost all of whom had worked the strike undoubtedly gave a collective sigh of relief. [535]

The Vietnam War, fought far away in the jungles of Southeast Asia, and the social turmoil that it caused across the nation may have appeared distant to many Rangers especially those with no personal connection to the conflict. The decision of President Nixon to expand the war into Cambodia, however, would bring the Rangers face to face with a counterculture that the older officers found hard to accept or even understand. On May 5 1970, the day after the tragedy at Kent State University, several thousand University of Texas students marched towards the Capitol building in Austin. The DPS swiftly ordered additional Rangers and Highway Patrolmen to provide security in case of violence. Senior Captain Clint Peoples, displaying the prejudice of the time stated that none of the hippies should be allowed to enter the Capitol unless it was over the dead bodies of Texas Rangers. In fact the demonstrators were able to gain access despite the presence of the Rangers. It took not only tear gas but also the assistance of the Austin city police to remove the 'hippies'. To their credit, however, no shots were fired suggesting that the Rangers, unlike the national guardsmen, showed considerable restraint.[536]

One year later, on May 22 1971, Austin, played host to President Nixon and Vice President Spiro Agnew. The President had come to Texas to witness the unveiling of the Lyndon B. Johnson Library constructed on the campus of the University of Texas. As the war was continuing to drag on with no determinable end in sight, Nixon's presence inevitably inspired a mass demonstration. Almost half the Ranger force, along with other federal and local lawmen, gathered in Austin to ensure stability. While the official ceremony took place on campus, large numbers of anti-war demonstrators gathered at the intersection of Red River and 26th streets. The Rangers, avoiding the urine filled bags and faeces hurled in their direction, formed ranks to combat any potential assualt by the sign waving protesters. Unsurprisingly, given the abuse they were enduring, the Rangers were apparently selecting targets from among the demonstrators in the event the crowd was to charge. Fortunately for all concerned, the anti-war protestors eventaully moved on avoiding a potentially deadly confrontation.[537]

Texan lawmen, especially the old time Rangers, grew increasingly frustrated during the sixties by federal court decisions that appear to both favor the criminal element and obstruct peace officers from effectively conducting their investigations and building cases against suspects. The 1966 Supreme Court decision in *Miranda v. Arizona* is perhaps the best example of the federal judiciary imposing an unpopular law on police officers across the nation. Chief Justice Earl Warren wrote an opinion that any individual in police custody had to be notified of their constitutional rights before any interrogation could take place. Rangers were thus obligated under federal law to inform all arrested suspects; "You have the right to remain silent, anything you say can and will be used against you in a court of law. You have the right to an attorney. If you cannot afford an attorney, one will be appointed for you. Do you understand these rights as they have been read to you?" Courts could and did reject perfectly solid cases due to a failure to 'Mirandize' the accused. Old school Rangers found the whole process exasperating and another example of the courts pampering potentially dangerous felons.[538]

The sixties and seventies were characterized by the battles for political, economic and social rights, neverethless, throughout the era Texan criminals continued their nefarious activities which inevitably attracted the attention of the Ranger corps. Homer Garrison, the long time DPS director, was intolerant of failure when dealing with the criminal element and when a Ranger fell short of his high standards he could expect be lose his job. Such was the case with Ranger Tully Seay of San Augustine.

On January 17 1962, a drunken bank robber named Marcus E. Carter held up the First National of Cushing in Nacogdoches County. On State Highway 21, Ranger Seay, noticed a vehicle similar in description to one involved in the robbery and forced it off the road. When Seay approached the car, however, Carter leapt out with a pistol in his hand taking the Ranger by surprise. The robber promptly disarmed the lawman and forced him into his car as a hostage. Eventually, after a four hour drive through East Texas, Seay persuaded the crook to release him near Beaumont. The Ranger reached the Beaumont DPS office later that evening, and subesequently placed an in depth description of the suspect's vehicle over the radio leading to an arrest that very night. In spite of the successful conclusion to the episode, Garrison found it unacceptable that an experienced officer could allow himself to be captured by a drunk. The DPS director had carefully developed the Ranger stereotype of a man who would die before backing down and now the public image had been shattered. Two weeks after the incident, on January 31, Teay was dismissed from the Ranger service.[539]

The most infamous murder in Texan history, occurred on November 22 1963 in downtown Dallas. President John F. Kennedy was fatally shot while travelling in the Presidential Motorcade. Texas Governor John Connally was also wounded by in the attack. The assassin was an ex-marine named Lee Harvey Oswald. The Dallas Police Department, not the Texas Rangers, played the principal role in the ensuing investigation. Rangers, however, were instrumental in protecting Governor Connally while he recuperated in Parkland Hospital.[540]

Alfredo Hernandez, born in San Luis Potosi, was an illegal Mexican immigrant with a penchant for burglaries. Based around Uvalde, Hernandez engaged in numerous robberies of both local businesses and private homes. After a failed home invasion, when an old man by the name of Rutherford not only beat up the robber but also took away his gun, Hernandez moved his base of operations to the tiny desert town of Dryden in Terrell County. On November 4 1965, Sheriff Bill Cooksey along with a former Border Patrolman and an eighteen year old youth headed out to a local arroyo following the sighting of a potential illegal alien. At the ravine they were joined by Alfredo Gallego, a ranch hand who had alerted the sheriff to the presence of a suspected illegal. Cooksey descended the arroyo and captured Hernandez. The sheriff, however, believing that he was dealing with a simple case of an immigration violation, gave Hernandez permission to collect his belongings. As he passed Cooksey, the

Mexican pulled out a Smith and Wesson M&P.38 and shot the sheriff in the leg and back. Hernandez then captured the others and forced Gallego to drive him from the scene.[541]

The outlaw boldly remained in the Dryden area engaging in his favored pastime of robbery. Sheriff Cooksey, who had fortuitously survived the shooting, noticed that the local store and gas station was being systematically burglarized every seven to ten days. Given that the items taken were basic rations, the sheriff suspected Hernandez of being responsible. In the summer of 1966, Cooksey and Ranger Alfred Allee Junior, the son of Captain Allee, began to stakeout the store in the hope of nabbing the fugitive. On August 19, Hernandez exited the store wearing a straw hat with tow sacks of provisions tied around his neck. When Cooksey demanded his surrender the bandit shot at him with his .38, the sheriff returned fire knocking off the straw hat and exploding the soda pop and canned chili con carne dangling in front of Hernandez. Allee then joined the shootout and a deflected bullet from the Ranger's gun shattered Hernandez's jaw causing him to faint from blood loss. The robber was sent to the state penitentiary and remained incarcerated until 1984. Following his deportation to Mexico, he was killed in unknown circumstances, according to information provided to the Rangers.[542]

In 1965, the 'See More Kid' resurfaced in the Hill Country. Brogdon had served three years in prison near Freeport before obtaining work at the Y.O. Ranch of Charles Schiener III. Ironically, it was Ranger Purvis, who led the pursuit of Brogdon, who found him the job. Brogdon continued to cowboy at several ranches before heading north to Montana in a stolen Pontiac Star Chief. In Montana, the outlaw confounded the local police with his backwoods skills but was eventually caught. Over the next few years, Brogdon served time in a number of penal institutions across several states, worked herding cattle and found employment in an oilfield near Aspermont. While in jail in Anson, Texas, Brogdon escaped during a prison breakout and headed west to California. The west coast, however, did not appeal to the 'See More Kid' who returned to the Medina Lake Country and resumed his life of hunting and burglarizing cabins deep in the Texas hills.[543]

In September 1966, Brogdon was arrested in the border town of Del Rio after a city policeman noticed him driving stolen jeep full of guns and saddles. Ranger Joaquin Jackson then tramsported the prisoner back to Medina County to await trial. The jail at Hondo did not hold the 'See More Kid' for long, several months later, Brogdon who had been appointed a trustee, widened the bars on a second floor window with simple tools, then naked and slicked head to foot with hair pomade squeezed himself out to freedom. Brogdon walked to Medina where he robbed a cabin taking possession of supplies including a Winchester pump rifle, a M-1 military carbine and several hundred rounds of ammunition. Ranger Jackson promptly gathered a posse and gave chase. After several days of fruitless searching the Ranger called for a pack of bloodhounds from the King Ranch. Brogdon continued to rob cabins and evade his pursuers before finally being cornered at the cabin of a Dr. Meyer by Jackson and Medina County Sheriff Miller with two of his deputies. The 'See More Kid' still possessed his formidable arsenal but fortunately for all concerned he was persuaded by the Ranger to surrender with a fight.[544]

On July 6 1967, Ranger Joaquin Jackson received a call from Morris Barrow, a deputy sheriff of Uvalde County. The partly decomposed body of a Mexican national by the name Leopoldo Ramos Flores had been discovered on the south Texas farm of Cecil Reagan. Flores had been a longterm worker on the farm and was noted for his loyalty to his employer. His killers were two Mexican migrant workers, eighteen year cousins Homero Morales Nino and Ramiro Nino Otero from the state of Coahuila. The two young men had murdered Flores for his three hundred dollar paycheck and also took a radio and dress shoes before fleeing back across the Rio Grande into Mexico.[545]

Ranger Jackson, however, was determined to apprehend the murderers who had committed a cold blooded crime on Texan soil. He sought the advice of Captain Allee who put him in contact with Felipe Zamora, a captain in the *Policia Judiciales de Estado* (PJE), a Mexican state police force responsible for investigating serious crimes. Jackson then drove into Mexico, crossing the Rio Grande at Piedras Negras, and made contact with the Mexican captain. Zamora, introduced the Ranger to Xicotencote Flores the *commandante* of city police in Nuevo Rosita, Coahuila. Flores offered to apprehend and handover the fugitives for the price three hundred dollars a head. Cecil Reagan had already agreed to provide funds to track down the killers of his employee and old friend. On July 27, the *commandante* delivered Ramiro Nino Otero into Ranger custody on the International Bridge at Piedras Negras. Four days later in Bandera County, Homero Morales Nino was arrested by a game warden. The boys were found guilty at trial and sentenced to thirty years in prison.[546]

The Medina Lake country, in Medina County, was a exclusive refuge for wealthy San Antonio residents who retreated there to relax including drinking, gambling and consorting with ladies of the night. In October 1968, the body of Henry C. "Champ" Carter was discovered lying against the fenceline of his leased property by the lake. He been killed by a blast from a shotgun loaded with buckshot. Carter was a renowned pimp and gambler who planned to turn his home into casino but was not known to have a history of violence. Two days after the body was discovered, county sheriff Charles Hitzfelder requested Ranger assistance. Ranger Jackson, stationed in Uvalde, led the investigation and working with the San Antonio Police Department built up a long list of potential suspects, violent underworld figures who had connections to Carter.[547]

In the spring of 1969, operating on a lead from SAPD Lieutenant Dave Keene, Jackson travelled to Louisiana. Jeannie Piper, an ex-girlfriend of the known gambling boss Bunny Eckert, had admitted to being a witness to the murder. Piper had fled Texas and was now living in New Orleans with a member of the Marcello family, part of the Sicilian Mafia. In exchange for immunity and pressurized by the Marcello family who didn't appreciate a Texas Ranger poking around their business, Piper agreed to give a statement. The night of the murder Eckert, Piper and Arnold McCoy had robbed Carter's residence hoping to slow down the opening of a casino by their business rival.

As they left the property the threesome encountered the owner driving his new Thunderbird. When Carter exited his vehicle, McCoy shot him with a twelve-gauge double barrled shotgun. The trio then dumped the stolen merchandise and fled at least temporarily to Mexico. On June 2, indictments were handed down by a grand jury, McCoy, however, was already dead after being shot in an Austin bar but Eckert was arrested in Temple four days later. Eckert was never brought to trial due a supposed lack of evidence but did not enjoy his freedom for long. Several years later he disappeared in suspicious circumstances.[548]

On April 3 that same year, fourteen inmates in the jail at Carrizo Springs decided that they had spent sufficient time in the crossbar hotel. The crooks overpowered the jailer and his wife before seizing weapons and ammunition. As the armed felons attempted to shoot their way to freedom they encountered several local peace officers as well as the belligerent old Ranger Captain A. Y. Allee. A hail of bullets from the lawmen forced the inmates back inside the concrete and steel jail where they chose to continue the battle from behind improvised fortifications. Taking heavy fire, Allee radioed for backup and within a short space of time Rangers' Tol Dawson, Jackson and Alfred Allee Jr. were on the scene along with local officers including Uvalde County Deputy Sheriff Morris Barrow.[549]

Captain Allee first attempted to end the standoff through the use of tear gas canisters. Unfortunately for the residents of Carrizo Springs, the old Ranger's aim proved to be lacking in accuracy, none of the 40 mm canisters made it through the jailhouse bars resulting in the area being shrouded in thick clouds of gas. Frustrated but undetered, Allee promptly led his men to the north wall of the jail. In response to shouts from the jail that the prisoners wanted to talk, the Captain yelled out "I'll give you sons of bitches till ten to lay down your arms and come out" and then promptly opened fire after three seconds. The Rangers and local lawmen burst through the entrance and swiftly cleared the bottom level. The armed inmates, however, remained in control of the second floor but the unwary criminals had clearly never experienced the wrath of Captain Allee. The sixty-four year old

Ranger, audaciously charged up the stairwell in a lone assault lighting up the jail with a bullet storm from a World War II era .45 submachine gun. By the time the gunsmoke settled peace had been restored to Carrizo Springs. The Rangers subsequently located all fourteen aspiring jailbreakers cowering in a corner cell.[550]

Charles Robert Mathis was a hardened gangster with a intimidating face and a long career in crime. In 1970, Ranger Glen Elliott, based in Longview, arrested Larry Fyffe for pilfering radios and televisions. Fyffe, an associate of Mathis's, struck a deal with the law, he would escape charges in exchange for information on his former accomplice. In December, Fyffe alerted the Rangers that Mathis intended to steal a bulldozer and the John Deere Company in Dallas was likely to be the target. On the date of the planned robbery, Rangers Elliott, Bob Mitchell, Red Arnold and Max Womack staked out the building. Around noon, Mathis materialized and swiftly hotwired a large truck designed to carry weighty construction equipment. As the gangster backed a bulldozer up a ramp onto the truck bed he was suddenly faced with four armed Rangers. Mathis pulled his pistol but this foolish action merely precipitated a barrage of shotgun fire which blew him high into the air. As he fell back the bulldozer crashed off the ramp onto his body crushing the felon.[551]

On the evening of October 13 1971, in Euless, located between Dallas and Fort Worth, police sergeant B. E. Harvell noticed a suspicious slow moving car. The peace officer infering that the driver might be looking for targets to rob promptly stopped the vehicle only to find himself confronted by a man with pistol. The officer exhanged fire with the suspect who then leapt back into his car and the chase resumed. At an intersection a woman jumped out of the car and shortly after the driver abandoned his vehicle and disappeared into a dark field. Upon questioning the female companion, Harvell learnt that his fugitive was fifty-three year old Huron Ted Walters, a career gangster with a forty year rap sheet dating back to the 1930s. Walters had just committed a hold up, robbing a liquor store and in the process shooting the owner.[552]

In response to the radio dispatch from Harvell, Ranger Sergeant Lester Robertson along with Rangers Tom Arnold and Howard "Slick" Alfred joined police and sheriff units in the hunt for Walters. The gangster had reached a house in Bedford where he took a couple and their daughter hostage and forced them into the family car, a 1969 Mercury. A second daughter, however, was able to escape and alert the Bedford police. Ranger Arnold spotted the stolen vehicle and together with police cruisers from both Bedford and Euless gave chase. When the Mercury attempted to turn onto State Highway 114 the lawmen were able to force the car off the road into a field where it was soon boxed in. Walters, however, held a twelve gauge sawed off shotgun against the head of one of the hostages and ignored the demands to surrender. Meanwhile Arnold, rested his 30.06 rifle on his car door, targeted Walters in the scoped sights and waited for his opportunity. As two officers cautiously approached along a creek, the robber turned to look momentarily lifting the shotgun. In that instant, Arnold ended the standoff with a single well aimed bullet.[553]

The 'Duke of Duval', seventy-four year old George Parr, remained in firm control of his south Texas fiefdom throughout the sixties. The federal and state charges brought against him in the 1950s had been reversed or dismissed. The Parr machine continued to plunder the county coffers in a display of unequaled corruption. In 1972, however, the IRS and U.S. Attorney's Office launched an investigation agianst Parr based on income tax evasion on the millions he had stolen from the county funds. This time the 'Duke' had met his match, despite brazen lying from local officials, disappearance of documents and lack of cooperative witnesses, he was indicted on April 6 1973. Eleven months later, in March 1974, the trial of George Parr was held in Corpus Christi. On the 19th of that month the jury found Parr guilty on all the charges of tax evasion and the 'Duke' received a five year prison sentence.[554]

Parr, remained free on bond, however, while his lawyers appealed the verdict. This stratagem had proved successful in the fifties in keeping him out of the penitentiary but on this occasion when the Fifth

U.S. Circuit Court of Appeals affirmed his conviction the prosecution sought the revocation of his bond. Although the 'Duke' still planned to take his case to the U.S. Supreme Court it was feared that he to abscond across the border. Following a hearing in Corpus Christi on March 31, Parr vanished, allegedly heavily armed. Over the next twenty four hours, federal and state lawmen including the Rangers combed Duval County for the former political boss. On the morning of April 1, a DPS helicopter located Parr's Chrysler parked on his *Los Horcones* Ranch south of Benavides. When Ranger Gene Powell reached the vehicle he discovered the 'Duke' had committed suicide by shooting a.45 bullet into his brain. Over the following three years Texas Attorney General John Hill led a task force which aggressively went after and destroyed the remnants of the Parr regime.[555]

Fred Gomez Carrasco, known to law enforcement as the 'Mexican Connection', was a brutal heroin trafficker who operated an extensive criminal network in Texas and northern Mexico. In the summer of 1974, the thirty-four year old Carrasco, who had apparently killed over fifty men, was serving time in the Walls Unit of the state prison in Huntsville. On July 24, Carrasco together with Rudy S. Dominguez and Ignacio Cuevas, armed with revolvers smuggled into the correctional facility, took control of the third floor library seizing seventy inmates and eleven prison employees as hostages. The sole goal of Carrasco was freedom, he sought to escape to Mexico and continue his narcotics trade south of the Rio Grande.[556]

Ranger Captain J. F. Rogers took command of the dozens of Rangers and Highway Patrolmen who had been swiftly dispatched to the scene. He was assisted by Captain G.W. Burks and together the Rangers plotted strategy with Jim Estelle, director of the Texas Department of Corrections (TDC). Although Carrasco and his two cronies, in exchange for various demandes, released the majority of the inmate hostages and several civilians over the course of the eleven day siege the situation remained highly volatile and commanded nationwide press attention. The Rangers considered various options including the use of explosives, tear gas and narcotics in the food deliveries but all were discarded due to impracticality and the uncertainty of the variables involved.[557]

It was hoped that the desire to escape would lure Carrasco and his men from their fortress and this proved to be the case. On August 2, Linda Woodward, a female hostage was released to inform the prison the peace officers and TDC officials of Carrasco's plan to end the standoff. The three convicts would leave the library in a homemade 'Trojan Horse' shield with four captives inside and surrounded by the remaining hostages. Carrasco demanded that an armored car be placed in the prison yard to facilitate the escape. The following evening the cumbersome 'Trojan Horse' slowly lumbered down the ramp towards the prison yard.[558]

At a predesignated point, the two Ranger Captains together with FBI agent Robert Wiatt and DPS intelligence officer Winston Padgett burst from hiding and demanded the felons surrender. At the same time hire pressure water hoses were turned on the shield and a corrections officer cut the rope tying the outside hostages to the shield. The attack quickly stalled as bullets struck the protective vests of the two Rangers and FBI agent temporarily incapacitating them, then the water hoses failed. For the next ten minutes, a firefight raged then using the restored hoses and an aluminium ladder the lawmen were able to finally overturn the shield. A heartbreaking scene greeted the Rangers, two female captives had been murdered before Carrasco shot himself in the head. Cuevas had fainted but Dominguez was still armed, when he thrust his pistol into the back of a third hostage DPS Agent Padgett placed two bullets in his head. The eleven day drama, the longest prison siege in U.S. history, had ended in tragedy despite the best efforts of the Rangers.[559]

John Webster Flannigan, born in 1923, never held a valid driver's licence from state of Texas yet he became in the words of Ranger Jackson; "the greatest bush pilot in the business."[560] Flannigan, from Crystal City, earned a law degree and subsequently opened a law firm in Austin representing a range of defendants including the madam of a whorehouse and the leader of a gang involved in drugs, robberies and white slavery. Perhaps inevitably, Flannigan himself crossed the line into criminality and was disbarred. The genial Flanigan returned to his roots in south Texas and entered into a new career as narcotics pilot supplying dope for his old confederates among the Dixie Mafia in Austin.[561]

Flannigan turned out to be an outstanding pilot. He was able to guide his often stolen planes through not over the mesquite thickets of the south Texas brush country and barely needed a landing strip making his movements hard to trace. In September 1975, a rancher near Crystal City alerted Ranger Joaquin Jackson to a suspicious single Cessna he had found on his property. The discovery of a single fingerprint would later allow Jackson was later able to tie Flannigan to the plane. While staking out the Cessna the Ranger and Drug Enforcement agents (DEA) learned that another plane had just dropped three hundred kilos of marijuana in a ditch before boldly landing at Crystal City airport. It was believed that Flannigan was the pilot. The lawmen raced to the airport but the crook had already left. When Ranger Jackson raided Flannigan's house in Crystal City he discovered a trove of stolen goods.[562]

The pilot himself had fled to Mexico and continued his illicit trade from south of the border. The Rangers finally caught the affable criminal several years later but at the request of the U.S. Attorney dropped the state charges to allow a federal prosecution. Flannigan was able make a deal with the feds for a short sentence to be served at a federal penitentiary in Florida. Incredibly, he soon 'escaped' federal detention by allegedly simply walking away from a receiving line. Back in Mexico he graduated to flying cocaine and possibly providing information to the DEA. Eventually he was busted flying cocaine into Kansas and on this occasion served out his sentence in prison.[563]

On May 29 1979, San Antonio federal judge John H. Wood was gunned down outside his condominium. 'Maximum John' was a courtroom dictator who habitually threw the maximum sentence on criminals unfortunate enough to be convicted in his courtroom. DPS swiftly dispatched Ranger Captain Jack O. Dean and three Rangers to the crime scene but were superseded by FBI deputy director James O.Ingram who descended from Washington with an army of agents. Nevertheless, Dean and his Rangers continued to make inquiries and passed on their findings to the feds.[564]

An anonymous tip off pointed Dean in the direction of Charles Harrelson, a contract killer and robber for hire as well as the father of future Hollywood star Woody Harrelson. The Ranger captain shared this information with Ingram who informed Dean that the FBI would take over the search. Harrelson was arrested by the Van Horn City Police in August 1980 and he was subsequently handed over to the FBI. In December 1982, he was convicted and given sentenced to time in federal prison. An upcoming case in Wood's courtroom involved Jimmy Chagra, a suspected El Paso drug dealer, who the FBI and DEA had been investigating for several years. Chagra, clearly had no intention of risking trial in front of 'Maximum John' and hired an assassin. The murder of a federal judge had made headlines in the national media. In the subsequent news coverage of the arrest and conviction the FBI took full credit yet the Texas Rangers, notably Captain Dean, had played a key role in the investigation.[565]

In June 1979, a well publicized incident led to humiliation for the Ranger corps and in particular Charles Cook of Company A. Lieutenant Governor William P. "Bill" Hobby ordered a 'call upon the Senate' to force a quorum and push through a controversial piece of legislation placing the presidential and state primaries on separate days. This was opposed by many liberal senators who saw it as benefitting the presidential hopes of former Texas governor John Connally. On the day of the quorum, May 18, twelve Democratic senators failed to show up in an attempt to delay the quorum and let the passage of time end the bill.[566]

Hobby, infuriated, called for DPS to track down the so called 'Killer Bees' and bring them to the senate. The Rangers and Highway Patrolman proved incapable of locating the missing senators much to the frustration of the lieutenant governor. On Sunday May 20, Ranger Cook arrived at the house of Houston senator Gene Jones and when a man exited the property who resembled the faxed photo of the 'Killer Bee' and answered to 'Senator Jones' the Ranger took him into custody and delivered him straight to Austin. In fact, the prisoner was Clayton Jones, the senator's brother, who allowed himself to be arrested to give his brother a chance to escape over the back fence. The 'Killer Bees' won the battle and only returned to the senate when it was too late to pass Hobby's bill. In so doing, however, the missing senators made the Rangers a laughing stock across the Lone Star State.[567]

While the escapade had made a mockery of the Rangers, the sixties and seventies saw the construction of a more positive and enduring monument to Ranger heroism. On April 15 1964, DPS Director Garrison accepted an offer from the Waco Chamber of Commerce to build a company headquarters and Ranger Museum on the Brazos River at a total cost of one hundred and twenty-five thousand dollars. In 1967, Garrison turned the first spade of dirt in the construction of the complex which would be known as Fort Fisher. The complex would be the home of Ranger Company F and also housed the Homer Garrison Memorial Museum dedicated to the history of the corps.[568] On August 4 1973, work began on a one million dollar addition to Fort Fisher. The Texas Ranger Hall of Fame would serve as a memorial to Rangers who died courageously in the line of duty or played a major role in the history and development of the Ranger Corps.[569]

Garrison himself, tragically, passed away from cancer on May 5 1968. The sixty-seven year old had served as DPS Director for almost thirty years and came to personnify the agency that he had shaped. Under his leadership the Rangers developed into highly professional peace officers well respected across the nation. During the Garrison era, the director earned not only the respect but also the love of the Rangers he commanded. If Garrison had lived for another twelve years his pride in the Texas Rangers would undoubtedly have remained unshaken. While the turbulence of the sixties, notably the Latino labor and political struggles in south Texas, led to sharp criticism of the Rangers and even calls to abolish the corps, by the mid seventies the storm had passed.

The retirement of Captain Allee in 1970 was symbolic of the change in the Ranger service. The grizzled old Ranger captain exemplified the finest attributes of the frontier Rangers. Allee was honest, loyal and possessed a complete absence of fear. His adherence to a simplistic black and white code of right and wrong was admirable but the Texas that he knew had changed. The time had come for a new younger generation of Rangers to take up the torch and guide the corps toward the twentieth century. The Ranger ranks, however, stayed virtually devoid of minorities remaining primarily comprised of white men. The acceptance of minority groups, especially women, into the Ranger service was an issue that many officers balked at especially when it appeared that the female candidates were chosen on the basis of their gender not ability. The issue of the Ranger corps becoming more reflective of the state demographics would develop into a topic of controversy and scandal over the ensuing decades.

15
Approaching the New Millenium

On November 4 1980, the charismatic California Republican, Ronald Reagan swept aside incumbent Jimmy Carter in a dramatic one sided presidential election. On election day, Reagan, a former governor of the the Golden State, achieved fifty-one percent of the popular vote compared to only forty-one percent for Carter. The number of electoral college votes for each candidates was even more reflective of the landslide Republican victory. Reagan won a staggering four hundred and eighty-nine votes while Carter could only carry six states for a total of forty-nine electoral votes.[570]

The decisive GOP win can be explained by a number of political factors. The failings of the undistinguished Carter presidency had disillusioned many Americans. The Democratic president, elected in 1976, had inherited slumping a economy. His mismanagement, however, only made the situation worse leading to both rising inflation rates and a heightened recession. Carter's drive for public acceptance over his unpopular energy-conservation iniatives demonstrated a grave failure in understanding the national mood. The image of the president as a weak national leader was compounded by his indecisive handling of the Iranian hostage crisis of 1979-1981.[571]

The election of Reagan, neverthless, also represented the revival of an American conservative political philosophy of antagonism to "big government", the reduction of the oversized federal bureaucracy, increased military spending and reaffirmation of Christian values and states' rights. The Reagan presidential campaign benifitted from a major evangelical religious resurgence characterized by the Moral Majority of Reverend Jerry Falwell. The perceived social permissiveness of the Democratic agenda, notably the Equal Rights Amendment (ERA) and gay civil rights, disaffected large numbers of white blue collar Americans who drifted into the embrace of the Republican Party.[572]

The conservativism of the eighties, exemplified by electoral victories for Reagan in two presidential elections, did not signal the end of the Civil Rights agenda including the goal of equal opportunities and representation in business, politics and law enforcement. In Texas, by 1993, the Lone Star State had elected a female governor, Ann Richards, only the second women in Texan history to ascend to gubernatorial office. Both the State House of Reprentatives and the Senate also contained a number of minority legislators. In terms of law enforcement, while the ranks of the State troopers included many African-American, Hispanic, and female officers the Texas Rangers remained dominated by white males leading one state congresswoman Karyne Conley to label the corps "the last bastion of the good-old-boy system".[573]

The historical relationship between the Texas Rangers and the *Tejano* population, notably in south Texas, had been marked by suspicion, tension and occasional outbreaks of violence. Given this uneasy legacy, it is unsurprising that the Ranger Division neither received a surfeit of Hispanic applications nor accepted large numbers of *Tejanos* into its ranks. Nevertheless, as noted earlier, in August 1969 Arturo Rodriguez Jr became the first Hispanic to wear the *cinco peso* in the modern Ranger force. In the 1970s, he was joined by Ray Martinez and Rudolfo Rodriguez, both of whom saw service in south Texas and were commended for their stalwart work.[574] By 2002, Hispanic Rangers comprised almost a quarter of the entire division.[575]

In the eighties, the National Association for the Advancement of Colored People (NAACP) agitated for the inclusion of African-Americans into the Ranger service. In July 1987, in a well publicized incident, Michael Scott a black Highway Patrolman, failed in his application to join the Texas Rangers. DPS Director Leo E. Gossett, however, dismissed the political criticism and pointed out that the successful applicant had simply scored higher than Scott in the selection process. Twelve months later Lee Roy Young Jr. became the first African-American Ranger in the twentieth century. Young, whose family could be traced back to a Seminole Indian scout, was a fifteen year veteran of DPS.[576]

In 1993, Company A Captain Earl Pearson ascended to the position of assistant commander of the Texas Ranger Division. In achieving the promotion, Pearson made history by becoming the highest ranking black officer in Ranger history. Nevertheless, a certain degree of prejudice remained within the service. Twelve months later, when Christine Nix, became the first female African-American Ranger Sergeant, two off duty Rangers were recorded using offensive racial slurs including *nigger* to describe their new colleague. The two men were given six months work probation for their actions.[577]

The question over the inclusion of women into the Ranger service proved to be far more controversial. While it was certainly true that a number of Rangers opposed the admittance of women into the division based on outdated sexist beliefs others expressed concerns that females would simply be unable to perform the harsh physical duties required of a Texas Ranger. Many in the Ranger Division claimed, with a degree of justification that potential female recruits would not be held to the same high standards as male applicants and would merely be appointed for political reasons.[578]

The political climate of the early nineties conspired against those who wished to keep the Rangers a masculine band of brothers. In 1993, Ann Richards was elected governor, Richards, a liberal, was clearly in favor of female Rangers and DPS Director James R. Wilson was left in no doubt as to her wishes. The Texas Legislature, which controlled the purse strings, also exerted significant pressure. In the summer of 1993, three new members of the House Appropriations Committee summoned Wilson and Senior Captain Maurice Cook to Austin to explain why the Rangers failed to reflect the demographic diversity of the Lone Star State. In a classic case of financial blackmail, unless the Rangers became more representative of minorities, it was clear that their budget would suffer severe cuts in the upcoming legislative session.[579]

In August of that year, it was announced that nine applicants would receive Ranger commissions the following month. The new Rangers included three Hispanics, one Asian-American, an African-American and most contentiously two women, Cheryl Steadman and Marrie Reynolds Garcia. The most serious criticism came from Rangers who argued that the two female candidates had been purely selected on the basis of their gender and lacked the necessary qualifications or background. There may have been more than a grain of truth in their grousing. Steadman was a state trooper in the warrants division while Reynolds Garcia served as sergeant in the driver's license service.[580] Several old hands, including Joaquin Jackson, a twenty-seven year veteran Ranger, retired that summer. Jackson commented that among the reasons for surrendering his badge was the hiring of unqualified women who were not held to the same high criteria as the male applicants.[581]

One of the first two female Rangers, former state trooper Steadman, lasted just over a year in the Ranger Division. In March 1994, Steadman had attended the Company A annual meeting at a hunting lodge in Tyler County. The Ranger claimed to have been subjected to inappropriate sexual jokes, was forced to work in the kitchen and objected to the excessive drinking and gambling. Steadman left the party in tears and alleged that her refusal to stay the night led to her being assigned only routine duties. On August 8, DPS Director Wilson approved her transfer to Motor Vehicle Theft Service and also promised an Internal Affairs Investigation. Eleven months later, in July 1995, the Public Safety Commission convened a meeting to consider her allegations of sexual discrimination. Among the Rangers who took the stand that day were Christine Nix and Marrie Reynolds Garcia who both testified that they enjoyed working as Rangers and had suffered no discrimination. The Public Safety Commission voted unanimously to find the Rangers not guilty of harassment of discrimination.[582]

The cloud of alleged sexual discrimination continued to hang over the Ranger Division. In 1994, Lisa Shepherd, a State Trooper, received the news that she had been selected to become a Texas Ranger. Shepherd, however, turned down the offer from Senior Captain Cook when she learned that she would be working in San Antonio in what she believed to be a demeaning and reduced position. Shepherd believed that she was discriminated against by Cook who sought to place her in a diminished role or have her turn down the job.[583]

In May 1995, former Ranger Steadman together with Shepherd lodged complaints of discrimination and prejudice against the Rangers with the Texas Commisssion on Human Rights. Seven months later, in December, the Ranger Division was named the defendant in a federal lawsuit brought by the two women who demanded millions of dollars in damages due to the emotional suffering that they had gone through due to supposed Ranger misconduct. The Texas Commission on Human Rights, however, in January 1996, ruled that the charges were baseless. On the federal level, the Steadman-Shepherd lawsuit was consistently dismissed by the courts and then appealed against by the plaintiffs. Finally, the U.S. Supreme Court, on January 18 2000, ruled against the final appeal thus ending the prolonged legal action.[584] Nevertheless, two days later DPS agreed to pay Steadman two hundred and fifty thousand dollars and grant her four weeks vacation to finally conclude the saga. The following day Shepherd agreed to the same financial settlement but received two extra weeks of vacation.[585]

While the DPS and the State of Texas agonized over the demographic makeup of the iconic lawmen and the crises that this caused, the Rangers continued their duties to the Lone Star State. Between 1980 and 2010, DPS faced a number of problems, both new and old. The U.S.-Mexican borderlands once again proved to a hazardous and dangerous region primarily due to the developing narcotics trade. Confrontations between law enforcement and armed cults or militia presented a fresh challenge for the Rangers. Meanwhile the criminal fraternity continued to engage in their nefarious activities.

In October 1980, Ranger Jackson, still stationed in Uvalde, was called to a trailer house deep in the cactus and mesquite studded hills. The Ranger met with Uvalde County Sheriff Kelly and a game warden at the trailer where the three men made a gruesome discovery. The partly decomposed bodies of a man and a woman were found in the dense brush behind the trailer. A Ranger presence had been requested after the man's boss had come to the trailer in search of his typically punctual employee and smelled the odor of decomposition. The sixteen year old son of the dead woman had previously returned the company truck and informed the employer that his mother and step father had gone on a world cruise. Ranger Jackson picked up the juvenile, whose real name could not be placed in the the investigative report due to his age, and the boy confessed to shooting his mother and stepfather with a.22 rifle. The sole reason behind the murders, according to the youth, was the fact that the couple would not allow him to drive the family car at weekends. He was placed in juvenile detention until the age of eighteen.[586]

The Texan oil industry had always been a hotbed of felonious activities. In the early eighties, oil field theft, whether the stealing of equipment or illegal siphoning of crude or natural gas, had escalated into a major problem. The Texas Independent Producers & Royalty Owners Association estimated that the financial cost of the pilfering totalled fifty million dollars annually. In the spring of 1981 the Texas legislature approved a law stating that oil field theft was deemed a second degree felony no matter what the monetary value of the stolen items. In the fall of that year, the Rangers with FBI assistance, broke up a band of thieves whose operations included several million dollars worth of oil patch thefts in Oklahoma and Texas. Overall, one fifth of Ranger investigations during this period related to property loss in the oil fields.[587]

In Texan history, Rangers had traditionally been renowned for the excellence of their shooting ability. In Wichita Falls, on May 19 1983, the skills of Ranger William Gerth Jr. were put to the test. Late that day, Gerth recognized the pick up truck of a wanted federal fugitive and radioed for backup. When the State Trooper appeared on the scene the felon promptly hit the gas leading the lawmen into a high speed car chase along the Southwest Parkway. Suddenly the truck hit the curb and the suspect leapt out and sprayed the patrol car with automatic rifle fire injured the trooper and trapping him inside the vehicle. As the armed crook approached the wounded trooper Gerth unloaded a 12-gauge shotgun blast into the man's chest. To the Ranger's astonishment, the suspect was merely knocked down and fired back at the Ranger before darting behind his truck. In the ensuing gun fight Gerth hit the suspect twice more before finally dispatching the man with a shot to the head. It turned out that the fugitive had been protected by body armor. For his bravery in protecting the life of a fellow officer, Gerth was awarded the first Medal of Valor ever given out by the Public Safety Commision.[588]

Henry Lee Lucas was a repugnant and monstrous serial killer whose first victim was his own mother, Viola, a sadistic and violent prostitute. In Jacksonville, Florida, Lucas met Ottis Toole, a homosexual transvestite arsonist who engaged in cannibalism and necrophilia. In the words of Ranger Joaquin Jackson; "each of these monsters was bad enough on his own, but when they traveled together, they were Halloween on wheels."[589] The sickening duo, based out of the house of Toole's mentally ill mother, crisscrossed the nation indulging their grotesque fantasies of murders, sex with dead bodies and other unimaginable horrors. Lucas, was finally arrested in Montague County, Texas, in connection with the disappearance of Kate Rich an elderly woman and Good Samaritan who had taken him in. Lucas had in fact killed the eighty year old lady, committed necrophilia with her corpse and cut up her body before burning it in a stove.[590]

On June 21 1983, Lucas was arraigned in court before District Judge Frank Douthitt. The detestable killer blurted out in open court that he had murdered hundreds of victims causing a major media feeding frenzy and generating interest from law enforcement agencies nationwide.[591] Lucas was convicted for the homicide of Kate Rich and the slaying of Becky Powell, Toole's slightly retarded niece, who had accompanied the vile pair on their journeys. He received sentences of seventy-five years and life in prison for the respective crimes. By this time, however, he had confessed among his many other crimes to the murder of a hitchhiker in Williamson County, whose body had been found naked except for a pair of orange socks. On April 2 1984, Lucas was placed on trial for the killing and was convicted and given the death penalty based on his confession.[592]

Under normal circumstances a prisoner would immediately be transfered to Death Row, but Lucas, due to the sheer number of his confessions was a suspect in hundreds of unsolved cases from across the country and was kept in the Williamson County jail which was more easily accessible to the investigators. Officers from five hundred and eighty-four agencies in the U.S. and Canada questioned Lucas regarding more than three thousand unresolved homicides. The killer also gave numerous media interviews. A Ranger task force headed by Sergeant Bob Prince coordinated the frenzied activity.[593]

It soon became apparent though that while Lucas had undoubtedly murdered dozens of victims he was also a cunning liar who enjoyed playing games with his interrogators and bartering confessions for jailhouse privileges. The media also began to question the validity of the confessions and the Ranger role in allegedly failing to investigate leads that would prove Lucas was lying in order to rapidly clear unsolved cases. The charade led to the most intense media assault on the honesty and professionalism of the Ranger Division since the Rio Grande Valley farm strike of 1966-67. The 'Orange Socks' conviction was also thrown into doubt by evidence that Lucas had been working for a roofer in Florida at the time. Eventually Governor George W. Bush requested that Texas Board of Pardons and Paroles review the case. When the board recommended leniency, the governor commuted his sentence to life in prison.[594] On March 12 2001,

Lucas died of a heart attack in prison, his accomplice, Ottis Toole had previously died in September 1996. Texas, America, and the world are better off without them.[595]

The fall of 1983 placed another frustrating case in the hands of the Texas Rangers. On the night of Friday 23 September, robbers struck the Kentucky Fried Chicken Restaurant in Kilgore. The crooks not only stole two thousand dollars but also kidnapped the four staff members and a friend who had dropped by to visit. Kilgore police requested Ranger assistance and the next morning, as Ranger Glenn Elliott examined the crime scene, five bodies were discovered off the highway in Rusk County approximately seventeen miles south of Kilgore. Four victims had been shot in the head, execution style, while the fifth had tried to flee and been gunned down. Elliott suspected that the motivation for the robbery was to find money for drugs. The killings could be explained by the need to remove any witnesses.[596]

The Rangers and local law enforcement questioned known drug users during the multi-agency investigation. Several suspects were identified including Darnell Hartsfield and Romeo Pinkerton. While the lawmen were convinced they knew who the culprits were they could not gather sufficient evidence to warrant a trial. Over twenty-two years later, in October 2005, Hartsfield was convicted of aggravated perjury, he had denied ever being in the KFC yet DNA from a blood spot proved that he had been present. One month later both Hartsfield and Pinkerton were indicted for the murders by a Rusk County grand jury. A third suspect in the case had died.[597] In 2008, both men were convicted of the KFC murders and sentenced to life in prison.

On January 11 1985, a routine Ranger Company F meeting was disrupted by a call from Ranger Bill Gunn based out of Cleburne, in Johnson County. Amy McNeil, the daughter of a director of the Alvarado State Bank had been seized at gunpoint while en route to school. Captain Bob Mitchell decided to dispatch the entire company to Alvarado to assist Gunn in the abduction case. While the Rangers headed towards Alvarado, Amy's father, Don McNeil, received a phone call from the kidnappers demanding one hundred thousand dollars in exchange for the life of his daughter. Later that day, Amy herself was allowed to call her anxious father to resassure him that she was still alive and well.[598]

The following afternoon, McNeil was ordered by the kidnappers to drive to a phone booth in East Dallas for further instructions. When the bank director arrived at the location he was then commanded to drive to another booth this time a hundred miles west of Dallas in the town of Tyler. At Tyler, McNeil was finally told to proceed to an abandoned service station near Mount Pleasant in Titus County. As McNeil headed towards Mount Pleasant he was shadowed by a DPS helicopter and fixed-wing plane in addition to the Rangers, FBI agents and Johnson County sheriff's deputies.[599]

At Mount Pleasant, Rangers' John Aycock and Brantly Foster concealed themselves close to the gas station and watched for any unusual activity. After a suspicious 1983 Buick twice slowly passed the target location the Rangers called it in and learned that the car had been stolen in Arlington earlier that night. Rangers Joe Wiley and Jimmy Ray attempted to stop the vehicle but were met with a hail of gunfire which punctured their car's radiator. The ensuing car chase meandered across three counties until the Buick ran out of gas in the small town of Saltillo. Two gunmen leapt out and opened fire on the lawmen but were swiftly out gunned by the powerful Ruger Mini-14 rifles used by the Rangers and were soon down having suffered minor wounds. Rangers' John Dendy and Howard "Slick" Alford raced to the car containing two other men and two women one of which proved to be the kidnapped girl Amy McNeil. The heroism and competence of the Rangers during the operation earned them accolades from all across America.[600]

Seven months later, in August 1985, Ranger Bob Prince, faced another potentially volatile hostage situation. In Meridian, located in Bosque County, a creepy looking man with a beard and long hair had attempted to capture a five year old boy and his teenage babysitter. The girl and child were fortuitously able to escape and alert the police. Several hours later the fugitive, after being spotted and pursued by a sheriff's deputy, was able to enter another house and take three hostages. By the eighties, each Ranger company had a trained hostage negotiator, a role that Prince held within Company F, over the next fourteen hours Prince would need all of his skills.[601]

The kidnapper was a dangerous midwestern crook named Jimmy R. Cooper who possessed a long criminal record. Ranger Prince of course had no idea who he was dealing with and was also unaware that during a previous hostage standoff in Indiana Cooper had enticed the negotiator to a window before shooting him twice in the face. During the prolonged and tense confrontation Prince was able to convince Cooper to release two of the captives in exchange for cigarettes and food. On each occasion, the Ranger had personally handed the items to Cooper through an open window. This left one remaining hostage, seventeen year old Jennie Davenport who had been repeatedly raped by Cooper, something that the Rangers were unaware of at the time. Finally, the kidnapper agreed to give up, on the sole condition, somewhat bizarrely perhaps, that he would be allowed to talk to his mother in Illinois. Cooper did speak with his mother that morning, he was also convicted of several charges including sexual assault and subsequently received a sentence of life in prison.[602]

In January 1987, Brent Beeler, a fugitive who was wanted for missing a parole hearing in Houston, broke into a house in Horseshoe Bay, a wealthy community near Marble Falls in Burnet County. The house belonged to William Whitehead, a wealthy rancher, and his family. Beeler abducted the family maid, twenty-two year old Denise Johnson and after raping and torturing her for a week he finally suffocated her and left her body to rot in a boathouse.[603] Eight days later he returned to the Whitehead property and kidnapped their two year old daughter Kara Lee Whitehead. The rancher then received a phone call, during which a cocky Beeler admitted killing the maid and demanded thirty thousand dollars as a ransom for the safe return of Kara Lee.[604]

Ranger Johnny Waldrip, stationed in Llano, had previously conducted a thorough investigation for the missing maid but had been unable to turn up any leads. Following the abduction of Kara Lee, he once again hustled to Horseshoe Bay. This time Captain Mitchell and a number of other Company F Rangers also showed up along with FBI agent Sykes Houston. Later that afternnoon, Beeler ordered Whitehead to drive his porsche and the cash to a location of his choosing.The sports car being too small for Rangers to hide in, the lawmen replaced the vehicle with a modified Lincoln Continental able to conceal two Rangers, John Aycock and Stan Guffey, behind the front seats. Regarding the change of cars, Whitehead was able to convince Beeler that his porsche was suffering from mechanical problems.[605]

A few hours later, Beeler demanded that the rancher park the Lincoln in the driveway of the house across the street and then leave the scene. Whitehead did as ordered leaving the two concealed Rangers to confront the murderous kidnapper. Within a minute Beeler appeared with Kara Lee and placed her in the front seat. As Beeler placed the case with the money on the backseat, in reality Aycock's chest and stomach, he must have noticed something was amiss. In the ensuing gunfight, Beeler put a bullet into head of Ranger Guffey as he rose from concealment before Aycock blasted him to death with repeated fire from his 9mm semiautomatic. Kara Lee had been rescued from the hands of a cold blooded killer.[606] Tragically, however, Ranger Guffey died from the headwound he had bravely suffered in the line of duty. At his funeral, in his hometown of Brady, Texas over seven hundred mourners paid their respects to a hero who had given his life for the State of Texas.[607]

Pablo Acosta Villareal was a Mexican-American drug lord who reputedly smuggled around sixty tons of cocaine into the U.S. annually. A billionaire who spread enough of his wealth among the local population to ensure his popularity, Acosta used Santa Elena, Mexico just across the border from the Big Bend National Park as his base of operations. In the winter of 1987, Park Rangers discovered a partly decomposed body on the American bank of the Rio Grande. The FBI along with Ranger Joaquin Jackson were called in to investigate. The corpse had been cut open and the organs removed before being filling with rocks to weight the body down. These actions were typically associated with the executions carried out by Colombian cartels.[608]

Ranger Jackson, however, suspected that the Mexican *cabron* was responsible. Through a contact in the Border Patrol, the Ranger was able to ascertain the identity of the victim, a *madrina* or reserve officer in the Mexican Federal Judicial Police. After the interrogation of two of the drug lord's henchmen Jackson was able to piece together the whole story. Acosta, who enjoyed close cooperation with the local state judicial police, was infuriated upon learning that his nephew had been arrested and tortured for information by the Mexican federal police. The *cabron*, kidnapped the reserve officer with the intention of 'interrogating' him to find out who had been responsible for his arrest of his nephew. Unfortunately the policeman had been killed by an accidental AK-47 discharge from one of his guards and Acosta's men placed the body in the river disguised as a Colombian execution. In April, the *commandante* of the Federal Judicial Police, incensed at the killing of one of their own, led a joint raid with the FBI and DEA on Acosta's headquarters at Santa Elena. At the end of the hour long gun battle, the infamous *cabron* was dead and his body was flown to the U.S. for an autopsy.[609]

Early in the morning of November 20 1988, Ranger Jackson, was once again requested to investigate a murder in the U.S.-Mexican borderlands. The previous day, Mike and Jamie Heffley accompanied by river guide Jim Burr of Far Flung Adventures had been enjoying a rafting trip through the scenic Colorado Canyon when they unexpectedly encountered billowing black smoke and hostile gunfire. In their desperate ensuing bid for survival both Jim Burr and Jamie Heffley suffered gunshot wounds although Burr was able to flee into the bush to seek help. Mike Heffley, however, was struck by a gut shot from a .44 caliber rifle and tragically died in the canyon. Ranger Jackson, alerted by Presidio County Chief Deputy Steve Bailey and accompanied by officers from the Border Patrol and U.S. Customs located the crime scene discovering the raft, numerous shell casings and the body of Mike Heffley. Burr had made it to County Road 170 where he was rescued. Jamie Heffley, more grievously wounded, was discovered and saved by a Black Hawk helicopter operated by U.S. Customs.[610]

As the story of the tragedy unfolded, the various federal and state law enforcement agencies on the American side of the border temporarily laid aside their typical squabbling and launched a determined effort to track down those responsible. The Mexican authorities were equally keen to resolve the case and locate the killers. A cynic might infer that the corrupt Mexican police were only concerned with the effect on the tourist trade but neverthless, they proved determined and reliable partners. Notably, *Commandante* Fernando Lozano of the Chihuahua State Judicial Police was a key player in the investigation.[611]

Ranger Jackson, following an invitation from the Mexican police, accompanied two Chihuahuan State Police Officers who were trailing the killers' movements along the canyon and through the desert beyond. The trackers eventually lost the trail in the rocky terrain but deduced that murderers had been moving towards a group of villages clustered along the Rio Grande east of Ojinaga. At the suggestion of the Texan, the Mexican lawmen agreed to focus their attentions on El Mulato, a notorious den of smugglers and drug mules. While the Mexican police pressured the residents of El Mulato for information, the Border Patrol, at the behest of Ranger Jackson, closed the crossing between Redford and El Mulato to place further strain on the Mexican village in the hope of coercing the citizens into yielding up the suspects.[612]

On the seventh day of the blockade, several anonymous calls to the Border Patrol provided the names of four suspects including a seventeen year old by the name of Eduardo Rodriguez Pineda. Due to the lack of probable cause needed for a state arrest warrant, it was decided to conduct a sweep of illegal aliens in the area using search warrants obtained from the Immigration Service. On November 29,

Pineda was arrested and confessed to being present during the shooting although he claimed falsely not to have been an actual gunmen. He was eventually sentenced to thirty years in a Texan penitentiary. His three accomplices, two of whom were only fifteen years old, were jailed in a youth prison in northern Mexico.[613] The four boys never gave a satisfactory reason why they had opened fire on the three Americans. Ranger Jackson, in One Ranger: A Memoir, simply states that "some black hearted boys...shot down three people to watch them die."[614]

The Rio Grande borderlands would continue to provide work for Ranger units up to the present day. In 1993, however, a violent standoff at Mount Carmel, Texas, made headlines across the world. A religious sect known as the Branch Davidians, led by David Koresh, who considered himself to be the new Messiah, owned a sprawling compound near Mount Carmel about ten miles east of Waco. The Bureau of Alcohol, Tobacco, Firearms and Explosives (ATF), based on information gleaned from former Davidians, believed that Koresh possessed a large cache of illegal weaponry and launched an inquiry. Sensational, though not necessarily inaccurate, allegations of polygamy and child abuse were also published by the press. Koresh, however, was aware of the investigation and offered to cooperate, to what extent is not clear, with the ATF officers. His approaches were rebuffed. On February 28, around eighty ATF agents assaulted the wooden compound. Koresh and his so called 'Mighty Men' repeled the federal attack leaving four agents and six Davidians dead.[615]

Captain Bob Prince, based in Waco, had previously offered to assist the ATF but had been turned down. In the wake of the shattering failed assault, ATF asked the Rangers to take command of the investigation on the grounds that while the killing of a federal agent was a federal crime, homicide was also a violation of state law. The FBI, however, moved in to manage the standoff. A veritable army of federal officers laid siege to the compound and conducted negotiations with the Davidians. The feds adopted a strategy of intense psychological warfare utilizing loudspeakers, bright lights and cut off electricity to the compound. Following the approval of U.S. Attorney General Janet Reno, the FBI-driven tanks, borrowed for Fort Hood destroyed Davidian vehicles and outbuildings.[616]

The Davidians, though, much to the frustration and embarrassment of the FBI, refused to give up. Koresh, through his attorney Dick DeGuerin, offered to surrender to the Texas Rangers but his peace offer was dismissed by the FBI who insisted that he submit to the federal agency. Finally, on the fifty-second day of the siege the FBI launched a massive attack on the compound. M728 combat engineering vehicles punched holes into the compound and injected CS gas. After Davidian gunmen opened fire at the federal agents, M3 Bradley armored cars entered the fray launching ferret missiles containing both the gas and a volatile chemical mix. By noon, the compound was engulfed in a massive fire which consumed the wooden structure within thirty minutes.[617] Seventy-six Davidians had perished during the attack, Koresh himself and a handful of accolytes had been killed by gunfire but the remaining men, women and children had succumbed to the smoke, fire or structural collapse of the building.[618]

As the burning embers of the Davidian compound began to settle the FBI relinquished control to the Texas Rangers. Captain David Byrnes from Company B was now in sole command of the battlefield and the investigation. The Rangers inventoried the seventy-seven acre compound recovering three hundred firearms including forty-eight illegally converted automatic weapons. The Rangers also recovered twenty-four thousand tons of debris and wreckage for potential use in the upcoming criminal trial. In June 1994, in a controversial trial, Judge Walter Smith ruled that the five surviving Davidians found guilty of carrying a firearm during a crime and conspiracy and three were sentenced for lesser crimes. The following year the U.S. Congress carried out hearings relating to the tragedy at Mount Carmel. Finally, in November 2000, John C. Danforth, appointed special counsel for a extensive inquiry into the events, presented his report. Danforth concluded that not only had the Davidians fired on the federal agents but they themselves had also set alight the compound thus causing their demise. Essentially the report absolved the FBI of any blame whatsoever. The issues of whether the ATF and FBI should have launched their attacks at all were not considered in the report.[619]

The Republic of Texas (ROT) was a militant group that adhered to a disproved separatist ideology. The ROT believed, falsely, that Texas had never been legally annexed to the Union and thus remained an independent republic. The group sought to restore Texan sovereignty through peaceful actions or if necessary by violence. Internal squabbling had led the group to divide into three factions. One splinter group, led by Richard McLaren was based in the mountains of Jeff Davis County. McLaren owned a house trailer, located deep in a rugged canyon, which served as the ROT 'Embassy'. McLaren and his associates refused to abide by state or county laws, filed liens against anyone who irritated them and engaged in war games on his property.[620]

On April 27 1997, Sheriff Steve Bailey of Jeff Davis County, arrested ROT 'chief of security' Robert J. Scheidt, after discovering firearms in his van. The ROT responded swiftly. Three militia members, attacked a neighboring property and took two hostages, Joe and Margaret Ann Rowe, who the group viewed as federal informers. On his ROT website, McLaren instructed militia members to deport federal authority figures including IRS agents and Governor George W. Bush. Captain Barry Caver, commanding Company E, ordered all of his Rangers to Fort Davis, the county seat. The following day, after lengthy negotiations, Scheidt, was freed after promising to ensure the release of the captives who referred to as 'prisoners of war' by the ROT. The 'chief of security' was as good as his word, the Rowes were freed and the hostage takers along with Scheidt retreated to McLaren's compound deep in the moutainous backcountry.[621]

The ROT compound was promptly besieged by the Rangers, Highway Patrolmen, sheriff's deputies and federal agencies including the FBI and U.S. Marshals. On this occasion, unlike the standoff at Mount Carmel, the Texas Rangers were in control and occupied the spotlight as the media broadcast the drama across the world.[622] For nearly a week the protracted negotations dragged on. Violence almost flared on the Friday evening when law enforcement officers closed the noose around the 'embassy' following indications that McLaren was calling for support from other militia groups. ROT solidarity, however, had already begun to fragment. Scheidt had surrendered earlier that day and later that night McLaren himself surrendered after Ranger Caver signed a formal ROT cease-fire document. Caver, however, had removed any unacceptable clauses before signing. Two ROT members, Richard Keyes and Mike Matson, refused to surrender and fled into the mountains. On May 5, Matson was shot dead by a TDC officer during a gunfight with lawmen. Keyes was later arrested north of Houston following a FBI tip off. [623]

In December 1998, Dr. Claudia Benton was found raped and murdered at her Houston home. Ranger Sergeant Andrew F. Carter Jr. took charge of investigation and swiftly received a hit on the fingerprints lifted from the scene. The suspect was a Mexican citizen, Rafael Resendez-Ramirez, a criminal with a history of assault and robbery nationwide. Resendez-Ramirez, however, had now gravitated towards rape and murder. In the spring of 1999, he continued his murderous ways. In May, in Weimar County, a pastor and his wife were killed in Weimar County, Texas. The woman had had also been raped. The DNA taken matched with the earlier murder in Houston. Ranger Carter also noticed the proximity of railroad tracks to both crime scenes and discovered that Resendez-Ramirez was known to frequently by ride the rails in freight trains.[624]

One month later, Resendez-Ramirez, was the prime suspect in four killings. Two women had been slain in Texas and an elderly man and his daughters were found murdered in Gorham, Illinois. In all the cases, evidence suggested that Resendez-Ramirez was the killer. All four victims also lived a stone's throw from railroad tracks. Sergeant Carter along with Ranger Brian Taylor travelled to Albuquerque to interview the suspect's half sister and ask for her help in getting the suspect to surrender. The two Rangers met with the woman and her pastor and joined them in prayer. In July, Carter received a phone call from New Mexico, informing the Ranger that Resendez-Ramirez wished to give himself up provided his safety could be guaranteed, he could receive family visits and he would receive a psychological examination. On July 13, the suspected serial murderer crossed the Zaragosa International Bridge linking Juarez to El Paso and surrendered to Ranger Carter.[625]

In 1994, George W. Bush, the son of the former U.S. president, George H. W. Bush, had vanquished the unpopular Ann Richards in the gubernatorial elections of that year. 'Dubya', as he was affectionately termed, proved to be a immensely well-liked and respected Republican governor who even proved popular among the heavily Democratic leaning *Tejano* electorate. In 1998, Bush, easily won re-election to the Governor's Mansion with tremendous support across the Lone Star State.[626] On June 12 1999, at a barbecue in Amana, Iowa, the Texas governor announced that he would be running as a Republican candidate for the the presidency of the United States.[627]

His candidacy provided the Rangers with a brief but new assignment. As Bush crisscrossed the nation on the campaign trail he was accompanied by a Ranger detail who protected the presidential candidate. Historically, providing security for the Bush campaign, was the first time that the Rangers had operated outside Texas for any length of time since the adventures of John 'Coffee' Hays and Ben McCulloch during the U.S.-Mexican War. The Rangers continued to provide protection for Governor Bush until he clinched the Republican nomination in the summer of 2000. At that point, the U.S. Secret Service took over the responsibility.[628]

Brian Burzynski, in 2005, was a Ranger Sergeant based out of Fort Stockton in southwest Texas. On February 23, he received a phone call from a volunteer math teacher at the Texas Youth Commission (TYC) correctional facility at Pyote, in Ward County. The volunteer informed the Ranger that several inmates had complained of the widespread sexual abuse at the hands of the TYC staff. Over the next two months, Burzynski assembled a strong case against the assistant superintendent and principal of the facility. The Ward County District

Attorney, however, delayed the prosecution for nearly a year and a half while the Ranger continued to gather evidence. In November 2006, Ranger Burzynski asked for help from the Attorney General's Office regarding the investigation. During the winter of 2007, the media got hold of the story which soon developed into a massive scandal amid public outrage. On March 6, Burzynski testified in Austin before the Joint Committee of the Operation and Management of the Texas Youth Commission where he received universal praise for his investigative work.[629]

That same month the Attorney General's Office began a joint inquiry with the Rangers into the allegations of sexual abuse within the TYC system. Rangers soon arrested the superintendent of a TYC prison in San Antonio for shredding incriminating evidence and a former guard who had worked another facility in Brownwood for sexual assault. Overall, the investigation launched by Sergeant Burzynski had far reaching results. The director and board of the TYC all departed the agency and many other senior employees were fired. Senate Bill 103 ordered major changes to TYC and Governor Rick Perry also placed the organization into conservatorship.[630]

The Fundamentalist Church of Jesus Christ of Latter-Day Saints (FLDS), led by Warren Jeffs, was a sectlike Mormon splinter group that continued to practice polygamy. In 2004, the secretive cult purchased a seventeen hundred acre property near to Eldorado, in Schleicher County. On the plot, the FLDS constructed a temple that closely resembled a fort in a strong defensive position. State and local law enforcement became concerned about sexual and physical abuse on the ranch, specifically of underage women by older 'husbands'. Ranger Brooks Long, stationed in Ozona, visited the property on several occasions to verify that no illegal activities were taking place. In March 2008, however, Child Protective Services, were called by a girl who claimed to be inside the FLDS ranch. Identifying herself as 'Sarah' she told CPS that she was sixteen years old, had been abused by her middle-aged husband and was pregnant.[631]

On April 3, thirty-five Rangers comprised part of a army of over two hundred lawmen which assembled around the FLDS property. The force was led by Ranger Captain Barry Caver. The officers feared a repeat of the Branch Davidian siege fifteen years before and the first Ranger team to enter the ranch were equipped with body armor and assault rifles. Fortunately, however, the FLDS members chose to avoid armed confrontation with law enforcement and allowed the police officers to enter the ranch without violence. Nevertheless, the FLDS attempted to thwart the investigation through peaceful means. The lack of cooperation and levels of deception eventually required the Rangers and CPS investigators to impose a form of martial law on the vast property. CPS, within the first four days, removed over four hundred minors from the FLDS ranch and placed them under the protection of the state of Texas. In December, CPS released a investigative report that stated that two hundred and seventy-five of those children had suffered abuse or neglect. Five months earlier, in July, Jeffs and four others were indicted by a grand jury for the sexual assault of a child.[632] In the summer of 2011, at the trial in San Angelo, Texas, Jeffs was convicted and sentenced to life in prison.

In the decades approaching the new millenium the legend of the Rangers continued to fascinate the public both in American and across the world. *Lonesome Dove*, written by renowned Texan novelist, Larry McMurtry, was first published in 1985. In the Pulitzer Prize winning book, two former Texas Ranger Captains, Augustus McCrae and Woodrow F. Call drive a herd of cattle from the Rio Grande to the grasslands of Montana. The bravery of the ex-Rangers is in little doubt, on one notable occasion McCrae single handedly dispatches a gang of bandits and renegades camped on the river. The Ranger Captain, however, frequently imbibes vast quantities of whiskey and enjoys 'poking' whores thus lowering the pedestal that the Rangers had historically been placed upon. Call, while generally holding himself to a higher moral standard, fathered an illegitimate son who he consistently refuses to acknowledge as his own. It is also worth noting that the cattle herd that the two Rangers and trail crew drive north were stolen from Mexican ranches south of the Rio Grande.[633]

During the nineties, McMurtry, authored three more novels in the saga of Call and McCrae. In *Streets of Laredo*, published in 1993, Call, following the failure of the Montana ranch is working as a bounty hunter paid to track down a vicious Mexican criminal. Two years later, *Dead's Man Walk*, explores the early years of the two Rangers as they battle Comanche Indians and participate in the fiasco of the Santa Fe Expedition of 1841. In 1997, *Comanche Moon*, the fourth novel in the epic series, was first published. The final book, to date, dealt with the middle years of the two Ranger Captains as they dealt with the Comanche, a Mayan *bandido* chieftain and the women who love them. All three novels continued to advance the theme of Ranger heroism mingled with a healthy dose of realism. The Ranger units are often bested by the Comanche war chief Buffalo Hump.[634] Blue Duck, the half-Mexican Comanchero son of the Comanche leader, evades capture for years and is finally apprehended not by a Ranger but a by fat deputy sheriff from New Mexico.[635] Call, unlike the traditional heroic Ranger who dies bravely in combat, suffers a less glamorous sunset of his life, in an ambush he loses both an arm and a leg, the famous Ranger ends his days sharpening tools in a barn.[636]

The popularity of McMurtry's epic series led to the filming of four TV miniseries adapted from the novels. In 1996, reality met fiction during the filming of *Dead Man's Walk*, while shooting the movie in south Texas, the Hollywood producers and stars were disquieted by the sudden appearance of a band of armed and mounted Mexican drug smugglers who had crossed the Rio Grande allegedly in search of a horse confiscated by the USDA. In reality the *bandidos* were aggravated by the filming which had dented their marijuana business. One of the leaders of the group was Roche Rodriguez a wanted federal fugitive, whose son Eduardo had been a shooter in the Colorado Canyon shootings. Former Ranger Joaquin Jackson, who was handling security on the set, notified Ranger Dave Duncan in Uvalde. A deputy U.S. Marshall and USDA agent were soon on the scene. Rodriguez was lured back across the river on the premise of the return of his horse but was promptly arrested and taken into custody.[637]

In April 1994, *Walker, Texas Ranger*, first aired on the CBS television. The show starring martial arts legend, Chuck Norris, as Ranger Cordell Walker, ran for eight consecutive seasons and was broadcast in over one hundred countries worldwide. While primarily noted for its action scenes and the use of martial arts as a tool of effective law enforcement, the series also proved to be illustrative of the changing demographics and nature of the Ranger Division. Walker, sporting a cowboy hat and boots, frequently chased villains down on horseback and relied more on intuition than technology when administering his brand of frontier justice. His sidekick, Ranger James Trivette, played by Clarence Gilyard, was an African-American former football player who represented the new breed of Texas Ranger. Trivette, utilized more sophististiced crime detection techniques yet frequently found himself out of his element when working in the back country.

One of the most famous Ranger Captains in history, John "Coffee" Hays, was honored in November 2001. On the courthouse square in downtown San Marcos, a nearly ten foot bronze statue of the mounted Ranger Captain brandishing a Colt revolver, was unveiled. The monument was paid for by a one hundred and twenty-five thousand dollar grant from the McCoy Foundation. During the dedication ceremony, witnessed by Hays' great-great grandson and great-great-great-grandson, the statue was unveiled from underneath a massive Texas flag. The times may have changed but Texas had not forgotten her heroes.[638]

At the dawn of the 21st century, the Texas Ranger Division stands as a powerful historical symbol yet also represents a modern effective and highly commended law enforcement agency. Although rocked in the eighties and nineties by accusations of racial and especially sexual discrimination by 2012 the Rangers had become far more representative of the demographic makeup of the State of Texas. The last decades of 20th century and early years of the 21st posed numerous challenges for the Ranger corps including confrontations with armed cults, violence along the Mexican border and the usual felonious mix of kidnappers, killers and robbers. Although justice was sometimes delayed and on occasion frustrated, the Texas Rangers, nevertheless, continued to put their lives on the line for the protection of the citizens of the Lone Star State.

Reflections: Deep in the Heart of Texans

The Texas Rangers have played an integral role in Texan history and deservedly remain an iconic symbol of the Lone Star State. The humble origins of the Rangers began with the settlement of the then Mexican province of *Tejas* by Anglo-American pioneers. The first Anglo-Texan settlers faced omnipresent danger of Indian raids and lacked military support from the Mexican authorities threatening the safety and very viability of the settlements. As early as 1823, the first *empresario*, Stephen F. Austin, called for a force of Rangers to guard the frontier against hostile Indians. The real *naissance* of the Rangers came during the fiercely contested Texas War of Independence from Mexico. As the flames of war licked over Texas, in 1835, the permanent council of Texas passed an ordinance calling for three companies of Rangers. The Rangers screened the fleeing civilian population from the Mexican army while simultaneously protecting the frontier from marauding Indians.

The powerful Comanche remained a potent threat to the nascent Texan Republic and the years after the revolution witnessed spiraling levels of bloody fighting between the Comanche and the Anglo-Texans. The Rangers served as the primary defenders of the young Texan nation and engaged in brutal and ferocious warfare with their native adversaries. Following annexation to the U.S., the ineffective federal military policies arguably led to an increase in Comanche raids and the subsequent brief federalization of the several Ranger companies to aid their state counterparts in protecting the borderlands.

The mutual animosity between Anglo-Texans and Mexicans stemmed from the atrocities committed by both sides including the Alamo and Mier Expedition. The conduct of the *Los Diablos Tejanos* during the U.S.-Mexican War, however, aptly amplified both the heroism and cruelty of the Texas Rangers. The Rangers demonstrated great skill and courage when dealing with both regular soldiers or guerrillas but also exposed their penchant for brutality and excessive retribution especially when stationed in Mexico City. Back home in Texas, the Rangers played a dual role as both lawmen and the enforcement tools of the Anglo elite.

When the deepening sectional divide finally tore the nation asunder in 1861, Texas and most Anglo-Texans chose to fight and die for 'Dixie', rallying in large numbers to the Southern cause. Texas Rangers enlisted in the Confederate forces seeing action on the eastern theater, New Mexico and along the Rio Grande. On the home front Ranger companies were required to protect Texans from Indian warriors, Union soldiers and Confederate deserters. Following the Union victory, the Rangers were disbanded, on the orders of the federal government. The subsequent chaos and increased lawlessness exacerbated by the incompetence of the new State Police however, prompted the reestablishment of the Texas Rangers.

In 1874, the turbulent frontier and the spiralling violence in the Rio Grande borderlands led Governor Coke to approve the creation of the Frontier Battalion and Special Force of the recreated Texas Rangers. The Frontier Battalion confronted the Comanche and their Kiowa allies, weakened by smallpox, but still a potent threat to travellers and the settlements. The Rangers should be credited for restoring security to the frontier although the ultimate defeat of the Southern Plains tribes was caused primarily by a reinvigorated U.S. military policy and was further precipitated by the catastrophic disappearance of the buffalo herds which removed a cornerstone of the Comanche economy and resources. The task of the Special Force was to pacify the borderlands and end the banditry. Led by Leander McNelly, the Rangers proved to be highly effective at combating the *bandidos* and cattle thieves of the Nueces Strip. McNelly and his men, however, achieved their success through morally questionable methods of frontier justice including intimidation, torture and summary executions.

In the last decades of the eighteenth century partisan feuds and outlawry remained a major source of instability within the Lone Star State. in Texas. The Rangers of the late 1800s began to function as lawmen instead of as an irregular military corps. The bandits and feuding factions attracted the attention of both the Frontier Battalion and the Special Force. During this era, it has also been observed, that the Rangers also served as a law enforcement tool of the primarily Anglo-Texan political and economic system at the expense of both *Tejanos* and poor whites. Following the birth of the Cattle Kingdom in the years after the Civil War the Ranger corps enjoyed close relations with the cattle barons, notably Captain Richard King, and frequently acted on their behalf. Equally, the big business interests controlling the mining operations and nascent industrial system could count on the Rangers to safeguard the interests of their various investments.

In south Texas, the relations between the *rinches* and the Hispanic communities remained tense. The violent historical legacy stretching back the Alamo remained vivid in the memories of both Anglos and *Tejanos* despite an acculturation through intermarriage and political alliances. Sporadic violence was apt to erupt with little warning and the arrival of the railroad and large numbers of Anglo farmers escalated the tensions. The discovery of the Plan de San Diego, and subsequent *sedicioso* insurrection sparked a brutal Ranger led counterinsurgency that may have killed up to five thousand Hispanics and left a dark stain on the history of the Texas Rangers.

During the nineteen twenties and early thirties, the Rangers confronted new challenges including taming the rowdy oil boomtowns, the enforcement of unpopular prohibition laws, the rise of the second

Ku Klux Klan and the 'iconic' gangsters of the 'public enemy era'. The weakness of the Ranger corps became clear when lawmen armed with Winchester rifles and Colt six-shooters and without official vehicles were confronted by criminals equipped with the latest in modern automobiles and weaponry. The polititization of the Ranger force, notably during the Ferguson years, not only affected the professionalism of the corps but also led to questions over the future of the organization.

On August 10 1935, the Department of Public Safety was born. It was comprised was of both the old Highway Patrol and the Texas Rangers. A merit system and intense training program ensured that competence not political connections would determine the career path in DPS. While the new agency suffered a few birth pangs, under the competent and visionary leadership of Homer Garrison Jr., the Texas Rangers developed into highly trained and professional lawmen. During the first decades of its existence the DPS confronted a host of problems; both small time criminals and villains linked to organized crime operated across Texas while racial and labor tensions became increasingly prevalent in the Lone Star State. American entry into a global war also brought new challenges for the Ranger Division. In the mid 1900s, the Rangers, also attracted the interest of academics whose work both enhanced and critiqued the legendary force.

In Texas, the social upheaval and Civil Rights movement of the sixties clashed with the deep conservativism of many citizens of the Lone Star State. The Texas Rangers, due to the perhaps misguided perception that they stood for Anglo supremacy and certainly due to their role in law enforcement, became key players in several well publicized crises leading to extensive criticism in the media. Many old time Rangers also became exasperated with a federal judiciary that appeared to coddle the criminal element and prevent lawmen from effective police work. By the 1970s, however, criticism of the Rangers had diminished and a new younger generation of Rangers had emerged to guide the corps into the last decades of the twentieth century.

At the dawn of the eighties, the Ranger Division remained primarily comprised of Anglo-Texan men. The question of the Rangers being forced to become more reflective of the state demographics was a divisive topic that embroiled the Rangers in a lengthy legal scandal. While Hispanic and African-Americans were accepted into the Ranger ranks with little tension many Rangers opposed the inclusion of women both due to sexist beliefs but also fears that they would simply be unable to enagage in the brutal physical aspects of Ranger work. The issue of the acceptance of women into the service was not helped by the sexual discrimination lawsuit filed by one of the first two female Rangers. In addition to the angst over Ranger demographics, the end of the twentieth century and beginning of the new millenium saw the DPS engaged in standoffs with armed militiamen, confronted by rising violence in the Rio Grande borderlands and the pursuit of a number of nefarious criminals. In 2012, at the time of writing, the Rangers deservedly remain a well respected and highly professional body of law officers who continue to serve and protect the citizens of the Lone Star State.

It is common, to look back on history with the benefit of hindsight and to judge historical actors or events by the social norms and morality of contemporary society. To do so, however, is to arrogantly assume that the social values and moral standards of our modern society can neatly be placed upon a society from a previous era which adhered to a different system of social values and whose citizens faced challenges and dangers that we cannot possibly comprehend. Among democratic countries, the majority of nations and peoples, arguably seek to install a legal, moral and social system which allows honest law abiding citizens the right to live their lives free from fear or danger. In a turbulent and volatile era, the imposition of law and order, required methods that fitted the place and the time.

The actions of the Texas Rangers should be fairly and impartially be judged within this criteria. During the long and bitter struggle with the Comanche, Ranger units attacked Indian villages killing men, women and children. While indisputably objectionable by the moral standards of modern warfare, one must remember that the Texan frontier had been ravaged by numerous Comanche raids during which the Indian warriors had raped and murdered settlers and their families. Those unfortunate enough to have been taken captive were often subjected to horrific forms of torture. It is unsurprising that the Rangers, many of whom had friends and kinfolk slain by the Comanche, developed a inherent animosity and loathing of the Comanche and a desire for a violent retribution.

In a similar fashion, McNelly and his 'Special Force', operating along the Rio Grande border in the late 1800s certainly violated the code of law as we know it today. The habitual hanging of suspects without a trial and use of torture to glean information would be entirely unacceptable in a modern civilized society. McNelly, however, did not live in the modern era, the south Texas of the late 1800s was a violent borderland region plagued by murderous bandits. His 'invasion' of Mexico during the Las Cuevas affair was foolhardy and caused uproar in Washington DC but in Texas he was praised for taking a strong line against cattle thieves irrespective of the legality of his actions. The Rangers, when dealing with the Comanche or Mexican bandits undoubtedly engaged in deeds of dubious morality yet in so doing they helped to end the intolerable violence that plagued the Lone Star State.

The performance of Ranger Captain Allee during the Latino political awakening and labor unrest of the 1960s also deserves examination. Allee, undoubtedly believed in Anglo-Texan control of the Lone Star State and was born in an era when Mexico was still considered the enemy. He may have also have considered *Tejanos* to be second-class citizens. To portray him, however, as an arrant racist not only fails to consider the world in which he was raised but also the actions that he undertook while serving as a Ranger. In Duval County, Allee confronted the Anglo political boss George Parr to defend the rights of the Hispanics who suffered under his regime. He also wrote a glowing recommendation for the first Mexican-American Texas Ranger. By the sixties, Texas had changed beyond comprehension and Allee along with many other Texans of his generation was unprepared for the the new realities of life within the Lone Star State.

It should be noted, however, that certain atrocities cannot be excused or justified. Such is the case with the so called 'bandit war' between 1915-16 in the Rio Grande borderlands. While the Plan de San Diego appealed for a race war and *sediciosos* did murder dozens of Anglo-Texans the insurrection never posed a serious threat to Texas or the U.S. The exceptionally violent response by the Rangers along with other lawmen was entirely unproportional to the initial insurrection. The sheer number of Hispanics killed and the fact that Ranger units continued to 'evaporate' suspects long after order had been restored clearly demonstrates that race played a more important role that the suppression of any actual threat to the Lone Star State.

The Anglo-Texans were a warrior people in the old Celtic tradition. The first frontiersmen and settlers who challenged the Comanche and the Mexicans had no noble aspirations they merely sought land and wealth. Like the *conquistadores* of Hernán Cortés, three centuries before, the Anglo-Texans, confident in their perceived moral and racial superiority, dispossessed the Mexican population and swept the feared Comanche from the southern plains. The Anglo-Texans displayed courage, valor and an incredible strength of character to achieve independence from a numerically superior enemy and conquer powerful native tribes who had confounded the Spanish and Mexicans for over a hundred years. Like most warrior societies, the Anglo-Texans respected courage even among their enemies and loathed cowardice. This frontier value system, however, led to a lack of empathy for the weak who were unable to protect themselves or make a success of their lives. This prejudice ensured that when the less fortunate banded together and agitated for aid or redress of grievances many Texans, raised with the concept of a frontier morality, looked on such groups with disdain.

The Texas Rangers in many ways represented the elite of the Anglo-Texan warrior society. Successful Rangers were exceptional men who typically commanded respect, possessed good judgement, tenacity and a complete absence of fear. In the nineteenth century, John 'Coffee' Hays, Ben McCulloch and 'Rip' Ford epitomized the very best of this warrior tradition. In the 1900s, this tradition was kept alive by Rangers including Frank Hamer, Manuel T. 'Lone Wolf' Gonzaullas and A. Y. Allee. Traditionally, the Rangers adhered to the the old moral code of the frontier and perhaps correctly viewed achieving justice as more important than abiding by bureaucratic legal technicalities. Leander McNelly is arguably the best example of this mentality. Rangers who dishonored the proud tradition had no future in the service. In the words of T. R. Fehrenbach, "Ranger bands were almost perfect microcosms of the Texan frontier concept of democracy. Leaders were leaders, because they first proved they could act."[639]

The dark side of the Rangers also stems from the ethos of the frontier warrior. Many nineteenth century Rangers, believing in their racial superiority viewed Mexicans as an inferior people and considered Indians to be primitive savages. The atrocities committed by Ranger units during the U.S.-Mexican War and subsequent oppression of the *Tejano* communities were significantly engendered by the racist outlook of Anglo-Texan society. Racism among the Rangers reared its ugly head once again during the brutal suppression of the Plan de San Diego. During the economic and political unrest of the sixties Ranger attitudes towards the Latino protesters were influenced by both a racial paternalism and the perhaps subconscious condescension of a warrior band looking down on a social group who had failed to help themselves.

The modern Rangers maintain the best traditions of their predecessors. The honor of wearing the *Cinco Peso* is only given to those lawmen who have demonstrated the requisite ability, strength of character and determination to uphold the laws of the Texas. The Rangers have adapted, however, leaving behind the racism and prejudice of their forefathers. The Rangers are no longer an elite band of Anglo-Texan brothers, they are now simply an elite band of Texans. The Texas Rangers are truly a breed apart.

At the beginning of the of second decade of the twenty-first century, the Texas Rangers face numerous challenges. The Mexican border remains plagued by the cross border trafficking of narcotics, guns and illegal immigrants. The spiralling violence as vicious drug cartels compete in turf wars and battle the Mexican government, threatens the safety and stability of Texan communities along the Rio Grande and beyond. Armed militia groups and religious cults are likely to pose further problems for law enforcement while criminals of every description will always be present in every society. Notably, the frontier crime of cattle rustling continues to pose problems in rural Texas.

The Rangers, in confronting these problems will undoubtedly demonstrate the same bravery, tenacity and strength of character as the most revered of their forebears did in very different eras. Each generation of Rangers has adapted to the new challenges and changes within the Lone Star State. At this point in history, the Texas Ranger Division represents both a highly professional and effective branch of law enforcement and a treasured symbol of Texan culture. The Rangers who currently wear the *Cinco Peso*, are very different in appearance, beliefs and methods from their predecessors yet they continue to serve as the vanguard of a proud and cherished legacy.

Glossary

Aztlan: The legendary homeland of the Nahua and Uto-Aztecan peoples of Mesoamerica. The American Southwest is one of many possible sites of *Aztlan*.
Alcalde: A Mexican municipal magistrate who possessed both administrative and judicial functions.
Bandido: The Spanish term for a bandit.
Brasada: A green/brown shrub from south Texas. In local usage it refers to the 'brush country' itself.
Cabron: An offensive Mexican-Spanish word with a number of meanings. Literally translates as 'Big Goat'. In this book, it refers to someone who is respected or feared due to their toughness of character.
Californio: A Spanish speaker, regardless of race, born in California before U.S. annexation in 1848.
Chaparral: An evergreen shrub found across southern Texas characterized by dense virtually impenetrable thickets.
Chicano: Traditionally a disparaging Hispanic term, it was transformed into a symbolic term representing ethnic pride and political consciousness for many Mexican-Americans during the Civil Rights era of the sixties and seventies.
Comancheria: The Comanche homeland from around 1700 to the mid 1800s. A vast region comprising of parts of modern day Colorado, Kansas, New Mexico Oklahoma and Texas.

Comanchero: Hispanic traders from New Mexico, often with Indian ancestry, who traded with the Comanche.

Corrido: A Mexican folk ballad or narrative song.

Cortinista: A follower of the Mexican-American bandit and politico-military leader Juan N. Cortina.

Empresario: A Spanish term whose literal translation is entrepeneur. During the early 1800s, it refered to a well-connected individual who was granted the right to settle on Mexican land in Texas. In return, the *empresario* would develop and administer the settlements, which in the view of the Mexican authorities, would provide a buffer zone against both the Indian tribes and the rapid spread of the American republic. The vast majority of *empresarios* were American.

Escoseses: A Mexican political faction of the 1830s who favored a strong centralized government.

Garzista: A follower of Catarino Garza during the rebellion of 1891.

Gringo: A pejorative Latin-American term for an individual from the United States.

Guerrilla: A combatant who engages in a form of irregular warfare in which highly mobile units use the tactics of ambush, raids and sabotage to harass a generally larger and more powerful enemy.

Hacienda: A Spanish term for a self-sufficient estate run for the benefit of the owner.

Mesquite: A shrublike deciduous tree found in the southwestern United States.

Mestizo: A traditional Latin American word for an individual of mixed ethnic heritage. In Mexico it was generally used to describe a person of both European and indigenous descent.

Patron: Literally translates from Spanish as boss. In south Texas, it was used to describe an individual who almost complete power over the economy, politics, land and people of a particular region.

Penateka: One of the largest Comanche bands, also known as the 'Southern Comanches' due to their location between the Edwards Plateau and the Cross Timbers.

Presidio: A fortified base built by the Spanish and Mexicans to protect their colonists and guard against hostile native tribes and rival colonial powers.

Pronunciamento: A public declaration of opposition to the current government as a prelude to a potential military rebellion. In Mexico, a *pronunciamento*, also known as a 'Plan', would often be a formal highly detailed written document.

Ranchero: Spanish word for a rancher.

Rinches: A pejorative Mexican-Spanish word for the Texas Rangers used by the *Tejano* and Mexican communities.

Sedicioso: A Spanish word for seditionist. In the context of this book it refers to the Hispanic raiders who robbed and murdered Anglo-Americans and elite Tejanos during the failed Plan de San Diego uprising.

Tejano: A Texan of Hispanic heritage.

Tequilero: A Mexican liquor smuggler during the Prohibition Era.

Vaquero: A Spanish, later Mexican, mounted herdsman. The style and language of the American cowboy originated to a large part from the *vaquero* tradition.

Yorkino: A liberal federalist Mexican political faction of the 1830s who supported greater autonomy for the regions.

Notes

Introduction
1. Walter P. Webb, *The Texas Rangers: A Century of Frontier Defence*, Austin:University of Texas Press, 1935 p.15
2. Ibid, p.79
3. Ibid, p.8
4. Julian Samora, Joe Bernal and Albert Pena, *Gunpowder Justice*, Notre Dame: University of Notre Dame Press, 1979 p.3
5. Benjamin Heber Johnson, *Revolution in Texas*, New Haven: Yale University Press, 2003 p.11
6. Ibid, p.11
7. Andrew R. Graybill, *Policing the Great Plains: Rangers, Mounties and the North American Frontier*, Lincoln: University of Nebraska Press, 2007 p.2
8. Ibid, p.21

Chapter I
9. Webb, op. cit, p.7
10. Martha Manchaca *Recovering History, Constructing Race: The Indian, Black, and White Roots of Mexican Americans*, Austin: University of Texas Press, 2001, p.196
11. Webb, op. cit, p.10

12. Josefina Zoraida Vasquez, "The Colonization and Loss of Texas: A Mexican Perspective", in Rodriguez O., Jaime E.; Vincent, Kathryn, *Myths, Misdeeds, and Misunderstandings: The Roots of Conflict in U.S.–Mexican Relations*, Wilmington: Scholarly Resources Inc. 1997 p.50
13. Robert M. Utley, *Lone Star Justice: The First Century of the Texas Rangers*, New York: Oxford University Press, 2002 p.14
14. Webb, op. cit, p.6
15. Utley, op. cit, p.15
16. Webb, op. cit, p.20-21
17. Utley, op. cit, p.17

Chapter 2

18. T. R. Fehrenbach, *Lone Star: A History of Texas and the Texans*, Cambridge: Da Capo Press, 2000 p.168
19. Ibid, p.168
20. Ibid, p.163-164
21. Ibid, p.165 and 169
22. Ibid, p.169
23. Utley, op. cit, p.18
24. Fehrenbach, op. cit, p.170
25. Ibid, p.192-193
26. Ibid, p.198
27. Ibid, p.214-215
28. Ibid, p.227
29. Ibid, p.229-233 and 240
30. Webb, op. cit, p.23-24
31. Utley, op. cit, p.19
32. Ibid, p.21
33. Webb, op. cit, p.25
34. Ibid, p.25
35. Ibid, p.35-38

Chapter 3

36. T. R. Fehrenbach, *Comanches: The Destruction of a People*, New York: Alfred A. Knopf, 1974 p.98-99
37. Brian DeLay, *War of a Thousand Deserts*, New Haven: Yale University Press, 2008 p.122 and 131
38. Fehrenbach, op. cit, p.133
39. Ibid, p.79
40. Ibid, p.275
41. Pekka Hamalainen, *The Comanche Empire*, New Haven: Yale University Press, 2008 p.290-291
42. Ibid, p.140
43. Utley, op. cit, p.22
44. Ibid, p.22 and 24
45. DeLay, op. cit, p.61
46. Ibid, p.95
47. Ibid, p.91
48. Ibid, p.65 and 80
49. Webb, op. cit, p.48-49
50. Fehrenbach, *Lone Star*, p.253
51. Webb, op. cit, p.54
52. Hamalainen, op. cit, p.179
53. Utley, op. cit, p.25
54. Ibid, p.26-27
55. Webb, op. cit, p.58-59
56. Utley, op. cit, p.32-33
57. Webb, op. cit, p.62 and 69
58. Utley, op. cit, p.4 and 8
59. Ibid, p.10
60. Ibid, p.12
61. Ibid, p.88
62. George E. Hyde, *Rangers and Regulars*, Columbus: Long's College Book Company, 1952, p.73
63. Ibid, p.99

64. Ibid, p.89 and 91
65. Webb, op. cit, p.127
66. Fehrenbach, op. cit, p.276
67. Utley, op. cit, p.93-94
68. Ibid, p.100
69. Ibid, p.90-91
70. Webb, op. cit, p.155-157
71. Utley, op. cit, p.102
72. Webb, op. cit, p.207 and 212
73. Utley, op. cit, p.120
74. Ibid, p.121
75. Ibid, p.122
76. Webb, op. cit, p.147

Chapter 4

77. Fehrenbach, op. cit, p.214
78. Utley, op. cit, p.39
79. Ibid, p.39
80. Ibid, p.38
81. Webb, op. cit, p.71
82. Utley, op. cit, p.41
83. Webb, op. cit, p.72
84. Utley, op. cit, p.41
85. Webb, op. cit, p.73
86. Utley, op. cit, p.43-45
87. Utley, op. cit, p.49-51
88. Utley, op. cit, p.46-48
89. Webb, op. cit, p.74
90. Utley, op. cit, p.52-54
91. Ibid, p.55
92. Webb, op. cit, p.77
93. Ibid, p.87
94. Utley, op. cit, p.55-56

95. George Brown Tindall and David Emory Shi, *America: A Narrative History 8th Edition*, New York: W.W. Norton, 2010 p.554
96. Fehrenbach, op. cit, p.269-270
97. Tindall and Shi, op. cit, p.554
98. Ibid, p.556-557
99. Ibid, p.557-560
100. Fehrenbach, op. cit, p.272
101. Webb, op. cit, p.93-95
102. Utley, op. cit, p.69-71
103. Ibid, p.73 and 76
104. Webb, op. cit, p.112-113
105. Utley, op. cit, p.77-79
106. Ibid, p.79
107. Webb, op. cit, p.115 and 118
108. Utley, op. cit, p.81 and 84
109. Samora, Bernal and Pena, op. cit, p.28
110. Ibid, p.29
111. Webb, op. cit, p.120
112. Utley, op. cit, p.83
113. Webb, op. cit, p.120
114. Utley, op. cit, p.85
115. Fehrenbach, op. cit, p.508
116. Graybill, op. cit, p.69
117. Utley, op. cit, p.94-95
118. Ibid, p.96-97
119. Graybill, op. cit, p.74
120. Samora, Bernal and Pena, op. cit, p.34-35
121. Webb, op. cit, p.182
122. Utley, op. cit, p.111
123. Ibid, p.112
124. Ibid, p.113 and 115
125. Ibid, p.117-119

Chapter 5

126. Tindall and Shi, op. cit, p.650
127. Ibid, p.261
128. Ibid, p.287
129. Fehrenbach, op. cit, p.328
130. Ibid, p.593
131. Ibid, 603 and 615-623
132. Ibid, p.640-642
133. Ibid, p.344-347
134. Ibid, p.345
135. Ibid, p.346-348
136. Ibid, p.354
137. Utley, op. cit, p.125
138. Ibid, p.124
139. David H. Rosenberg, "Confederate Manifest Destiny in New Mexico", *America's Civil War*, July 2000, (Volume 13, Number 3) p.53
140. Donald S. Frazier, *Blood and Treasure: The Confederate Empire in the Southwest*, College Station Texas: Texas A & M University Press, 1995 p.230
141. Fehrenbach, op. cit, p.368
142. Ibid, p.374-375
143. Ibid, p.376
144. Ibid, p.374
145. Ibid, p.379-385
146. Ibid, p.389-391
147. Utley, op. cit, p.125-126
148. Ibid, p.126-127
149. Ibid, p.128
150. Ibid, p.128-129
151. Ibid, p.130-131
152. Webb, op. cit, p.219
153. Fehrenbach, op. cit, p.416-417 and 424

154. Utley, op. cit, p.136-137
155. Ibid, p.138-141

Chapter 6
156. Ibid, p. 142
157. Webb, op. cit, p.397
158. Fehrenbach, op. cit, p.533
159. Webb, op. cit, p.309
160. Ibid, p.309-311
161. Utley, op. cit, p.147
162. Webb, op. cit, p.313
163. Utley, op. cit, p.150
164. Webb, op. cit, p.317-318
165. Utley, op. cit, p.151
166. Fehrenbach, op. cit, p.546-547
167. Ibid, p.547
168. Ibid, p.548-549
169. Ibid, p.550
170. Elliott West, *The Way to the West: Essays on the Central Plains*, Albuquerque: University of New Mexico Press, 1995 p.72
171. Hamalainen, op. cit, p.294-297
172. West, op. cit, p.53
173. Graybill, op. cit, p.48
174. Utley, op. cit, p.213
175. Graybill, op. cit, p.49
176. Utley, op. cit, p.214-215
177. Graybill, op. cit, p.50
178. Utlcy, op. cit, p.215

Chapter 7
179. Fehrenbach, op. cit, p.573-574
180. Utley, op. cit, p.161
181. Ibid, p.160
182. Webb, op. cit, p.233

183. Utley, op. cit, p.161
184. Fehrenbach, op. cit, p.575
185. Graybill, op. cit, p.96
186. Utley, op. cit, p.162
187. Fehrenbach, op. cit, p.576
188. Graybill, op. cit, p.95
189. Fehrenbach, op. cit, p.576-577
190. Ibid, p.577
191. George Durham, as told to Clyde Wantland, *Taming the Nueces Strip: The Story of McNelly's Rangers,* Austin: University of Texas Press, 1962, p.130
192. Utley, op. cit, p.162
193. Fehrenbach, op. cit, p.578
194. Ibid, p.578-579
195. Webb, op. cit, p.259
196. Utley, op. cit, p.165
197. Fehrenbach, op. cit, p.581
198. Utley, op. cit, p.166
199. Ibid. p.582
200. Fehrenbach, op. cit, p.582-583
201. Ibid, p.584
202. Utley, op. cit, p.167
203. Ibid, p.170
204. Graybill, op. cit, p.96
205. Fehrenbach, op. cit, p.585

Chapter 8
206. Webb, op. cit, p.319
207. Fehrenbach, op. cit, p.571
208. Webb, op. cit, p.319
209. Utley, op. cit, p.158
210. Webb, op. cit, p.236
211. Utley, op. cit, p.159
212. Webb, op. cit, p.290

213. Utley, op. cit, p.171
214. Ibid, p.155-157
215. Ibid, p.181-182
216. Webb, op. cit, p.334-335
217. Utley, op. cit, p.183
218. Ibid, p.191-192
219. Webb, op. cit, p.352-353
220. Graybill, op. cit, p.98
221. Webb, op. cit, p.358-362
222. Utley, op. cit, p.201-203
223. Ibid, p.205
224. Ibid, p.179
225. Webb, op. cit, p.330
226. Ibid, p.330-333
227. Ibid, p.286-287
228. Utley, op. cit, p.176-177
229. Webb, op. cit, p.371-372
230. Utley, op. cit, p.183-184
231. Ibid, p.184
232. Webb, op. cit, p.377
233. Utley, op. cit, p.186-187
234. Ibid, p.210-211
235. Ibid, p.211-212
236. Ibid, p.172-173
237. Ibid, p.172-173
238. Ibid, p.175

Chapter 9
239. Graybill, op. cit, p. 112
240. Ibid, p.71
241. Ibid, p.112-113
242. Dee Brown, *The American West*, New York: Touchstone, 1994, p.296-297, and Graybill, op. cit, p.114
243. Graybill, op. cit, p. 113

244. Ibid, p.108
245. Webb, op. cit, p.275-278
246. Utley, op. cit, p.170
247. Americo Paredes, *"With His Pistol in His Hand": A border ballad and its hero*, Austin, University of Texas Press, 1958, p.29
248. Utley, op. cit, p.276
249. Graybill, op. cit, p.106
250. Utley, op. cit, p.277
251. Paredes, op. cit, p.30
252. Graybill, op. cit, p.119 and 124
253. Fehrenbach, op. cit, p.607-608
254. Graybill, op. cit, p.125-126
255. Ibid, p.127 and Utley, op. cit, p. 233-234
256. Graybill, op. cit, p.129-130
257. Ibid, p.140-142
258. Ibid, p.144
259. Utley, op. cit, p.237
260. Graybill, op. cit, p.163-165
261. Ibid, p.166-167
262. Ibid, p.171-172
263. Ibid, p.177 and 182-185
264. Utley, op. cit, p.259-260
265. Graybill, op. cit, p.193-194

Chapter 10

266. Benjamin Heber Johnson, *Revolution in Texas*, New Haven: Yale University Press, 2003 p.9
267. Fehrenbach, op. cit, p.690
268. Utley, op. cit, p.244-245
269. Ibid, p.245-246
270. Heber Johnson, op. cit, p.25
271. Utley, op. cit, p.255
272. Ibid, p.269-270
273. Paredes, op. cit, p.55

274. Paredes, op. cit, p.56 and Utley, op. cit, p.274
275. Utley, op. cit, p.274-275
276. Heber Johnson, op. cit, p.21
277. Utley, op. cit, p.275
278. Heber Johnson, op. cit, p.26
279. Ibid, p.13 and 15
280. Ibid, p.27-32
281. Ibid, p.39
282. Ibid, p.71-72
283. Ibid, p.83-98
284. Utley, *Lone Star Lawmen: The Second Century of the Texas Rangers*, New York: Berkley Books, 2007 p.28
285. Ibid, p.35-39
286. Utley, op. cit, p.33-34
287. Heber Johnson, op. cit, p.123
288. Samora, Bernal and Pena, op. cit, p.65
289. Utley, op. cit, p.46
290. Heber Johnson, op. cit, p.169
291. Utley, op. cit, p.53
292. Ibid, p.61
293. Heber Johnson, op. cit, p.152 and 163
294. Utley, op. cit, p.75
295. Fehrenbach, op. cit, p.693

Chapter 11
296. Tindall and Shi, op. cit, p.1023-1030
297. Utley, op. cit, p.90
298. Ibid, p.92
299. Ibid, p.92
300. Robert Cox, *Time of the Rangers*, New York: Forge Books, 2009, p.108
301. Utley, op. cit, p.93-94
302. Ibid, p.93
303. Ibid, p.94-95

304. Cox, op. cit, p.110
305. Cox, op. cit, p.111 and Utley, op. cit, p.95
306. Cox, op. cit, p.111-112 and Utley, op. cit, p.95
307. Cox, op. cit, p.111-112
308. Utley, op. cit, p.96
309. Ibid, p.115-116
310. Ibid, p.116-117
311. Cox, op. cit, p.131-132
312. Utley, op. cit, p.123
313. Ibid, p.123
314. Ibid, p.129-130
315. Ibid, p.130-131
316. Ibid, p.132
317. Cox, op. cit, p.141
318. Utley, op. cit, p.133
319. Cox, op. cit, p.145-146
320. Utley, op. cit, p.144
321. Ibid, p.144-145
322. Cox, op. cit, p.147
323. Ibid, p.147
324. Utley, op. cit, p.147-148
325. Ibid, p.148
326. Cox, op. cit, p.151
327. Richard F. Hamm, Shaping *the Eighteenth Amendment: temperance reform, legal culture, and the polity, 1880-1920*, Chapel Hill: University of North Carolina Press, 1995, p.228
328. Charles M. Robinson III, *The Men who wear the Star: The Story of the Texas Rangers*, New York: Random House Press, 2000, p.281-282
329. Cox, op. cit, p.106-107
330. Webb, op. cit, p.553
331. Utley, op. cit, p.97
332. Cox, op. cit, p.107
333. Utley, op. cit, p.98

334. Ibid, p.104
335. Ibid, p.104
336. Ibid, p.104-105
337. Cox, op. cit, p.115-116
338. Utley, op. cit, p.106 and 111
339. Ibid, p.106-107
340. Tindall and Shi, op. cit, p.1023-1024
341. Ibid, p.1026-1028
342. Ibid, p.1025
343. Fehrenbach, op. cit, p.645
344. Tindall and Shi, op. cit, p.1026
345. Cox, op. cit, p.100-101
346. Ibid, p.112
347. Fehrenbach, op. cit, p.645
348. Utley, op. cit, p.87-88
349. Cox, op. cit, p.113
350. Utley, op. cit, p.100-101
351. Ibid, p.102-103
352. Ibid, p.103-104
353. Cox, op. cit, p.142-143
354. Ibid, p.143
355. Utley, op. cit, p.137-139
356. Ibid, p.133
357. Ibid, p.133-134
358. Cox, op. cit, p.101
359. Ibid, p.101
360. Ibid, p.102-103
361. Utley, op. cit, p.98-99
362. Cox, op. cit, p.113-114
363. Ibid, p.114
364. Ibid, p.114
365. Utley, op. cit, p.100
366. Ibid, p.157 and 160
367. Ibid, p.114

368. Ibid, p.115
369. Cox, op. cit, p.129-130
370. Ibid, p.134-136
371. Webb, op. cit, p.538-539
372. Utley, op. cit, p.161
373. Cox, op. cit, p.158 and 161
374. Ibid, p.158-159
375. Utley, op. cit, p.162-164
376. Webb, op. cit, p.543
377. Cox, op. cit, p.136
378. Webb, op. cit, p.533
379. Cox, op. cit, p.137
380. Utley, op. cit, p.128
381. Webb, op. cit, p.533-534
382. Utley, op. cit, p.157
383. Cox, op. cit, p.139
384. Utley, op. cit, p.158
385. Cox, op. cit, p.140
386. Utley, op. cit, p.103 and 107-108
387. Ibid, p.119 and 140-141
388. Ibid, p.142
389. Cox, op. cit, p.89
390. Fehrenbach, op. cit, p.638-639
391. Utley, op. cit, p.109-112
392. Fehrenbach, op. cit, p.647
393. Ibid, p.651
394. Utley, op. cit, p.152-153
395. Cox, op. cit, p.158
396. Ibid,, p.155
397. Utley, op. cit, p.158-160
398. Ibid, p.166-167

Chapter 12
399. Ibid, p.166

400. Cox, op. cit, p.164-167
401. Ibid, p.167-169
402. Utley, op. cit, p.171-172
403. Ibid, p.172
404. Ibid, p.171
405. Ibid, p.179-180
406. Ibid, p.180-181
407. Ibid, p.181-182 and 184
408. Cox, op. cit, p.170-172
409. Ibid, p.174-175
410. Ibid, p.176-177 and p.183
411. Utley, op. cit, p.187-188
412. Ibid, p.189
413. Ibid, p.173-174
414. Ibid, p.193-194
415. Bern Keating, *An Illustrated History of the Texas Rangers*, Chicago: Rand McNally and Company, 1975, p.186
416. Cox, op. cit, p.226-227
417. Keating, op. cit, p.188
418. Ibid, p.188
419. Cox, op. cit, p.235
420. Samora, Bernal and Pena, op. cit, p.81
421. Cox, op. cit, p.187
422. Utley, op. cit, p.194
423. Keating, op. cit, p.188
424. Utley, op. cit, p.174
425. Cox, op. cit, p.171
426. Utley, op. cit, p.199
427. Cox, op. cit, p.181
428. Utley, op. cit, p.200

Chapter 13
429. Ben Proctor, *Just One Riot: Episodes of Texas Rangers in the 20th Century*, Austin: Eakin Press, 1991, p.65-66

430. Ibid, p.68
431. Ibid, p.71-73
432. Utley, op. cit, p.177-178
433. Cox, op. cit, p.190-191
434. Ibid, p.180
435. Ibid, p.182
436. Ibid, p.200-201
437. Tindall and Shi, op. cit, p.1151-1153
438. Fehrenbach, op. cit, p.653-654
439. Cox, op. cit, p.187
440. Fehrenbach, op. cit, p.654
441. Cox, op. cit, p.194 and 197
442. Ibid, p.194
443. Ibid, p.197-198 and 203
444. Ibid, p.199-200
445. Ibid, p.196
446. Ibid. p.204-206
447. Utley, op. cit, p.217
448. Tindall and Shi, op. cit, p.1159-1160
449. Ibid, p.1241
450. Cox, op. cit, p.213-214
451. Ibid, p.223-224
452. Ibid, 216-217
453. Utley, op. cit, p.230
454. Cox, op. cit, p.227
455. Utley, op. cit, p.230-231
456. Ibid, p.232
457. Ibid, p.233
458. Ibid, p.234
459. Joaquin H. Jackson, *One Ranger: A Memoir*, Austin: University of Texas Press, 2005 p.85-91
460. Ibid, p.92-93
461. Proctor, op. cit, p.96-98
462. Ibid, p.98-101

463. Ibid, p.79-82
464. Ibid, p.82-84
465. Cox, op. cit, p.235-236
466. Utley, op. cit, p.210
467. Ibid, p.211
468. Ibid, 211-212
469. Cox, op. cit, p.242-243
470. Ibid, p.242-244
471. Utley, op. cit, p.219-220
472. Cox, op. cit, p.248-249
473. Utley, op. cit, p.176-177
474. Ibid, p.177
475. Ibid, p.226
476. Ibid, p.226
477. Cox, op. cit, p.222-223
478. Ibid, p.202 and Utley, op. cit, p.225
479. Tindall and Shi, op. cit, p.1291-1292
480. Fehrenbach, op. cit, p.684
481. Cox, op. cit, p.237
482. Ibid, p.238 and Utley, op. cit, p.227-228
483. Utley, op. cit, p.228-229
484. Ibid, p.220
485. Cox, op. cit, p.172
486. Utley, op. cit, p.220
487. Ibid, p.221-222
488. Fehrenbach, op. cit, p.658
489. Utley, op. cit, p.222
490. Ibid, p.222-223
491. Webb, op. cit, p.8 and 14-15,
492. Paredes, op. cit, p.24-25

Chapter 14
493. Tindall and Shi, op. cit, p.1341-1343 and 1346
494. Ibid, p.1310-1311, 1319 and 1326

495. Ibid, p.1352-56
496. Ibid, p.1327, 1335,1342 and1344
497. Ibid, p.1356 and 1360-1361
498. Fehrenbach, op. cit, p.666, 687-688 and 697
499. Utley, op. cit, p.236-237
500. Jackson, op. cit, p.67
501. Samora, Bernal and Pena, op. cit, p.89-91
502. Ibid, p.96-97
503. Utley, op. cit, p.237
504. Samora, Bernal and Pena, op. cit, p.96-101
505. Cox, op. cit, p.261-262
506. Samora, Bernal and Pena, op. cit, p.113-116
507. Cox, op. cit, p.263-264
508. Ibid, p.269
509. Joaquin H. Jackson, *One Ranger Returns,* Austin: University of Texas Press, 2008 p.3
510. Samora, Bernal and Pena, op. cit, p.132
511. Jackson, op. cit, p.3
512. Samora, Bernal and Pena, op. cit, p.132
513. Ibid, p.133-136
514. Cox, op. cit, p.270
515. Jackson, op. cit, p.6
516 Ibid, p.4-6
517. Ibid, p.9
518. Utley, op. cit, p 240-241
519. Jackson, op. cit, p.13 and 15
520. Utley, op. cit, p.241
521. Samora, Bernal and Pena, op. cit, p.153-154
522. Utley, op. cit, p.242-243
523. Ibid, p.244-245
524. Samora, Bernal and Pena, op. cit, p.125-128
525. Utley, op. cit, p.248-249
526. Jackson, *One Ranger: A Memoir,* p.63 and 70-74
527. Utley, op. cit, p.251-253
528. Samora, Bernal and Pena, op. cit, p.91-92

529. Jackson, op. cit, p.152
530. Samora, Bernal and Pena, op. cit, p.93
531. Jackson, op. cit, p.152
532. Cox, op. cit, p.279
533. Jackson, op. cit, p.152
534. Utley, op. cit, p.223
535. Ibid, p.223-224
536. Cox, op. cit, p.282-283
537. Ibid, p.283-284
538. Ibid, p.273-274
539. Ibid, p.255-257
540. Ibid, p.264
541. Jackson, *One Ranger Returns*, p.102-106
542. Ibid, p.107-108 and 111
543. Jackson, *One Ranger: A Memoir*, p.93-96
544. Ibid, p.98-105
545. Ibid, p.43-45
546. Ibid, p.46-53
547. Jackson, *One Ranger Returns*, p.134-135 and 139
548. Ibid, p.139-142
549. Jackson, *One Ranger: A Memoir*, p.147 and 153
550. Ibid, p.149 and 152-154
551. Utley, op. cit, p.268-269
552. Ibid, p.266-267
553. Ibid, p.267-268
554. Cox, op. cit, p.300-301
555. Ibid, p.301-302
556. Proctor, op. cit, p.102-105
557. Ibid, p.108-117
558. Ibid, p.127-137
559. Ibid, p.137-140
560. Jackson, op. cit, p.212
561. Jackson, *One Ranger Returns*, p.124-125
562. Ibid, p.125-128
563. Ibid, p.130-131

564. Utley, op. cit, p.278-279
565. Ibid, p.279-280
566. Ibid, p.280 and Cox, op. cit, p.307
567. Utley, op. cit, p.280-281
568. Ibid, p.270-271
569. Cox, op. cit, p.292-293

Chapter 15

570. Tindall and Shi, op. cit, p.1394-1395
571. Ibid, p.1385-1387 and 1390
572. Ibid, p.11392-1394
573. Quoted in Cox, op. cit, p.340
574. Utley, op. cit, p.315
575. Jackson, op. cit, p.75
576. Cox, op. cit, p.334-336
577. Ibid, p.348 and 366
578. Utley, op. cit, p.315-316
579. Ibid, p.315
580. Ibid, p.316
581. Jackson, *One Ranger Returns*, p.171
582. Cox, op. cit, p.347-352
583. Ibid, p.347-349
584. Utley, op. cit, p.316-317
585. Cox, op. cit, p.363
586. Jackson, op. cit, p.113-114 and 117
587. Cox, op. cit, p.316-317
588. Ibid, p.318-319
589. Jackson, op. cit, p.91-92
590. Ibid, p.93
591. Cox, op. cit, p.319
592. Utley, op. cit, p.297-298
593. Cox, op. cit, p.321-324
594. Utley, op. cit, p.299-300
595. Jackson, op. cit, p.99

596. Utley, op. cit, p.283
597. Ibid, p.284-285
598. Cox, op. cit, p.309-310
599. Ibid, p.311
600. Ibid, p.311-313
601. Utley, op. cit, p. 285-286
602. Ibid, p.286-288
603. Jackson, *One Ranger: A Memoir*, p.179-180
604. Cox, op. cit, p.332
605. Jackson, op. cit, p.180-181
606. Ibid, p.182-183
607. Cox, op. cit, p.333
608. Jackson, *One Ranger Returns*, p.162-163
609. Ibid, p.163-165
610. Jackson, *One Ranger: A Memoir*, p.119-133
611. Ibid, p.134
612. Ibid, p.134-137
613. Ibid, p.137-139
614. Ibid, p.146
615. Utley, op. cit, p.304-307
616. Ibid, p.307-308
617. Cox, op. cit, p.343-344
618. Utley, op. cit, p.309
619. Ibid, p.309-314
620. Ibid, p.319-320
621. Ibid, p.320-321
622. Cox, op. cit, p.357
623. Utley, op. cit, p.322-326
624. Cox, op. cit, p.358-359
625. Ibid, p.359-361
626. Fehrenbach, op. cit, p.705
627. George W. Bush, *Decision Points*, New York: Crown Publishers, 2010 p.35-37
628. Cox, op. cit, p361-362

629. Ibid, p.369-370
630. Ibid, p.370-371
631. Ibid, p.372
632. Ibid, p.373-375
633. Larry McMurtry, *Lonesome Dove*, London: Pan Books, 1985 p.192, 238, 499 and 833
634. Larry McMurtry, *Dead Man's Walk*, New York: Pocket Books, 1996 p.79 and 239-240
635. McMurtry, *Lonesome Dove*, p.934-935
636. Larry McMurtry, *Streets of Laredo*, New York: Simon and Schuster, 1993 p.541
637. Jackson, op. cit, p.229-230
638. Cox, op. cit, p.367-368

Conclusion
639. Fehrenbach, op. cit, p.719

Bibliography

Ball, Larry D. *Desert Lawmen: The High Sheriffs of New Mexico and Arizona 1846-1912*. Albuquerque: University of New Mexico Press, 1992.

Brogan, Hugh, *The Penguin History of the United States of America*, London: Longman, 1999.

Brown, Dee, *The American West*, New York: Touchstone, 1994.

Bush, George W., *Decision Points*, New York: Crown Publishers, 2010

Cox, Robert, *Time of the Rangers*, New York: Forge Books, 2009

DeLay, Brian, *War of a Thousand Deserts*, New Haven: Yale University Press, 2008

Durham, George, as told to Clyde Wantland, *Taming the Nueces Strip: The Story of McNelly's Rangers*, Austin: University of Texas Press, 1962

Fehrenbach, T.R., *Comanches: The Destruction of A People*, New York: Alfred A. Knopf, 1974.

Fehrenbach, T.R. *Lone Star: A History of Texas and the Texans*, Cambridge: Da Capo Press, 2000.

Frazier, Donald S. *Blood and Treasure: The Confederate Empire in the Southwest*. College Station, Texas: Texas A & M University Press, 1995

Graybill, Andrew R. *Policing the Great Plains: Rangers, Mounties and the North American Frontier*. Lincoln: University of Nebraska Press, 2007.

Hamalainen, Pekka, *The Comanche Empire*, New Haven: Yale University Press, 2008

Hamm, Richard F. *Shaping the Eighteenth Amendment: temperance reform, legal culture, and the polity, 1880-1920*, Chapel Hill: University of North Carolina Press, 1995

Heber Johnson, Benjamin. *Revolution in Texas: How a forgotten rebellion and its bloody suppression turned Mexicans into Americans.* New Haven: Yale University Press, 2003.

Hyde, George E. *Rangers and Regulars*, Columbus: Long's College Book Company, 1952.

Jackson, H. Joaquin, and David Marion Wilkinson. *One Ranger: A Memoir*, Austin: University of Texas Press, 2005.

Jackson, H. Joaquin, with James L. Haley. *One Ranger Returns*, Austin: University of Texas Press, 2008.

Keating, Bern. *An Illustrated History of the Texas Rangers*, Chicago: Rand McNally and Company, 1975.

Manchaca, Martha. *Recovering History, Constructing Race: The Indian, Black, and White Roots of Mexican Americans*, Austin: University of Texas Press, 2001

McMurtry, Larry. *Comanche Moon*, New York: Pocket Books, 1998

McMurtry, Larry. *Dead Man's Walk*, New York: Pocket Books, 1996

McMurtry, Larry. *Lonesome Dove*, London: Pan Books, 1985

McMurtry, Larry. *Streets of Laredo*, New York: Simon and Schuster, 1993

Paredes, Americo. *"With His Pistol in His Hand": A border ballad and its hero.* Austin: University of Texas Press, 1958.

Prassel, Frank Richard. *The Western Peace Officer.* Norman: University of Oklahoma Press, 1972.

Proctor, Ben. *Just One Riot: Episodes of Texas Rangers in the 20th Century.* Austin: Eakin Press, 1991.

Rosenberg, David H. "Confederate Manifest Destiny in New Mexico." *America's Civil War*, July 2000 (Volume 13, Number 3)

Samora, Julian, Bernal, Joe, and Pena, Albert. *Gunpowder Justice: A Reassessment of the Texas Rangers.* Notre Dame: University of Notre Dame Press, 1979.

Tindall, George Brown and Shi, David Emory. *America: A Narrative History 8th Edition*, New York: W.W. Norton, 2010.

Utley, Robert M. *Lone Star Justice: The First Century of the Texas Rangers*. New York: Oxford University Press, 2002.

Utley, Robert M. *Lone Star Lawmen: The Second Century of the Texas Rangers*. New York: Berkley Books, 2007.

Vasquez, Josefina Zoraida. "The Colonization and Loss of Texas: A Mexican Perspective", in Rodriguez O., Jaime E.; Vincent, Kathryn, *Myths, Misdeeds, and Misunderstandings: The Roots of Conflict in U.S.–Mexican Relations*, Wilmington: Scholarly Resources Inc. 1997

Webb, Walter Prescott. *The Texas Rangers: A Century of Frontier Defence*, Austin: University of Texas Press, 1935.

West, Elliott. *The Way to the West: Essays on the Central Plains*. Albuquerque: University of New Mexico Press, 1995